OLIVIER MESSIAEN
and the Music of Time

OLIVIER MESSIAEN
and the Music of Time

PAUL GRIFFITHS

Cornell University Press
ITHACA, NEW YORK

First published 1985 by Cornell University Press

Library of Congress Cataloging in Publication Data

Griffiths, Paul.
Olivier Messiaen and the music of time.

Bibliography: p.
Includes index.
1. Messiaen, Olivier, 1908–   Works.
I. Title.
ML410.M595G7   1985   780'.92'4   84–45797
ISBN 0–8014–1813–5

Printed in Great Britain

For Rachel
and the seven years

Contents

Illustrations

ACKNOWLEDGEMENTS

Grateful acknowledgement is made to Messiaen's publishers in Paris, Editions Durand S.A., Alphonse Leduc et Cie, Editions Salabert, and their London agent, United Music Publishers Ltd, for permission to reproduce the music examples. The publisher responsible for each work is given in the Catalogue of Works on p. 257.

old chains of cause and effect have been forgotten, and that chords can be moved about in a symmetrical universe that imposes no single flow of time.

There is a nearer connection with Stravinsky, whose music is also often free from diatonic pressure, strongly pulsed and conveyed in repetitive forms. But Stravinsky never missed keeping his eye on his watch. If the imperative of diatonic harmony was lost, then some causation had to come from elsewhere, usually from metre (hence the importance of dance in his work). Messiaen does not dance his way onward, except on rare occasions when his concern is with the imperfection that separates man from the eternal, unchanging divinity. And it is of course his unswerving focus on God that gives his music its reason to be, and to be as it is. It is a truism that Western music since the Renaissance has been about man, about beings whose existence in time is short, directed and hopefully progressive. The capacity to speak of God comes only when the march of time is forgotten, as it is forgotten in plainsong, in a very few composers within but beyond the central tradition (Bruckner outstandingly) and in a great deal of music from other cultures, where the main purpose of music may be to address the divine. It is not surprising, therefore, that the most potent influences on Messiaen should have come not so much from Debussy and Stravinksy as from plainsong and from exotic music: from the rhythms and modes of ancient Greece and India, from the resonant heterophonies of Bali, from the ululations of birds.

All these may seem at some remove from the terms of Catholic devotion in which Messiaen most frequently presents his works. However, it is precisely the nature of his religiousness that has been responsible for so much misunderstanding of his music: Catholic observers have often been appalled at the vulgarity with which the truths of their faith are projected, non-Catholics mistrustful of the scent of incense carried, it must be admitted, not only by Messiaen's titles and verbal expositions but also by his inheritance from a French musical tradition of piety stemming from Gounod. But vulgarity is only a sign of innocence, and of piety too: it is the willingness to use any material, even added-sixth chords sweetly scored for strings, without a flicker of anxiety about that material's history. Time is, once more, not at issue.

It is, moreover, the denial of forward-moving time that is the generative and fundamental substance of Messiaen's music: the matter of his verbal commentaries is no more than an explanation of the music, referring to one particular system of religious belief, and conducted in terms other than those of the music. The music is not tied to that system, as Messiaen has suggested in his willingness to adapt concepts from other traditions of religious thought, especially Hindu: he is not the first Western religious thinker to recognize that the essence of spirituality is universal, to be found as readily in an Indian temple as in a Gothic cathedral, in the Upanishads as in the Gospels. Of course, he has been powerfully stimulated by the most marvellous events and imaginings of Judaeo-Christian tradition: the Nativity, Transfiguration, Resurrection and Ascension of Christ, the glories of the resurrected existence and the affiliation of all humanity to God. However, the basic truth enshrined in all of these is a truth peculiarly amenable to musical expression: it is the presence of the eternal within the temporal, the unmeasurable within the measured, the mysterious within the known. It is the truth of everything Messiaen has written.

CHAPTER 1
Childhood and Before

Enigmas of time start before the beginning. For most individuals there is no knowing how genetic and environmental conditions have already begun to shape personality in the womb, but in Messiaen's case there is something to be said about his uterine existence, since his mother, the poet Cécile Sauvage (1883–1927), made her pregnancy the subject of a collection of twenty poems, *L'âme en bourgeon*.[1] Obviously these convey her experiences and not those of her son, but they are addressed to him, whether as embryonic child or new-born baby, and they must have affected his later view of himself. Indeed, he has confessed as much. In a book of conversations with Antoine Goléa that is one of the major sources for his early life, he admits that his mother's poems 'certainly influenced my character and my whole destiny',[2] and he interprets one line even as a prophecy that he would be an artist.[3] Much later, in a note for a record of twelve poems from the collection recited with discreet interludes played at the organ by himself in 1977, he declares that 'this is his purest pride: to have inspired *L'âme en bourgeon*'.[4]

Some idea of Sauvage's effusive imagery and her affectionate. if proprietorial manner in these poems may be had from one of the shorter ones, 'La tête':

O mon fils, je tiendrai ta tête dans ma main,
Je dirai: j'ai pétri ce petit monde humain;
Sous ce front dont la courbe est une aurore étroite
J'ai logé l'univers rajeuni qui miroite
Et qui lave d'azur les chagrins pluvieux.
Je dirai: j'ai donné cette flamme à ces yeux,
J'ai tiré du sourire ambigu de la lune,
Des reflets de la mer, du velours de la prune
Ces deux astres naïfs ouverts sur l'infini.
Je dirai: j'ai formé cette joue et ce nid

De la bouche où l'oiseau de la voix se démène;
C'est mon oeuvre, ce monde avec sa face humaine.

O mon fils, je tiendrai ta tête dans ma main
Et, songeant que le jour monte, brille et s'éteint,
Je verrai sous tes chairs soyeuses et vermeilles
Couvertes d'un pétale à tromper les abeilles,
Je verrai s'enfoncer les orbites en creux,
L'ossature du nez offrir ses trous ombreux,
Les dents rire sur la mâchoire dévastée. . .

Et ta tête de mort, c'est moi qui l'ai sculptée.[5]

If Messiaen had not been Messiaen, then no doubt this poem and its nineteen companions would have fallen with the rest of Sauvage's work into obscurity. But if his music has saved her verse, it may be also that her poetry played some part in making him a composer in the first place. Uncountable aspects of inheritance and experience must go into the production of artistic creativity. One of them in Messiaen's case could hardly fail to have been a garland of poems that so welcomed him as special.

The child of whom they speak was born in Avignon on 10 December 1908 and christened Olivier Eugène Prosper Charles, but soon afterwards the family moved to Ambert in the département of Puy-de-Dome, the birthplace of Chabrier. There the boy learned to read, and there he acquired a brother, Alain, born in 1913 and apparently not greeted by a second set of maternal poems from Sauvage. Even so, he, like Olivier, inherited or otherwise imbibed something of his mother's poetic gift, becoming the author of verbal interpretations of music, including his brother's, published as Cortège d'Euterpe. Pierre Messiaen, the boys' father, was a man of letters too – a lycée teacher of English and translator of Shakespeare – but his part in their intellectual formation has generally been underplayed (perhaps justly: the composer never learned to master English). He was, inevitably, an absentee parent during a crucial period of his elder son's life, for before Olivier was 6 the First World War had broken out and the English teacher become a soldier.

Sauvage took the two boys to her brother André's house in Grenoble. He was a surgeon, and also involved in the war effort; the boys were therefore in the charge of their mother and of her mother, Marie Sauvage, and they were brought up, according to the composer's account, 'in a climate of poetry and fairytales . . . such as enormously develops a child's imagination and leads him towards thinking in immaterial terms, and so to music, the most immaterial of the arts'.[6]

From fairytales to music, though, the route lay through drama and religion. Messiaen has recalled how at the age of 8 he recited the whole of Shakespeare from an edition 'decorated with romantic woodcuts'[7] (this was before his father published his own translation), with his brother as participant or audience. He even went further and made a toy theatre: 'For the back of the stage I used Cellophane wrappings that I found in sweet boxes or patisserie bags and then painted with Indian ink or quite simply with water-colours; then I put my sets in front of a window, and the sun coming through the coloured Cellophane projected coloured light on to the floor of my little theatre as well as on to the characters.'[8]

These childhood Thespian endeavours may be of small consequence, but what is significant is that Messiaen should have remembered them decades later and thereby given the hint that they were important to the development of his creative mind: one can hardly miss the suggestion of stained-glass windows, so potent an image in his artistic world. At the same time his mind was learning to work musically. Having taught himself to play the piano, he began composing canons at the octave when he was 8, and only afterwards was sent to his first teacher, a Mlle Chardon. Between the ages of 7 and 10 he demanded operatic vocal scores for his Christmas presents: *Don Giovanni* and *Die Zauberflöte*, Gluck's *Alceste* and *Orfeo*, *La damnation de Faust*, *Die Walküre* and *Siegfried* were duly left by Père Noël, and these he sang and played through at the piano.[9] His repertory also included, astonishingly for a child so young, Debussy's *Estampes* and Ravel's *Gaspard de la nuit*,[10] so that at an early age he was in touch not only with the magic realm of an opera of the mind but also with some of the most significant of recent French music.

Not surprisingly, given this musical precocity, he began to compose. *La dame de Shalott*, a piano piece after Tennyson's poem, is mentioned from 1917, and described by the composer of fifty years later as 'a very childish piece, but not altogether stupid and not entirely without sense, a piece I still regard with a certain tenderness'.[11] Another observer has found 'in the little allegro describing Lancelot's ride ... a distant premonition of the "Intermède" from the *Quatuor pour la fin du temps*'.[12]

At this stage, though, one might have thought the boy was preparing himself for a career as an operatic composer, were it not that his theatrical preferences were all imaginary and fantastic: there is no account in his reminiscences of ever visiting a real theatre, and his favourite Shakespeare plays, like his chosen operas, were those with a strong element of the supernatural, *Macbeth*, *A Midsummer Night's Dream* and *The Tempest*. In fact, the theatre was a second best. It was in the Catholic faith – which he adopted for himself, his parents not being particularly religious – that he found something to touch his sense of the mysterious much more deeply. For if Shakespeare offered him 'super-fairytales',[13] he discovered in his religion 'this attraction of the marvellous multiplied a hundredfold, a thousandfold'.[14]

Speaking thus has, however, brought him much misunderstanding. A faith that regards the Gospels and the Apocalypse as a sort of ultimate Hans Christian Andersen must appear lacking in adultness, and it is hardly enough to insist, as Messiaen has insisted, that the difference between Shakespeare and Christian belief is simply that between 'a theatrical fiction' and 'something true'.[15] But such naïveté can only be admired: to question Messiaen's sincerity and his motivation is as unprofitable as it is improper. The most it can yield is a fake reason for dismissing his music, whereas it may be more productive to examine ways in which the contemplation of divine things has led him to take up musical and philosophical issues of interest to all.

Much of the remainder of this book will be concerned with these matters, but the territory can be quickly charted here. In the first place, quite straightforwardly, the wish to display Christian mythology in music has given Messiaen a reason to compose: something vouchsafed to few of his contemporaries in an age when music is no longer much prompted by patronage, commercial interest or, except in some instances, self-advertisement. Secondly, he has given himself the challenge of attempting to describe in music the most awe-inspiring figments of the human mind – the Incarnation, the Resurrection of the Body, the Celestial City. But thirdly, and most crucially, to meditate on religion has been for him pre-eminently to meditate on time.

There are good reasons for that. Religious truths are unique in being presumed to operate throughout all eternity; to contain them in music may therefore require a new conception of time, one less bound by the pressure of forward motion that has been a chief characteristic of Western music since the Renaissance. Many mystics have spoken of the experience of being transported 'outside time' during a state of heightened religious awareness, when long periods may pass very swiftly or brief times hugely extend. In rather the same way, music that is unusually slow in its harmonic movement – that of Bruckner, for example – has readily been regarded as religious in its subject matter. It is therefore to be expected that Messiaen, who has concentrated on religious subjects more than any other great composer since Palestrina, should find the experiencing of time of special interest.

But we had left him in 1918. With the war over, Pierre Messiaen rejoined his family and took them across the country to Nantes. The young composer could take with him his Shakespeare and his vocal scores, his missal and his manuscript paper, but he could not take the mountains of Grenoble that had surrounded him during his first years of self-discovery. He was to return to those alps of the Dauphiné in order to compose there many of his most important works, was to call himself 'not a Cartesian Frenchman but a Frenchman of the mountains, like Berlioz',[16] was several times to write music for or about mountain summits.

In the Loire city of Nantes, however, his time was not wasted. He had piano lessons with various local teachers (Gontran Arcouët, Robert Lortat and the Véron sisters). He also began the formal study of harmony with Jehan de Gibon, who remained in touch with his pupil until he died, and who gave him, at the age of 10, a score of *Pelléas et Mélisande*, another 'super-fairytale' to be played over again and again in imagination. It was, Messiaen has said, 'a revelation, a thunderbolt', and 'probably the most decisive influence on me'.[17] His brief childhood was over. After only a few months in Nantes his father accepted a post at the Lycée Charlemagne in Paris, and at the age of 11 Messiaen was admitted to the Conservatoire.

CHAPTER 2
The Conservatoire

There is a feeling of immediate familiarity to the decade of Messiaen's studies at the Conservatoire: this was Paris in the twenties, the age of Stravinsky and clean-cut neoclassicism, of jazz and cabaret, of Cocteau and Les Six, of the chic second phase of the Ballets Russes. Here again, though, our conceptions of time may differ from Messiaen's, for that whole culture affected him hardly at all. He was impressed by Milhaud's *L'homme et son désir* and by a Stravinsky triple bill of *The Rite of Spring, The Wedding* and *Pulcinella*,[1] but as he later expressed it: 'I had no time for that so-called simplification that started out from Gounod to founder in 'returns to Bach' and such like.'[2] In his Paris there were other things going on.

There was, first of all, a living tradition of religious music that was bound to affect the young Catholic composer, with Louis Vierne to be heard at Notre Dame, Charles-Marie Widor at St Sulpice and Charles Tournemire at Franck's church of Ste Clotilde. Tournemire, composer of symphonies with such titles as *Les danses de la vie* (1918–22) and *La symphonie du triomphe de la mort* (1920–4) as well as of a vast cycle of meditations on plainsong contained in his *L'orgue mystique* (1927–32), must stand high among Messiaen's musical godparents, but there were also other and quite different sources of influence. Like many others, Messiaen was powerfully struck by the dynamic orchestral brilliance of Villa-Lobos,[3] who lived in Paris between 1923 and 1930, and who gave sensational concerts there in 1924 and 1927: the fast movements of Messiaen's early works for orchestra, up to and including even the *Turangalîla-symphonie*, taste the same frenzy and vividness. Another American, Varèse, was back in his home city between 1928 and 1933, composing his *Ionisation* for percussion.

There were also visitors from the east, emigré Russians like Nikolay Obukhov (1892–1954) and Ivan Vishnegradsky (1893–1979), who brought with them a line of harmonic and mystical venturing that emanated from Skryabin. Both had performances in Paris, and their music was discussed in the *Revue musicale*.[4] Of the two, Obukhov would seem particularly close to Messiaen in his Christian testimony and also his scoring – such works as *Le pasteur tout-puissant règne* for female voice with ondes martenot and piano (1930) promise to be irresistibly Messiaenic – but the influence is hard to gauge, partly because Obukhov's few published works date from a later period, when it might have been that he was learning from Messiaen, and partly because Messiaen may have been drawing directly on similar harmonic and philosophical indications in Skryabin.

Other features in the landscape of his student mind were poetic and musicological. Quite distinct from the urbane world of Les Six, there was in Paris a widespread understanding of music as a spiritual discipline, an art concerned with human and eternal time. Of course, Stravinsky himself, never entirely at ease with the modishness of his supporters, recognized this in his dictum of 1935 that: 'The phenomenon of music is given to us with the sole purpose of establishing an order in things, including, and particularly, the co-ordination between *man* and *time*.'[5] That same co-ordination was also a subject of concern to, for example, the plainsong scholar Dom André Mocquereau, whose *Le nombre musical grégorien* (1908–27) dealt with the rhythmic performance of chant in patterns of 'arsis' (upbeat) and 'thesis' (statement): Messiaen learned much from Mocquereau's work.[6] He also learned from, or at least shared in, the speculations of such writers as Romain Rolland and Paul Claudel, both of whom felt that music was immensely larger than its European heritage and that its principal purpose was precisely as Stravinsky described.

Meanwhile, if from a different point of view, the surrealists were indicating how art might penetrate beyond the material world, for it was during the same decade of the twenties that André Breton, Paul Eluard and Pierre Reverdy published their most radical work. Nor can one ignore the mental sustenance that came from a level less bound by particularities of epoch, from Messiaen's regular attendance at the church of St Leu.

Nevertheless, it was within the walls of the Conservatoire that the adolescent composer learned most of his art. First he studied the piano with Georges Falkenberg; then harmony with Jean Gallon (second prize, 1924); counterpoint and fugue with Georges Caussade (first prize, 1926); piano accompaniment with C. A. Estyle (first prize, 1927); organ and improvisation with Marcel Dupré (first prize, 1928); history of music with Maurice Emmanuel (first prize, 1928); composition with Paul Dukas (first prize, 1929); and timpani and percussion with Joseph Baggers, this last an unusual study, suggesting that Messiaen was already, perhaps stimulated by *The Wedding*, looking beyond the norms of Western musical presentation. Meanwhile his excellent academic record in the more normal disciplines suggests how well he got on with his teachers, and he has spoken warmly of what he learned from them.

Jean Gallon (1878–1959) and his brother Noël (1891–1966), who was Messiaen's tutor throughout his Conservatoire career, gave him 'the sense of natural harmony and a harmonic technique of which I am very proud'.[7] It was also Jean Gallon who had the idea of sending him to Dupré to learn the organ, not because he was a devout Catholic but rather because he had shown gifts as an improviser when studying piano accompaniment.[8] Jean Gallon was the outstanding harmony teacher of his generation at the Conservatoire, succeeded in that eminence by Messiaen himself; he foreshadowed too his pupil's iconoclasm in introducing Debussy and Ravel into the syllabus. In earlier life he had had some success as a composer of sacred music, but it was the younger brother Noël who was the more fluent composer, his works ranging from opera to piano music and songs.

Marcel Dupré (1886–1971) was, in Messiaen's words, 'the Liszt of the organ'. 'His music', Messiaen goes on, 'is the reflection of his extraordinary virtuosity; he has pages of extreme difficulty and great brilliance in the toccata manner, and he initiated the ultra-staccato style.'[9] His influence on Messiaen becomes clear in the latter's big show-pieces for the organ, but as the pupil of Vierne, Widor and Alexandre Guilmant he was also responsible for passing on to Messiaen a tradition of French organ playing and composition that went back to Franck, Vierne's teacher. The link to Guilmant is also tantalizing, for Guilmant was one of Messiaen's great predecessors at the organ of La Trinité in Paris, and it was hearing Guilmant improvise on that organ that made Dupré work at fugal improvisation, to an effect that perhaps bore most fruit in the music of his pupil.

Dupré also encouraged in Messiaen an interest in the metres of Greek poetry, though the principal expert in that field was Maurice Emmanuel (1862–1938). And it was again Dupré and more especially Emmanuel who set the young composer in search of unconventional modalities.[10] Emmanuel wrote much on ancient Greek rhythm and music, including a long article in Lavignac's encyclopedia, which would have been Messiaen's principal source for this and other exotic information. Indeed, Emmanuel shared altogether the fascination with Greece and the East felt by very many French artists of his generation, not excluding Debussy, but his manner was more scientific: his Cello Sonata, Op. 2, (1887) is in the Phrygian mode (compare Debussy's Phrygian-tinged String Quartet of 1893), and his Piano Sonatina No. 4, Op. 20, (1920) used Indian modes. When he was the subject of a special issue of the *Revue musicale* in 1947, Messiaen contributed a short appreciation of his *Trente chansons bourguignonnes*, Op. 15, of 1913, recalling how after a performance of these folk-song arrangements he 'was amazed –

and at once converted to modal music'.[11] It would of course be interesting to know exactly when this took place. Messiaen says he was 'still a young student at the Conservatoire' but remarks also that this was fifteen years ago, which would give a date of 1932, after he had left the academy and written a good few modal works of his own. However, if the article was written at the time of Emmanuel's death, the date would be 1923, a much better fit.

As for Paul Dukas (1865–1935), Messiaen remembered that 'he developed in me a sense of artistic probity and gave me an orchestral technique of which I am, once more, very proud'.[12] Certainly a joyous deployment of the resources of a full symphony orchestra is very much a feature of Messiaen's early music, whether it came from Dukas or from Villa-Lobos or from somewhere else. Artistic probity, perhaps, is a less demonstrable quality. In the case of Dukas himself, arduous self-examination had caused him to suppress any major work for many years, but his earlier achievement was definitely a model of compositional integrity and prowess for the young Messiaen, particularly his opera *Ariane et Barbe-Bleue* (1899–1906). Just as he was to do in the case of Emmanuel, Messiaen contributed to the special issue of the *Revue musicale* published in 1936 to commemorate Dukas: indeed, he contributed as both fellow composer and student, the number including a *Pièce pour le tombeau de Paul Dukas* for piano and an essay on *Ariane*. Dukas's opera appealed to him for its orchestral magnificence, but also, and possibly more so, for its philosophical content, his article freely acknowledging respect for a composer who was always in search of the most profound truth, and who projected that restless inward search into his largest work.

By the time Messiaen completed his studies with Dukas, in 1930, he had a respectable number of compositions in his portfolio: three orchestral scores, a set of songs, a group of preludes for the piano and a handful of organ pieces. Most of these, however, were recent. His official lists[13] include only one work from his early Paris years, a pair of Villon settings for voice and piano made in 1921 (Debussy's three Villon ballades, one may recall, were only 11 years old, Messiaen himself only 12). The next piece mentioned similarly unpublished, is *La tristesse d'un grand ciel blanc* (1925), a piano composition which, to judge only from its title, could well have fitted into the book of preludes written four years later.

In between Messiaen composed his first orchestral works, *Le banquet eucharistique* (1928) and a Fugue in D minor from the same year, as well as his first pieces for his own instrument, the organ: an *Esquisse modale* (1927), *Le banquet céleste* (1928), *L'hôte aimable des âmes* (1928) and, somewhat oddly, a set of *Variations écossaises* (1928). Of these, only *Le banquet céleste* has been published, making it the earliest piece of

Messiaen in print. Like *Le banquet eucharistique* and *L'hôte aimable des âmes*, it was composed during a summer holiday on his aunt's farm at Fuligny in the département of Aube, east of Paris, and the three works evidently had shared subject matter. For if the fugue and the unimaginable Scottish variations must have been done as conservatory tasks, the Fuligny works assail the very personal theme of meditating on the Eucharist, which is for the Catholic the primary day-to-day evidence of the intervention of the eternal: the mass is not merely the memorial of Christ's sacrifice but the actual repetition, the declaration that a single event is not tied to a single time but can occur again and again in perpetuity. It is this opening of linear progressive time to contain the omnipresent, this vision of the eternal in an instant, that *Le banquet céleste* conveys, and we can guess that *Le banquet eucharistique* did so as well, since we know that the organ piece took material from the orchestral,[14] which was performed at the Conservatoire by the student orchestra under the director, Henri Rabaud (1873–1949), but has not been seen or heard since.

Messiaen has given his view that *Le banquet céleste* is 'a very charming, tender, soft and spring-like piece that has nothing extraordinary about it'.[15] Like many of his comments on his own music, however, this needs to be treated with some caution. The work is in fact very extraordinary indeed, despite its modest scope; and if it is 'spring-like' it is so only by virtue of announcing the Messiaen to come. Certainly there is nothing particularly vernal about music of such slow pace and dense harmonic weave as example 1, from the start of the composition. This

Ex. 1   Le banquet céleste

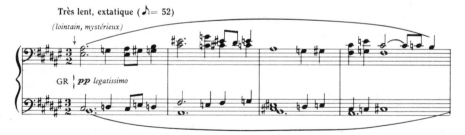

is, however, very much Messiaen's spring as a musical personality, even though he was only 19 when he wrote it (some sources, including certain printings of the music, give a date two years earlier still, but this would appear to be erroneous). Among composers of the twentieth century, perhaps only Britten and Shostakovich have announced themselves so fully so young.

The newness of *Le banquet céleste* is, for the moment, one of substance rather than purpose, since the piece has a very natural place during the communion of a mass, a conventional moment for organ music, most especially in France. The 'heavenly banquet' is of course the Eucharist, and the music's intention is made clear, as so often in Messiaen, by an explanatory superscription from the Bible, here taken from St John: 'He that eateth my flesh, and drinketh my blood, dwelleth in me, and I in him' (6:56). As a statement about time this is clear. The eternal is present. And the music of Messiaen's invention relates quite directly to this perception.

In the first place, the piece is uncommonly slow. The metronome marking, and with it a doubling of the rhythmic values, was introduced with the new edition of 1960, but apparently this was simply because organists were taking the piece too fast: after all, the music looks as if it ought to be going at several times the notated speed, which is to say that this is the tempo a Western musical mind would feel appropriate for music of this rate of harmonic change. Of course, at such a speed *Le banquet céleste* would sound trivial, its phrases answering one another in far too pat a fashion. The given tempo is essential in order that the harmonic progressions be estranged, which they are because the standard interval between chords is something more than two seconds. At that rate events are just slipping out of being perceived as belonging to the same present,[16] so that harmonic tendencies are considerably dissipated. Simply by virtue of their duration – the first chord's length of seven seconds is surely unprecedented among Western musical openings – the chords are beginning to function as images of eternity rather than as moments in a time flow. However, the actual nature of the chords is not wholly insignificant to the effect.

Messiaen here introduces what he calls his 'second mode of limited transpositions', which, in the form used in the first bar of *Le banquet céleste*, can be given as C sharp–D–E–E sharp–G–G sharp–A sharp–B. Transpositions of this mode are limited because of its regularity. There is a repeating unit of a minor third, divided always into minor-second and major-second intervals; and so every fourth chromatic transposition of the mode produces the same set of notes as the first. Thus whereas the major scale, for example, exists in twelve different transpositions, this mode has only three. (Messiaen's harmonic thinking is very much in terms of keyboard instruments, so that enharmonic equivalences can be regarded as real identities.)

However, Messiaen's terminology may be slightly unhelpful, since the important thing about his second mode is not that its transpositions are limited but rather that its construction is symmetrical, since this is the root cause of the limitation on transposition and also of the tonal instability that he musically exploits. The same is true of his other 'modes of limited transpositions', among which the first is the whole-tone scale, little used by him because, as he has said: 'Claude Debussy, in *Pelléas et Mélisande*, and after him Paul Dukas, in *Ariane et Barbe-Bleue*, have made such remarkable use of it that there is nothing more to add.'[17] However, his own practice in such works as the *Quatuor pour la fin du temps* belies this, and one may surmise that he has been less attracted to the whole-tone mode because it offers fewer points of contact with diatonic harmony.

One cannot, for instance, make a triad with the notes of the whole-tone scale, since it contains no fifth. The second mode, on the other hand, includes not only a fifth on four of its degrees (C sharp, E, G and A sharp in the version given above) but also both major and minor thirds, the major sixth and the flattened seventh, while its whole symmetry is that of the diminished-seventh chord, one form of which is instanced by the four diatonic centres mentioned. The second mode therefore lends itself to the dominant-seventh, diminished-seventh and added-sixth chords that are the main pillars of Messiaen's harmony in *Le banquet céleste* and much later music, as well as to the equally characteristic establishing of the tritone, not the fifth, as the interval of highest structural importance. Obviously one is bound to suppose that the chords and the tritone movement came first. Since Messiaen has said that Dupré helped him 'to discover myself by making me work methodically at improvisation', it could well be that he came upon the second mode as an abstraction from chordal combinations he found to his taste, perhaps from the pairing of two added-sixth chords a tritone apart (e.g. C sharp–E sharp–G sharp–A sharp and G–B–D–E).

The second mode is not, however, Messiaen's invention, as he has readily acknowledged in noting its appearance in Rimsky-Korsakov, Skryabin, Stravinsky and Ravel.[18] To those names one might add also that of Liszt,[19] but in none of these composers is the mode used in anything like Messiaen's manner. Normally it arises not from the mingling of diatonically distant triadic harmonies but from that of diminished-seventh chords (e.g. C sharp–E–G–A and D–F–G sharp–B), though what is possibly the very earliest suggestion of this mode does come in a couple of bars startlingly alive to harmonic possibilities that Messiaen was to take up more than a century later. Example 2 is from the twentieth of Beethoven's *Diabelli Variations*, and it includes all but one of the notes of the second mode. Of course, it is not necessary to suppose that Messiaen was directly influenced by this transient

Ex. 2   Beethoven: Diabelli Variations, *variation 20*

moment; the point is rather that the most searching musical mind in our culture came upon areas that could be fully explored only at a later stage in musical history. Other commentators have found adumbrations of serialism in Beethoven; no doubt there are hints too of musical worlds yet to be revealed.

More immediate, and intriguing, is Messiaen's connection with Stravinsky. His own statements have tended to concentrate on Stravinsky's rhythm as being that master's major contribution,[20] but it cannot escape notice that his second mode is identical with the 'octatonic scale' that some analysts have seen as a central aspect of Stravinsky's thinking throughout his creative life,[21] and Messiaen himself is perhaps taking a sideways look at his Parisian contemporary when he speaks of his modes as belonging 'in the atmosphere of several tonalities, *without polytonality*'[22] (his italics). What he means by this, one may guess, is that he avoids diatonic conflict within a polytonal field, partly because his oppositions are successive rather than simultaneous (e.g. C sharp and G in the first bar of *Le banquet céleste*), and partly because his chords enfold rather than expose different harmonic consequences: the added-sixth chord, for instance, can be heard as a major triad in root position or as a triad of the relative minor in first inversion, and the first chord of *Le banquet céleste* tends, just because it is so long sustained, to substantiate a C sharp root quite as much as it looks for an F sharp resolution.

If much of Stravinsky shows the same mode being used to very different purposes, it must be obvious that to describe *Le banquet céleste*, or any other Messiaen composition, as being 'in the second mode' is hardly more helpful than to describe the *Diabelli Variations* as being 'in the diatonic mode' (though this has not prevented Messiaen from using such generalized terminology, and will not prevent us). What matters is how the mode is employed. In the case of the opening of this short organ piece, there are two transpositions alternating in operation: that already mentioned (odd-numbered bars) and a form best regarded as displaced from this upwards by a fourth, and so starting on F sharp (even-numbered bars). In either modality the music confines itself to triadic harmonies, which means, as has been shown, moving among keys at minor-third intervals and ignoring the fifth that is of primary importance in the diatonic system. Thus the first bar moves from C sharp to G by way of E and the second from F sharp to C by way of A: rhythmically the same, each is the mirror of the other, and is so even on a narrower scale, since in each the tritone jump is first made all at once and then with an intervening step – an early instance of a classic Messiaen technique for achieving growth, by following an idea with its decorated repeat.

Dominant sevenths and triads are thus ranged on the steps of diminished-seventh chords, and thereby floated beyond the gravitational forces they would normally imply, for the need for a dominant seventh to resolve ceases to be felt when resolution is so long and so repeatedly refused. Messiaen enhances the effect of flotation by avoiding chords in root position, except where he would seem to be intending to introduce a shaft of light from a more normal musical world: this happens in the ninth bar of *Le banquet céleste*, where triads descend in whole tones as if opening a window on to Debussy.

Nevertheless, and even outside such moments as these, *Le banquet céleste* cannot wholly break with diatonic expectations: certainly not when it uses such chords as it does. Messiaen has stated his regret at his use of key signatures in his early music,[23] and clearly their meaning, like the entire meaning of the diatonic system, is changed by his practice. But if *Le banquet céleste* cannot be said to be 'in' its notated key of F sharp major, then quite definitely F sharp major is the key that it is not in, the key towards which it aspires. It starts with a dominant seventh of that key, but, very typically, Messiaen substitutes a tritone for the conventional fifth of the dominant–tonic relation, and so G appears to jam the wanted descent to F sharp. In fact that descent is impossible, for one of the nice features of the second mode is that it permits the construction of dominant sevenths for the very four keys whose tonics it does not contain. When F sharp does arrive, in the second bar, it is itself within the context of a seventh chord, with the E sharpened (and therefore introducing a note foreign to the second mode in this transposition) in order, so Messiaen suggests, to give a 'very intense tonal impression'[24] of F sharp major, shutting off the aspiration towards B major that would simply lead the music around the circle of fifths. In no sense, however, is even this 'very intense' F sharp a resolution of the opening chord of the piece, being so elevated, inverted and arriving by a chromatic movement of harmony and bass from the immediately preceding chord. Later appearances of F sharp major harmony are also much undermined, whether by being placed fleetingly on weak beats (if one may still speak of beat at this speed) or by inversion.

The slow swing in the first two bars between different transpositions of the mode continues in very similar fashion throughout most of the first part of the piece (bars 1–11). Then in the eleventh bar a melody appears in the pedals, keeping to the notes of the mode and preparing a return to the opening music. Briefly this opens out into the transposition of the mode not used so far (bar 16) before the scalewise descent of bar 8, F sharp–E–D sharp–C sharp, is slowly and repeatedly affirmed, reversing the standard dominant–tonic cadence and bringing the music back to rest in dominant-seventh harmony on C sharp. It is at the end as it was at the beginning, with only the sixth degree removed from the initial chord and the fifth inserted in its place. Without wishing to read too much into Messiaen's début composition, which lasts in all for only twenty-five bars (but six minutes at the marked speed), the frustrated nature of the harmony is evidently at one with the extreme tempo: both serve to contradict progression, as again does the small-scale and large-scale repetition. Right from the first, therefore, and even quite decisively, Messiaen abandons the attunement to measured progress that had been a feature of almost all Western music since the Renaissance. Moreover, he does so already by using the principal techniques for countering arrowed time in much of his later music: those of withholding diatonic resolution, proceeding with extraordinary slowness and moving through greater and smaller cycles of repetition within a single harmonic field, though one containing a great variety of chords organized in some other way than that of diatonic hierarchy.

Meanwhile, next summer at Fuligny, he completed the eight *Préludes* for the piano that he dedicated to Henriette Roget, a fellow student at the Conservatoire; she gave them their first public performance in Paris in 1931 at a concert of the Société Nationale. Here Messiaen was writing for the concert audience and not for the communicating congregation, besides which the piano is simply not capable of the sustained changeless sonorities on which *Le banquet céleste* so much depends. Accordingly the *Préludes* are a lot more brilliant and extrovert, but their basic harmonic axioms are the same, as is their simplicity of form.

At the same time a reference to Debussy is inescapable, in the title of the collection as a whole and in those of individual pieces from it, as well as in the sensitivity to keyboard resonance and qualities of texture. Sometimes the music comes so near Debussy as to verge on quotation, as when the second piece arrives at mellowed bass chords recalling the 'lointaine sonnerie de cors' of Debussy's Prelude 'Les sons et les parfums tournent dans l'air du soir', or when the third, for its subsidiary material looks out on 'Jardins sous la pluie'. However, Messiaen himself has pointed out that rhythmically he was 'very far from Debussy's divine liberty',[25] and the same is true on the formal plane, where his preference, as in *Le banquet céleste*, is for repetitive and symmetrical shapes. It is tempting to see these squarenesses of rhythm and form as being allied, even interdependent, but Messiaen's view would appear to be different. When Claude Samuel suggested in interview that Debussy's formal and rhythmic innovations were related, Messiaen insisted that they were 'two distinct domains',[26] giving a clue to that separation of the elements of music – mode, rhythm, instrumentation, form – that is one of the principal marks of his divergence from the Western tradition. And indeed later works, with rhythms much more various than those of the *Préludes*, will be contained in forms similarly static and reiterative.

The real justification for such structures is to be found in the notion of time they embody, and also perhaps, on the level of material, in

Messiaen's choice of pitch structures that invite permanence rather than progression: his modes of limited transpositions, and harmonies made to sound like natural resonances. Repetition is the enemy of progress, and as such it was gradually extinguished during the development of Western music from Bach to Schoenberg, in keeping with an almost universal principle that though music might vary its rate of motion, that motion must always be experienced as forward-directed (the rise of accurate chronometry during the same period is presumably not unrelated). By contrast, even Messiaen's very earliest published compositions, *Le banquet céleste* and the *Préludes*, forgo the directional movement of diatonic-symphonic music in favour of the stasis of symmetrical modality and the circular return of repetitive form. Where we observe most Western works as single threads of time drawn through the loop of the perceptual present, Messiaen's first works invite us to see the thread as being stopped (first chord of *Le banquet céleste*) or else circular, so that the same events recur unchanged.

For example, the first and shortest of the *Préludes*, 'La colombe', simply has two five-bar sections which are both repeated before a tiny coda brings the music to rest in its tonality of E major coloured by mode 2. And this coda is not a resolution but rather an explanation of stasis in that it exemplifies Messiaen's imitation, again following Debussy, of natural resonance (see example 3). The staccato chord in the bass

Ex. 3   Préludes   *1 'La colombe'*

provides the fundamental and the first overtone while the next five overtones are sounding in the sustained chord, and though it ought to need a piano tuned in just intonation for the resonances to be properly activated, the nearness of even temperament is enough to deceive the mechanism of the instrument and the ear. Moreover, if resonance is the model for harmony, as so often in Messiaen it is, then dissonances can be accommodated as high partials: that happens here in the diminished double octaves in the high treble, which more reinforce than disturb the grounding on E.

The preludes that follow are neither structurally nor harmonically so straightforward as 'La colombe', but formal symmetry continues to operate. The third and fourth, 'Le nombre léger' and 'Instants défunts', are both in varieties of ABABA form; the fifth, 'Les sons impalpables du rêve', expands this to ABACABA with a change to the minor for the middle section, and the second, 'Chant d'extase dans un paysage triste', completes the triune division with a CDC middle section, this time in the major within a minor context. One may reasonably assume that this centrepiece, in the favoured key of F sharp major turned by mode 2 towards dominant interests, is the ecstatic song and the outer sections its landscape, just as the title of the sixth prelude, 'Cloches d'angoisse et larmes d'adieu', seems to apply quite literally to a two-part structure. The seventh piece, 'Plainte calme', has the simple symmetrical pattern AABBA, and it is only the last, 'Un reflet dans le vent . . .', that essays a more developing kind of form. Messiaen calls it, indeed, a sonata,[27] but the sections are quite baldly set off from one another, and the use of the key a fifth above for the secondary material does not have the same effect in Messiaen's harmonic world.

One reason why has already been indicated in much of the set, as it has also in *Le banquet céleste*: it is the substitution of the tritone for the conventional dominant. At the start of 'Cloches d'angoisse', for instance, the key signature and the tolling pedal (out of Ravel's 'Le gibet') prepare for C minor, but the piece prefers a ninth chord on D flat, an augmented fourth below the pedal, and to be understood not as a dominant itself but as an assertion of a modal tonic. Example 4 introduces a new mode of limited transpositions, Messiaen's third, which consists of pairs of semitones alternating with whole tones, so that the repeating unit is the major third and the underlying structure the augmented triad, not the diminished-seventh chord as it is in the second mode: once more, though, this underlying structure is a tonally unsettling one. In the *Préludes* the third mode shares the arena quite evenly with the second: Nos. 1, 2, 3 and 7 are largely occupied with mode 2 and Nos. 4 and 8 with mode 3, while in Nos. 5 and 6, the two pieces the mature Messiaen finds most attractive,[28] both modes are important. Altogether the eight preludes can be seen as a first compendium of harmonic and melodic traits connected with these two modes – which gives them a flavour wholly different from Debussy's – with some slight interference from other modes Messiaen has described; they testify to how he had 'acquired a very quick familiarity' with his modal system 'while improvising daily on my modes at the organ class'.[29]

There are in sum sixteen modes that qualify under Messiaen's

Ex. 4 Préludes 6 'Cloches d'angoisse et larmes d'adieu'

definition as being 'of limited transpositions', but some of them can be discounted: the chromatic scale, with its single transposition, offers no melodic or harmonic limitations whatsoever; the diminished-seventh chord and the augmented triad are both much too limited, as indeed is the mode consisting simply of a tritone. That leaves the twelve shown in example 5, which also indicates the number of different transpositions, the name (if any) given to the mode by Messiaen, and the triads that can be formed with the notes of the mode.

Messiaen's omission, and neglect, of the mode alternating semitones and minor thirds might seem curious, particularly in view of its interesting provision of triads on the steps of an augmented triad; but no doubt he would regard it as a truncated mode 3, which has this property in double measure. Of the modes he does distinguish, the second and third are far and away of greatest importance, in his output as a whole as well as in the *Préludes*. Modes 4 and 5 are exotic rarities, not found in these piano pieces, but mode 6 crops up in 'Instants défunts' (especially bars 23ff.), 'Les sons impalpables' (bar 16)[30] and 'Cloches d'angoisse' (bar 5 etc.).[31] Mode 7 is so chromatic as to be of dubious usefulness, though it may perhaps be implicated at points where Messiaen's harmony is most uncertain. The most striking example of this in the *Préludes* comes at the start of 'Instants défunts', whose first two bars can be understood as operating within mode 7 (see example 6).

However, the ear is more likely to register semitonal shift (implying a change of mode, not a continuation within the same area) and the interval of a tritone, followed by a very hesitant expression of D minor and then a characteristically unorthodox route to A major (an answering phrase ends in D major). Also characteristic is the flowering of consonance after a section of boxed-in chromaticism, while the use in the first bar of a symmetrical arrangement of note values presents us with a first example of what is, in Messiaen's self-confessedly ungainly terms, a 'non-retrogradable rhythm': one that reads the same forwards and backwards. There is clearly a link of symmetry between the modes of limited transpositions and the non-retrogradable rhythms: not for nothing is the first chapter of Messiaen's compositional treatise concerned with the 'charm of impossibilities'.[32] 'This charm,' he there states,

> at once voluptuous and contemplative [i.e., as timeless as sexuality or religion], resides particularly in certain mathematical impossibilities of the modal and rhythmic domains. Modes which cannot be transposed beyond a certain number of transpositions, because one always falls again into the same notes; rhythms which cannot be used in retrograde, because in such a case one finds the same order of values again – these are two striking impossibilities.

It seems likely that the attractiveness of non-retrogradable rhythms for Messiaen resides not only in this charm but also in the way such rhythms might appear as images of the reversibility of time. However, there are difficulties here. Rhythms such as that in the first bar of example 6 are non-retrogradable in their durations but not in their attack points: their palindromic, reversible nature may therefore be more apparent when they are played on an instrument that tends to bring out duration, such as the organ, rather than on the piano, which emphasizes attack point. Here the effect is more likely to be of a stumbling division of the 3/4 bar, in keeping with the chromatic harmony just as the even crotchets of the third bar accord with triads.

In the modal area, the 'charm of impossibilities' must lead, as has already been well noted in the case of mode 2, to a harmony that is circuitous and static rather than, as in the diatonic system, progressive. The modes give rise to triads related not by dynamic fifths but by more ambivalent entities: the diminished-seventh chord (mode 2), the augmented triad (mode 3) and the tritone (modes 4 and 6). Correspondingly, the tendency is for music founded on these modes to remain in one ambiguous area, and then perhaps to shift to another, but not to modulate and so develop. That raises problems when Messiaen makes an exceedingly rare attempt at sonata form, as he does in the last prelude, but it has its consequences too when he comes to write any music of long duration.

Ex. 5   Modes of Limited Transpositions

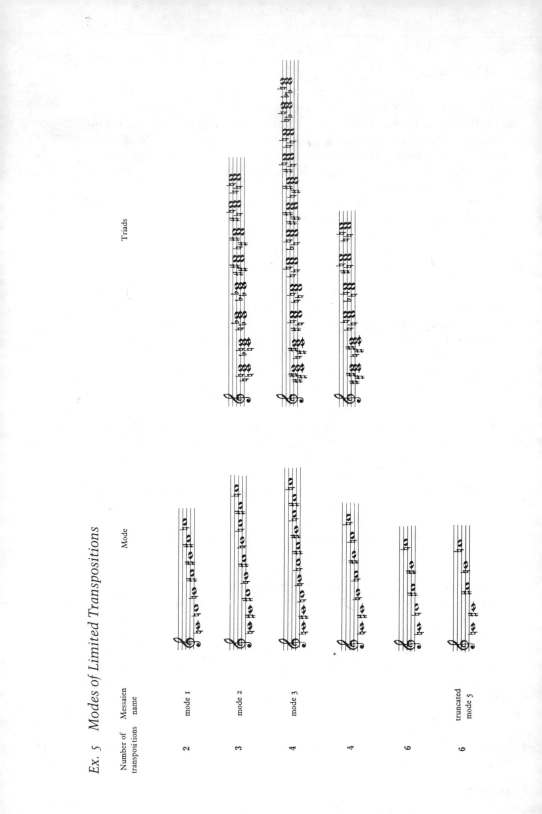

| Number of transpositions | Messaien name | Mode | | Triads |

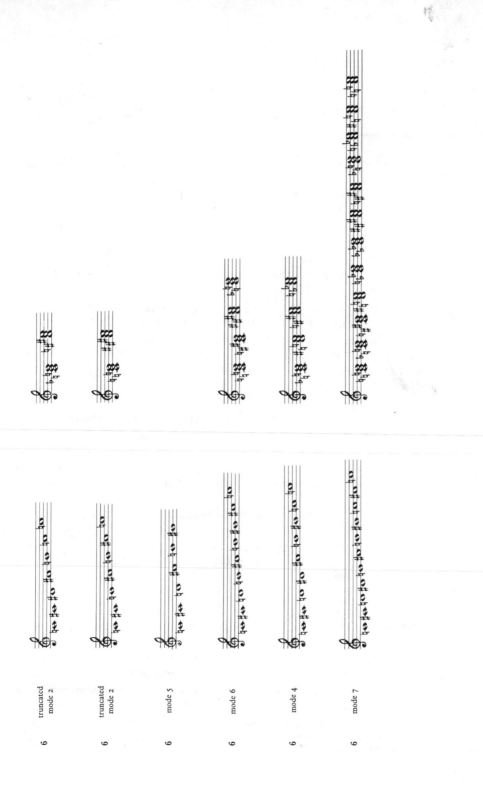

Ex. 6   Préludes   *4 'Instants défunts'*

Inevitably, therefore, the lack of development is most powerfully felt in 'Cloches d'angoisse', which, playing for about nine minutes, is the longest piece in the volume. The whole composition can be understood as a vast expansion of the diminished-seventh chord. In the first half the embrace of G and D flat is joined by chains of chords in mode 6 (right hand) and mode 2 (left hand), the transpositions chosen so that the two triads held in common by the modes are those of B flat (A sharp) and E, completing the diminished-seventh chord (see example 4). The second half takes up a four-chord fragment from the first and disposes it in radiant B major inflected by mode 2 towards the dominant and also towards, once more, the diminished-seventh chord (see example 7). The slow tempo here is essential to the atmosphere of total *naïveté* that makes such usage of cheapened harmonies not only permissible but even right and powerful, which it becomes because it brings into being the new conception of time. The diminished-seventh chord is no longer a moment of thrilling uncertainty in a passage of progress: it is the whole event, lengthily elaborated. When the end arrives, all that has happened is that the opening tritone has been shifted from G–D flat to B–E sharp as the bells of anguish have been transformed into the tears of farewell.

The simultaneous use of two different modes, seen briefly in 'Cloches d'angoisse', is more substantial a feature of 'Les sons impalpables', where a principal harmonized voice in mode 2 is heard against a chiming ostinato of chords in mode 3. Any transpositions of these two modes will share just two triads a minor third apart; in this case the triads are those of A and F sharp, and the choice is not accidental, since A major is the central key of the piece,[33] which ends with all the notes of mode 3 piled into a chord on A that again suggests natural resonance.

A major is also the central key of the set. Its dominant, E major, is the key of 'La colombe' and 'Le nombre léger', and its subdominant is that of 'Instants défunts' (rather nominally) and of 'Un reflet' (much more definitely). Its relative minor of F sharp underpins the 'Chant d'extase', and B major, its dominant's dominant, is of prime importance in 'Cloches d'angoisse'. The only outsider is 'Plainte calme', which hovers

Ex. 7   Préludes   6 *'Cloches d'angoisse et larmes d'adieu'*

in Skryabinesque fashion within the diminished-seventh chord on F. There are therefore seven preludes grouped around A major, just as there are seven chief modes of limited transpositions, and one may wonder whether in both cases Messiaen was influenced in his numbering by the perfection traditionally associated with the number seven and by Newton's (similarly influenced) seven colours of the rainbow. Certainly the decision to number some modes and not others appears a little arbitrary, and Messiaen has said that at the time of the *Préludes* he was already speaking of a 'rainbow of chords'.[34] This is very much how the polymodality of a passage such as example 4 is to be understood, the different chords splashing different tints on to a screen of sustained colour. And if we are to follow Messiaen in his association of particular harmonies with a real sense of particular colours, then the *Préludes'* basic screen of A major is a screen of intense blue.

There was also other compositional business to be done in this year of 1929. Messiaen entered for the Prix de Rome, writing a fugue on the given subject by Georges Hüe and a choral setting of 'Sainte Bohême' from Banville's *Odes funambulesques*. These were not judged worthy for him to go forward to the final round, but the next year he did, and composed the regulation cantata, *La mer*. Following many other distinguished French composers, however, he failed to win the prize, and he made no further attempt, for in 1931, having left the Conservatoire, he was appointed organist of La Trinité in Paris. He may also have felt the academic constraints of the Prix de Rome to have become redundant in view of the other music he had composed in 1930: the *Diptyque* for organ, the cantata *La mort du nombre*, the *Trois mélodies* and the first orchestral score he was to publish, *Les offrandes oubliées*, this last the fruit of another Fuligny summer, whereas the smaller works were done in Paris.

The *Diptyque* is subtitled 'essay on earthly life and blessed eternity'; it is also dedicated jointly to 'mes chers maîtres Paul Dukas et Marcel Dupré', and though it would be invidious to apportion the two segments to the two masters, the first part is distinctly indebted to Dupré, much more so than is anything else in Messiaen's organ music. Moreover, the debt is precisely to the staccato toccata manner that Messiaen was to single out in his appreciation of his teacher: a moto perpetuo of close chords in a very chromatic C minor is subjected to variation, first around G minor and then around F minor, before coming to a crisis in canon at the octave.

There are simple canons in the *Préludes*, too, including one by inversion (in the middle section of 'Instants défunts'), for canon in these terms is essentially a technique of repetition, and it is the young Messiaen's only alternative to homophony or to the inactive counterpoint where one voice is simply the background for another, as in all the quotations above from the *Préludes*. Any more engaged intertwining of parts would inevitably lead towards development, which can have no place in his music except when it appears in a section of compartmentalized alteration: a decoration of an initial image, or a paraphrase. This is what happens in the opening section of the *Diptyque*, though the material is so ostinato-obsessed and so tonally wavering that the sections join to produce a static continuum, whose disruption the canon announces.

Dupré at this point, if he had countenanced music where virtuosity of performance is so inwardly directed by the closeness of the harmony, might have launched into a fugue. Messiaen now parts company with him completely by discovering a kind of music that will reappear in his works, an exceedingly slow melodic ascent through the sweet vapours of added-sixth and diminished-seventh chords arranged on the circular steps of mode 2. The feeling is both rapt and wrapped: ecstatic in its denial of the flow of time (the principles are essentially as in *Le banquet céleste*), and warmly enclosed in its harmonic nature, particularly in its use of the added-sixth chord, where the tonic is partly felt to be enclosed as mediant within its relative minor.

A decade later Messiaen arranged this second part of the work for violin and piano to make it the finale of his *Quatuor pour la fin du temps*, transposing it up to E major. That key he had already proved suitable for such music in the last section of *Les offrandes oubliées*, a triptych to set beside the *Diptyque* of the same year, having three elements whose meanings are explained in a poetic prologue to the score:

Les bras étendus, triste jusqu'à la mort,
sur l'arbre de la Croix vous repandez votre sang.
Vous nous aimez, doux Jésus, nous l'avions oublié.

Poussés par la folie et le dard du serpent,
dans une course haletante, effrénée, sans relâche,
nous descendions dans le péché comme dans un tombeau.

Voici la table pure, la source de la charité,
le banquet du pauvre, voici la Pitié adorable offrant le pain
*   de la Vie et de l'Amour.*
Vous nous aimez, doux Jésus, nous l'avions oublié.[35]

Clearly the 'forgotten offerings' of the title are God's redemptive sacrifice and the adoration due to him in return; and it may seem odd that Messiaen should have wished to introduce such religious teaching into the orchestral repertory. But symphonic meditations on sacred things had long been acceptable in France from organist-composers, who were expected to be religious. Messiaen, too, was responding to what he has always seen as his purpose, that of presenting the truths of the Catholic church in a musical form: it is the set of *Préludes* where no religious subject is to be found, that constitutes the exception in his output.

It is no surprise, therefore, that the three little stanzas of the poem should correspond closely with the three sections of the piece. Like the two parts of the *Diptyque*, they are united by a common melodic motif, but this is in both works less a theme than a signature, not the fount of the music but an inscription upon it: that, of course, is a function of Messiaen's being a non-developmental art, and it leads to one's perception of the theme as an indicator of musical changes for which it is not responsible, a litmus paper inserted from outside in order to render different musical states comprehensible. In the first part of *Les offrandes oubliées* it is played by strings and high woodwind, and later by low strings and bassoons, with harmonic support from clarinets and horns (example 8(a)). In the second it is thrown out by a solo trumpet across heaving chords (example 8(b)). And in the last, exactly as in the last part of the *Diptyque*, it becomes the starting point for a long melody, with the E minor connotations of the first part now replaced by

E major luminously coloured by mode 2: Christ's sacrifice has been
recognized in the Eucharistic celebration, and the circle of love rejoined
(example 8(c)).

Ex. 8   Les offrandes oubliées

(a)

(b)

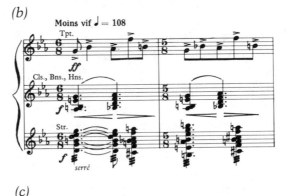

(c)

Meditation on the mass, or meditation on the eternal's presence, has
already appeared as essential to Messiaen's thought, but the earlier
sections of *Les offrandes oubliées*, illustrating Christ's passion and the
headlong rush of sin, are altogether less typical. The first has something
of the character of Bartók. Strings in octaves play a modal chant divided
irregularly into groups of one, two or three quavers: Messiaen was later
to describe them as 'neumes',[36] indicating the importance of plainsong
to him as a model of melody. Here the neumatic melody is twice
interrupted by contrary scales in mode 3, which Messiaen, characteristically hearing harmony as colour, describes as 'long grey and mauve

wailings'. The second of these wailings is followed by the theme as shown in example 8(a).

The middle section, marked 'fierce, desperate, panting', is a savage presto of weightily scored and irregular shapes, a race into the abyss for which Messiaen learned much from *The Rite of Spring* and also from *L'apprenti sorcier* of his composition teacher. The style is not one he was to find much future use for, and this passage is the one that indicates most clearly its composer was still only 21. It is also problematic as an image of sin, which one might think more enticingly pictured in the sweetness and opulence of the finale, even if Messiaen was here thinking of divine love expressed in the Eucharist. The problem of interpretation is one that will recur, as could hardly fail to be the case when a composer in a godless age elects to understand his music as explanatory of his Catholic faith; and Messiaen's awareness that there is a difficulty here is suggested by his commentaries and textual inscriptions, which become ever more detailed from this point onwards. Nor is it odd that the issue of intention should be raised by what was the first of his works designed for the larger concert public, who had a first chance to hear it when Walter Straram, a great champion of new French music, conducted it at one of his concerts in Paris on 19 February 1931.

The alternative to giving his works verbal explanations was for Messiaen to provide them with sung texts, as he did in the two other compositions of 1930, the *Trois mélodies* and *La mort du nombre*. Like all his later published vocal works, these set words of his own: the only piece in which he has set another poet, apart from the very early Villon songs, is the central number of the *Trois mélodies*, which takes a short lyric from Sauvage, though not from her maternal collection. Thus doubly enfolding his mother, within his music and then within his songs, Messiaen may have intended the *Trois mélodies* as a remembrance of her, for she had died in 1927, too soon to see the flowering of the artistic gifts she had predicted for her son. In the first song, 'Pourquoi?', the singer asks why the delights of nature have lost their appeal for her (and this is definitely a soprano cycle, a first intimation of the larger works Messiaen was to write for soprano before the end of the decade). The Sauvage setting, 'Le sourire', is a pianissimo expression of love's tender fragility, breathed by the singer over diminished-seventh harmony. Then 'La fiancée perdue' joyfully exults in the pleasures of the beloved, which are the pleasures of nature (the Song of Songs will be a repeated poetic influence on Messiaen), before moving inwards from E major to D major for a final prayer that she may have rest.

La mort du nombre is equally concerned with death and eternal life. It is a dialogue of two souls, soprano and tenor, accompanied by a piano and joined also by a violin, which starts the work muted and alone with a line of melody. The key signature here suggests D minor, but the music belongs rather in the Aeolian mode on A, and the opening tenor recitative is also modal in the old sense, beginning in Dorian D. The tenor sings of the flight of his beloved's soul as a brilliant light; there is then a return of the violin melody, after which he sings in more agitated, chromatic style of his distance from his beloved. She then sings a consolatory sentence in D major coloured by mode 2, after which the tenor repeats his anxieties and she repeats her gentle encouragement, now in E major influenced by mode 2, a warm area familiar from 'La colombe' and Les offrandes oubliées. The tenor follows this with a longer statement of his desperation and hopelessness, at the end of which the soprano simply bids him wait and hope, to chords of F major and D major. The violin returns, now with piano accompaniment and in untroubled B major (the first fourteen bars have no accidental: the longest such stretch in Messiaen). What it introduces is a concluding aria for the soprano in which she sings of joy in the resurrected body and then of the 'song of our conjoined soul', given out by the violin in a slow high flight that ends the cantata, still in B major with the usual added sixth. Messiaen's choice of key here has led some[37] to suggest a parallel with Tristan und Isolde, but if there is a connection with another work it is more closely with the prelude 'Cloches d'angoisse et larmes d'adieu', where again B major is important, and where the 'tears of farewell' seem to be tears of joy in release from earlier travails. Less exceptionable is the notion that La mort du nombre resembles Bach's conversation of souls in his cantata O Ewigkeit, du Donnerwort (BWV 60), though any direct influence is unlikely when poetically and musically the piece belongs so firmly with Messiaen's other works of the period.

Indeed, the 'death of number' must have been one of his most conscious preoccupations around 1930, for it is the death of counting, the death of time: something to be encountered in the resurrected eternity of the Diptyque, the Trois mélodies and La mort du nombre itself, or else tasted in the communion celebrated in Le banquet céleste and Les offrandes oubliées. In all these works the image of eternity is, very reasonably, one of harmonic stasis, accentuated either by repetitive figuration, as in the two vocal works, or else by extreme slowness: the choice is, of course, largely a matter of medium, since the piano of the songs and cantata cannot manage the organ's or the orchestra's sustained sounds. The final section of Les offrandes oubliées is particularly demanding in this regard. Both the earlier sections avoid metrical regularity, the Bartókian changing bar lengths of the first being followed by Stravinskyan oppositions in the second (especially at the end, where one kind of music in progressive diminution, from six beats to five to four to two, is interleaved with another in progressive augmentation, from one beat to three to five). It is, however, in the closing pages that the rule of regularity is most completely destroyed. At the notated tempo here the smallest duration is over a second and a half, and each bar lasts for more than thirteen seconds.

Under such circumstances no sense of pulse or of metre is possible. Instead the melody of the violins moves when it wills over what Messiaen calls its 'carpet of pianissimo chords, with reds, golds and blues (like a distant stained-glass window), in the light of muted string soloists'.[38] And the final chord, which might well have been written as a full bar with a pause, is instead carefully marked to last for thirteen quavers, providing an early instance of Messiaen's self-confessed 'marked predilection for the rhythms of prime numbers'.[39] It is also an early instance of his delight in number symbolism and other conceits that are bound to remain latent, behind the existence of the music as sound. One may wonder whether this secretness, this essential independence from the music, is a property too of its theological substance.

CHAPTER 3

La Trinité

The second of Messiaen's orchestral works to reach the concert public, a year later, was *Le tombeau resplendissant* (1931), the product of another summer at Fuligny. The orchestra is the same as that of *Les offrandes oubliées*, and so too is the basic structural principle: again there are three different kinds of music signed with motivic connections, but now the first, hectic like the middle part of the earlier work, reappears to make a four-part form A (*vif*) – B (*modéré*) – A' (*vif*) – C (*lent*). The ending is even again in modally perfumed E major and scored for muted strings, though this time the image is simpler: a melody for the violas and cellos in unison rises up to join a high E major chord sustained in violin harmonics throughout.

One might well conclude that the work is another meditation on the Eucharist, and that the 'resplendent tomb' is the tabernacle on the altar. Henri Martelli's report on the first performance duly confirms this by reproducing a poem by Messiaen said to be inscribed on the score, which begins, 'I sing the gift of the divine essence, The body of Jesus Christ, His body and his blood.'[1] However, the present score has a rather different poetic preface, making the work very much more autobiographical, and seeming to fit the music much better because, like the poem of *Les offrandes oubliées*, it is in sections corresponding to the musical form. The first begins, 'My youth is dead' and speaks of 'anger like a volley of blood, anger like a hammer blow. . . . Despair and tears!' Looking back to that lost youth, the second remembers a 'music of flowers' and a 'joyously melancholy' melody (perhaps the oboe solo fixed on the diminished-seventh chord on C). The third returns to the theme of the first in even more violent language, just as the music of the third part is still more tempestuous than before, and the fourth identifies the 'resplendent tomb' as the 'tomb of my youth', though in quoting from the Beatitudes it makes it quite clear that repose has been found in acceptance of God.

Perhaps embarrassed by this soul-bearing programme, which one might conclude he suppressed at the time of the first performance, Messiaen preferred for many years to seal up the work in the tomb of his publisher's library, and it was only in the 1980s that it began to be regularly performed again, revealing it as one more expression of that stinging intemperate anger that erupts occasionally in the music of the young Messiaen, and that in this very work he shows himself mastering in acquiescence in the divine will. Musically it is a matter of intense chromaticism being diverted into something serenely diatonic: one of the most important aspects of the modes of limited transpositions is that they provide avenues for that tactic.

But if Messiaen had by now thoroughly mastered his modal style, some future experiences were still to be decisive. Among them may probably be counted his first encounter with the Balinese gamelan, at the Exposition Coloniale held in the Bois de Vincennes in 1931, the year of *Le tombeau resplendissant*. One singles this out not only because of a pleasing symmetry with Debussy's discovery of Javanese music at the Exposition of 1889, but also because of a close kinship of technique and even aim between Messiaen's and Eastern music. For though the actual sound of the gamelan was not to enter his orchestra until the *Trois petites liturgies* of a dozen years later, he had already been instructed in Indian rhythmic formulae as catalogued in the Lavignac encyclopedia, and also, much more importantly, the whole tenor of his work had suggested a dissatisfaction with European progressive time and with Western views of music as polite social entertainment, emotional confession or abstract recreation of the mind. Very little in Messiaen is polite; almost nothing is abstract; and though the subjectiveness of his music is open to debate, in conscious intention it is objective, concerned only with the conveyance by the most suitable means of holy truth, or, more rarely, secular verities which again have the force of myth and therefore of feelings not personally defined but presumed to be general.

His enthusiasm for the music of Bali and India (and later Japan) may therefore be understood not only as a longing for the East common among French composers since the Middle Ages, but also as an acknowledgement of a shared feeling for time as static or circular and of shared goals in the presenting of mythical stories, the achievement of contact with mental material that has passed unchanged through generations, transcending time. There are, however, difficulties with this parallel, and they go to the heart of Messiaen's music. In the first place, Messiaen cannot presume his subject matter to have any widespread spiritual significance for his audience: the case is utterly different from that which obtains when Balinese musicians and dancers gather to enact a ceremonial. And even if we discount Messiaen's theological intentions, there are still problems connected with his belonging to a musical culture that has grown to serve a quite different notion of time, and a quite different notion of the nature of composition. For though Balinese music also has its composers, the culture is much stronger than any individual ego. Messiaen is by contrast working within an exceedingly weak culture, where a great many of his decisions have to be his own, and where his personality will be invoked whenever his music is performed, heard, discussed or written about. To create religious, and therefore supra-personal art in such a culture goes against the grain, exactly as it goes against the grain of Western music for progressive time to be abandoned. In both cases the costs are high. Messiaen's wish to encapsulate a circular or stationary experience of time drastically reduces his formal options to the repetitive and symmetrical, while as a religious artist he has had to contend, as the literature amply shows, with widespread incomprehension from both detractors and supporters. Indeed, it may be that at this stage of Western culture religious art is impossible except as a spiritual exercise for the creating individual.

The problems of religious intention in art have of course been felt in Western church music ever since composers began to emerge as individuals, a phenomenon which one may place in the twelfth-century school of Notre Dame. Messiaen's awareness of those problems is surely at the root of his view that the only proper liturgical music is plainsong,[2] but he is equally adamant in stating the religious dimension of his own music:

> The first idea that I have wanted to express . . . is the existence of the truths of the Catholic faith. . . . That is the first aspect of my work, the most noble, doubtless the most useful, the most valuable, the only one, perhaps, that I will not regret at the hour of my death.[3]

To accept that this is Messiaen's intention, however, is not to accept that it is, or need be, a primary route towards the understanding of his music. We may do better to consider his as a mental rather than a spiritual art, one providing experiences for the imagination that go beyond the natural in ways suggested by his religion and his ornithology: experiences of weightlessness, great clarity and timelessness, of flight and joy (hence the great number of works dealing with resurrected existence). Moreover, to understand Messiaen in terms of his religious intentions would seem to be going at things the wrong way round. If Messiaen's is a religious art, then its subject is vastly more important than its substance, and it would seem an exercise of doubtful value to bring the whole theology of sin and redemption to bear on the analysis of *Les offrandes oubliées*, for example. At the same time, religious elements can hardly be ignored when they become so numerous and operate in such a variety of ways. Firstly, there are the titles, superscriptions and programme notes with which Messiaen's music is increasingly supported from *Les offrandes oubliées* onwards.

Secondly, there are the messages inserted directly into the musical substance in the form of quotations from plainsong. Thirdly, there are more concealed messages, sometimes amounting to a language of symbols, in which number and motif can be endowed with quite precise meanings, even if one may argue that those meanings can be understood only with reference to the composer's notes. And fourthly there are matters of style, which become much more difficult to define as religious.

One might have supposed, for instance, that the contemplation of the divinity could not be noisy, harsh or vigorous, were it not that Messiaen has shown repeatedly that it can be. Indeed, one of his great efforts has been to enlarge the scope of religious music by responding, as he sees it, to sacred texts that may hugely challenge the imagination to the extent that they are appalling or awe-inspiring: he is scornful of those who would expect instead something 'saccharine, vaguely mystical and above all soporific',[4] though it could be said he has found it possible to write exactly this kind of music in such movements as the finales of the *Diptyque* and *Les offrandes oubliées*. However that may be, certain criteria of musical spirituality do seem to remain. Most notably, the diatonic system is by long convention, if not by inherent nature, a humanist language. Music that would speak of the divine has to wield its triads in other ways or else avoid them altogether, which is perhaps because we accept the major–minor system as some sort of musical reality and associate excursions from it with experiences beyond the normal. Messiaen himself may be thinking in these terms when he says that music can encompass 'an opening towards the beyond, towards the invisible and the unsayable, which can be made with the help of *sound-colour* and amounts to a sensation of *dazzlement*' (his italics).[5]

Unarguably a composer is likely to produce such a sensation when his mind is on the wondrous rather than the monitory, which must at least partly explain Messiaen's concentration on what is most miraculous in the Christian faith: the birth of Christ, his Transfiguration and Ascension, his reappearance on earth in the Eucharist, the promised resurrection of all faithful souls, and the apocalyptic vision of St John. It is also fairly clear that his creative focus on what is strange and spectacular in his faith has opened him to discoveries of what is strange and spectacular in his art, and it is surely here that discussion must begin. Indeed, Messiaen's own very apt appeal to the phenomenon of 'dazzlement' might presuppose as much, for if the mind is dazzled, it is dazzled by it knows not what: the music makes its effect in the first place by virtue only of what it parades in sound and time, not by the intentions that may crowd around it. And there is considerable evidence that the music does make its effect in this way. After all, it would be absurd, or worse, to have to conclude that Messiaen had become one of the most admired composers of his age by virtue of his creative adherence to a faith in which only a minority of his audience had any belief.

This is not, of course, to question the very profound character of his own belief. If we cannot with confidence see that belief as being expressed in his music, it is indisputably expressed in his music's intentions, as it is in his work as a practising musician in the worship of the Church, this continuing ever since his appointment as organist in the north Parisian church of La Trinité. The basilica of La Trinité was one of several churches in Paris to be endowed with organs by Aristide Cavaillé-Coll (1811–1899), and all of Messiaen's organ works are intended in the first place for the sort of grand romantic instrument that builder created: his precise stipulation of stops, following in French tradition, is an indication of this. Composing, however, is the least of the church musician's duties. Except for interruptions due to the war (1940–1) and then to a rebuilding of his instrument (1964–6) Messiaen has played regularly on Sundays at La Trinité at vespers and at three masses, accompanying plainsong at high mass, playing 'classical and romantic music' at the 11 o'clock mass, and performing his own works at the midday office.[6]

Among those works, however, there are few that are suitable for liturgical use. Unlike Tournemire, who composed his way through the church year, Messiaen has written only one organ mass, the *Messe de la Pentecôte* (1949–50). Instead he has preferred the medium of the organ recital, to which he first contributed some small pieces, the *Diptyque* and *Apparition de l'église éternelle* (1932), but which he then made the forum for works big enough to constitute whole programmes in themselves, forming personal liturgies of meditation: *La Nativité du Seigneur* (1935) and *Les corps glorieux* (1939). During this period his only more conventionally liturgical composition – and his only sung contribution to the liturgy at all – was the simple communion motet *O sacrum convivium!* of 1937, a brief presence at the mystery considered from further off in *Les offrandes oubliées* and many later compositions of this period and beyond.

Of course, *La Nativité* and *Les corps glorieux* differ from *Les offrandes oubliées* in that they have their natural home in church, since that is where organs are normally to be found. It is, however, the instrument rather than the building that seems to be of the essence. To begin with, Messiaen started writing for the organ at a time when its attractiveness to contemporary composers was small: since the turn of the century only Reger had found much use for it at all. Messiaen therefore had the opportunity to bring to the organ for the first time a modern feeling for varieties of timbre, and his preface to *La Nativité* shows how proud he was of this innovation. But the very nature of the organ was also important, for it allowed him to experiment directly with combinations of timbre: the only parallel is Cage's prepared piano, developed at very much the same time.

Two more aspects of the organ lent themselves to Messiaen's musical needs. The first was its immateriality. Generally, and specifically at La Trinité, one hears organ music without being able to see the organist, and so the musical experience is divorced from any visual experience of its performance. Not only may this bodilessness enhance the music's spiritual aura, it also acts more demonstrably to change the way the music is perceived: the invitation is that one should feel oneself to be passing through the music as it happens, rather than observing its passage at some point in one's consciousness. It is the difference between being a participant and being an observer; it is also the difference between liturgy and drama; and it is fundamentally, once more, a difference in the perception of time, a difference between opening oneself to the music's measurement of time and checking that measurement against one's internal time sense. And though this is only tangentially to do with actual durations, the organ's ability to furnish long changeless durations is unique, and important enough to count here as a final point in its usefulness to Messiaen, as already demonstrated in the first chord of his first published composition.

All that has been said in general terms about La Nativité and Les corps glorieux applies equally to L'Ascension in the organ version Messiaen made in 1933–4 from his orchestral original of 1932–3 – and the fact that he made such a transcription of his first big orchestral work (Les offrandes oubliées he had transcribed in the more normal way for the piano) is some indication of the primacy of the organ in his musical thinking during the eight years between his appointment to La Trinité and the outbreak of the Second World War. After that he was to write for the organ much more infrequently, adding two more large works to the repertory in 1950–1 and then another only in 1969. But during the thirties he was very much an organist-composer.

The first piece he wrote at La Trinité, Apparition de l'église éternelle, is conceived entirely in chords moving very slowly but with the utmost determination. Their harmony is unusual, the basic image being an implacable growth from chromatic tritonal darkness to the strong light of bare fifths, this typically taking place on groupings of three chords that double in value from quaver to crotchet to minim (hence a sevenfold, prime-number rhythm). Harmony and rhythm together provide an emblem of the unalterable edifice appearing out of confusion: in Messiaen's own words, the piece is an 'enormous and granite-like crescendo',[7] in which the church comes ever nearer until it is bathed in a C major chord long sustained by both manuals and pedals; there is then a corresponding departure.

L'Ascension, essentially composed in the same year, is a work of much more complex form, which therefore demands much fuller explanation of its meaning, or so Messiaen's movement titles and inscriptions would seem to imply. There are four 'symphonic meditations' (the term is the same he had used for Les offrandes oubliées), and they all, though this is not precisely indicated, have texts relating to the Ascension Day office. The first, 'Majesté du Christ demandant sa gloire à son Père', and the last, 'Prière du Christ montant vers son Père', have words from John 17, of which the quotation above the latter movement is said at First Vespers of the Ascension: 'Father ... I have manifested thy name unto the men. ... And now I am no more in the world, but these are in the world, and I come to thee.' Between these musical voicings of Christ's solemn prayer come two exclamations on the Ascension as seen from earth: 'Alléluias sereins d'une âme qui désire le ciel' and 'Alléluia sur la trompette, alléluia sur la cymbale', the first inscribed with a prayer for resurrection that comes from the Collect of the Ascension mass, the second having a text from Psalm 47 – 'God is gone up with a shout, the Lord with the sound of a trumpet' – that occurs more than once in the liturgy for Ascension Day.

The first movement, bearing the words 'Father, the hour is come; glorify thy Son, that thy Son also may glorify thee', is scored only for wind instruments, these reinforcing a tone of festal solemnity that suggests Berlioz's Grande symphonie funèbre et triomphale. Like the Berlioz, this is outdoor music, presaging the bold, big design of a much later work, Et exspecto resurrectionem mortuorum, which Messiaen was to imagine performed among high mountains (and it is surely no accident that his first large-scale work should be concerning itself with a miracle on a mountain). Christ's prayer in this movement would seem to be carried in alternation by the trumpets, and the presence throughout of a strongly modal trumpet melody rather suggests the influence of plainsong, perhaps of the plainsong setting of the prayer of Christ reported by St John (see example 9(b)).

Example 9(a) shows the start of the work. The first sound is a G sharp minor chord with an added A, a dissonance relieved by the melodic fall to E sharp that produces a whole-tone chord instancing one of Messiaen's preferred interval patterns (two–four–two semitones: see, for example, examples 19, 26 and 41, pp. 81, 96 and 128, for some contrasted melodic expressions). After this nesting of two tritones the melody rises through a tritone, which interval then finds itself in conflict with the fifth as the B is underlined by a chord of F major. The inclination of the melody is to treat B as the dominant of E sharp, but the harmony insists that the real dominant of E sharp, or F, is C, and then that if B is to be understood as a dominant, it can be only as the dominant of E: hence the massive E major chord with which the first phrase ends. This dispute, between a melodic feel for the tritone as natural dominant

Ex. 9   (a) L'Ascension   *1 'Majesté du Christ demandant sa gloire à son Père'*

(b) *Magnificat Antiphon, First Vespers of the Ascension*

and a harmonic convention that the fifth has this function, is central to *L'Ascension* as to much of Messiaen. It seems to matter rather less that the whole first phrase is couched in the third mode of limited transpositions.

The second phrase is an extension of the first. The melody again rises through a tritone, from B to F, and again the harmony presses the claims of normality in affirming F sharp. After this there is a slip to A major agreed by both, but then the melody strikes in its original B, substantiated once more by a massive access of diatonic force, which now works to establish B as tonic rather than as dominant. The whole process is immediately repeated, and repeated again in enlarged form after a middle section that completes the diminished-seventh harmony of the opening by adding D to the B, F (E sharp) and G sharp already prominent. Structurally, then, the movement is as monumental as it is in instrumentation, the form being ABABCCABB.

Even more straightforward is the shape of the second movement, where the 'serene alleluias' are alternately extrovert and introvert in an ABABA pattern. Again the wind instruments are much to the fore. They alone play in the first section, joined in its repetitions by an increasing tissue of decoration, and the two 'trios' are pastoral interludes featuring solo woodwinds over a drone of string harmonics and then, in extension, over a more elaborate background.

The main subject (see example 10) suggests an artificial chant. This is in pure mode 3, which ought to mean, given the symmetry of that mode, the absence of any defined tonal centre. As usual, however, diatonic is subsumed into modal usage, and here in an exemplary manner, since the key signature of F major proposes a flattening not actually observed in the mode. The melody begins, of course, closer to F minor, and can be understood as a working out of the conflict contained in the first idea between a seventh arpeggio on F, with its augmented triad upper part, and B as the modal dominant – a conflict not far distant from that of the first movement. The first part of the melody centres itself on different notes from the initial rise: first F, then C (bar 4), A flat (enharmonic transposition of the mode in bar 5) and E (end of bar 5). The second part simply affirms thrice the authenticity of a cadence from B to F. Rhythmically this latter part gives the odd impression that time has softened, while the more abrupt motifs of the first part provide a classic instance of Messiaen's regard for Dom Mocquereau's theory of arsis and thesis.

Ex. 10   L'Ascension   2 *'Alléluias sereins d'une âme qui désire le ciel'*

The tonal centre of F persists in this movement throughout the drone-based interludes, and throughout the repetitions of the opening melody, despite its festooning with scales in the third mode. So far, therefore, *L'Ascension* has executed a semitonal rise from the E major ground of its first movement, and this process continues. The 'Alleluia on the trumpet' begins as a lively dance in F sharp minor, duly led by the trumpets, and, like the quick movement in *Les offrandes oubliées*, recalling *L'apprenti sorcier* in its relentless energy and growth, even though the feeling here is more exultant than exasperated. However, the final section of the movement, beginning rather curiously as a quasi-fugue, is centred on E flat, a semitone down from the E of the first movement, and the finale fulfils both upward and downward longings, since it is notionally in G major (hence the four movements execute the pattern E–F–F sharp–G) while resting decisively, as *Le banquet céleste* had done, on the dominant-seventh chord (hence E–(F)–E flat–D).

But as far as the material of the finale is concerned, the image of ascension is pre-eminent. The most frequently repeated idea is a rise of chords owing something to processes foreshadowed in the first movement, for again the first sound is a triad with the addition of a minor second. This time, though, the semitone-raised stranger is played in the bass and joined by its submediant; it therefore has a more strongly felt presence, and it causes the music to rise in steps until the process has been weakened by changes of modality, first from minor to major, and then to whole tone, reaching from that point the dominant-seventh chord central to this movement (see example 11).

Ex. 11   L'Ascension   *4 'Prière du Christ montant vers son Père'*

The effect is of the first movement's prayer being answered. Where before ascent had been frustrated, with the insistence on the tritone instead of the expected fifth as the goal of the melody, here there is no decisive end to the harmonic ladder but only a resting point on an unstable chord, the dominant seventh. And in the latter part of the movement, the rise of example 11 is repeated in ever higher transpositions: there is a sense of mounting into the ether, and, just as in *Les offrandes oubliées*, Messiaen conceives such music as belonging to a small group of strings.

This contrast between the appellant wind instruments of the first movement and the spiritualized strings of the finale is one of the losses when the work is played in its organ version. The 'serene alleluias', too, sound more human when their reedy solos belong to woodwind instruments rather than organ pipes, and Messiaen's uncertainty about the arrangement is suggested by his remark that the task of transcription was 'so troublesome that I had to recompose most of the movements'.[8] This is something of an exaggeration as far as the first, second and fourth movements are concerned, since the changes are slight, but the third movement is wholly replaced, possibly because Messiaen considered the 'Alleluia on the trumpet' too much an orchestral expression, possibly because he had, even though only a year had passed, outgrown the rampant Dukas influence.

The new organ movement, 'Transports de joie', retains the ascending key scheme by placing itself in F sharp major (the E flat is now

suppressed), but there are no thematic links with its orchestral predecessor. Indeed, the voice is quite new. This is the first Messiaen quick
movement that does not have a certain awkwardness, whether because
the propulsive means are unsuitable (the sonata principle in the last of
the *Préludes*) or because Stravinsky and Dukas are too readily heard
pushing in the background. No doubt Messiaen was still thinking of
Dupré's virtuosity, but the energy of 'Transports de joie' is his own,
gained from sharply profiled rhythmic motifs, and from syncopations
and changes of time signature that upset the sense of time quite as much
as does the endlessness of such slow movements as the finale of
L'Ascension.

One might, indeed, hazard that he had been in search of a quick style
that would work in the absence of regular metre, for his taste for
irregularity had already become apparent. Of course, 'Transports de joie'
does not take irregularity very far, but it does point the way towards the
rhythmic speculations that were suddenly to flower the next year in *La
Nativité du Seigneur*. And since 'Transports' is both more typical of
Messiaen and more striking than the 'Alleluia on the trumpet', there is a
case for considering the authentic *L'Ascension* as consisting of the first,
second and fourth movements of the orchestral version with the inter-
polation of the third from the organ. In whatever form it is heard,
however, the work gains consistency from its upward tonal movement
and from the different interpretations of ascension embodied in the
thematic material of its outer movements. Messiaen's material does not
lend itself to development, and this is acknowledged in the verse–
refrain forms common to all five movements; but if it is not a symphony, *L'Ascension* is a suite that finds in the ascension theme a
stimulus towards new and striking musical images.

La Nativité du Seigneur is different in that the images are more
symbolic than structural, which is partly why the work requires not
only movement titles and biblical inscriptions but also an explanatory
preface. This is a fascinating document. Predating the *Technique de
mon langage musical* by several years, it is Messiaen's first published
account of his modes of limited transpositions, of which he draws
attention to five: the first, second and third, numbered thus, and two
'fourth modes', one being the definitive fourth mode and the other the
sixth. He also draws attention to their use in the work, though not
exhaustively: he makes no mention, for instance, of the fact that the
long final section of the fourth movement, 'Le Verbe', is in the second
mode. However, he does give a very fair indication of how much of the
music hinges on these modes, particularly on the second and third.

The modes of limited transpositions form the first of five 'principal
means of expression' which he lists in his preface, the others being
'enlarged pedals, decorations and appoggiaturas', the 'added dot', the

'progressive widening of intervals' and the 'chord on the dominant'. An example of the 'enlarged pedal' has been noted in 'Les sons impalpables du rêve': it is Messiaen's term for an ostinato, though normally one that shifts chords up and down scales, as in that prelude, and as too in the example he chooses here from the second piece, 'Les bergers'. Similarly, the 'enlarged decorations and appoggiaturas' are melismatic embellish- ments, while the 'chord on the dominant' is a harmony including all the notes of the diatonic major scale, one that may have a dominant flavour when, as in 'Le Verbe', the fifth degree is in the bass and, uniquely, accompanied by its fifth. (More generally the 'chord on the dominant' emblematically represents the great variety of chords Messiaen uses to shade his unchanging harmony.) As it appears in 'Le Verbe', the chord precipitates a fortissimo descent in the pedals, and that is all. Messiaen's preface alerts one also to its use in the eighth piece of the cycle, 'Les mages', but it is not at all as central a feature of the music as the modes, and the same may be said of the 'progressive widening of intervals', which is used only in the seventh piece to generate (or perhaps simply to explain) a fan-like opening and closing of chords in music of melancholy joy to express the idea of 'Jésus accepte la souffrance'.

By contrast, the third of Messiaen's five 'means of expression', the 'added dot', quietly heralds a massively important innovation in his music. The most characteristic moments of earlier works, such as the serene alleluias of *L'Ascension*, had already shown a liking for irregular rhythm but now that taste affects every movement very conspicuously. At its most elementary, the 'added dot', or added half-value, upsets a conventional metre, as happens, for instance, with the unbalanced 3/4 heard right at the opening of the first piece, 'La Vierge et l'Enfant' (see example 12).

Ex. *12*   La Nativité du Seigneur   *1 'La Vierge et l'Enfant'*

This technique, however, is evidence of something deeper in Mes- siaen's rhythm: a sense of time pulsed in individual units, not grouped in the larger metrical entities that give most Western music a feeling of progression due to regular pattern. Slow movements, like 'Desseins éternels', may remove themselves from the time-measuring of pulsa- tion because so long a time elapses between sound and sound, as had been the case with the ending of *Les offrandes oubliées*, but anything like the sustained scherzo of that work, or of the orchestral *L'Ascension*, is now out of the question. Instead, with the aid of his added values and other imbalances, Messiaen discovers varieties of fast motion that are all his own. *La Nativité* is full of them, and they range from perpetually different overlays on a 3+3+5/8 ostinato in the middle section of 'La Vierge et l'Enfant' to the introduction of semiquaver hiccoughs into a dance of charming *naïveté* for the shepherds in the next piece.

No doubt Messiaen's conception of rhythm in terms principally of quantity owed something to what he had learned of Greek metre and of the rhythmic formulae, the 120 deçî-tâlas, listed in the Lavignac encyclopedia and copied there from the most prestigious treatise of north Indian music in the thirteenth century, the *Saṅgīta-ratnākara* attributed to Sarṅgadeva. It is important to note that these deçî-tâlas were already antiquated conceits when they were tabulated in the *Saṅgīta-ratnākara*, and that they bear as much relation to modern Indian music as the Mogul miniature does to the Bombay cinema. Messiaen's fascination with what he calls 'Hindu rhythms' is an abstract fascination, concerned with the formulae and not with any musical embodiment they might once have had, or might now retain in contemporary Indian practice. Indeed, it is arguable that the Lavignac list errs in notating as a dotted semiquaver what ought to be read as a semiquaver followed by a semiquaver rest, so that many of the irregularities Messiaen specially cherishes are spurious.[9] There may be some justice, therefore, in retaining here the French forms of the deçî-tâlas' names.

For the moment Messiaen's use of the deçî-tâlas is limited. One of them, with the auspicious name of *turangalîla*, is notated in the preface but not in the music, while other features, such as the alternation of 3/4 and 7/16 in 'Les mages', suggest the Śarṅgadeva patterns without exactly repeating any of them. There are also cases where modal phrases begin to take on Indian contours, for by turning the pages of Lavignac a little beyond the deçî-tâlas Messiaen would have encountered the eighteen játis, or fundamental melodic formulae. The most striking example, admitted by him,[10] comes in the long concluding slow section of 'Le Verbe', where constant rhythmic unpredictability within a framework of regularity parallels the melodic and harmonic variety within phrases that settle always on G (see example 13).

This demonstrates Messiaen's discovery of a rhythmic technique as powerful and individual as his modal system, and with similar leanings towards unorthodox manoeuvres with orthodox units: metrical patterns in the one case, common chords in the other. At the same time he had discovered an important new kind of musical expression, for if irregular rhythmic grouping in a quick tempo may boost excitement,

Ex. 13   La Nativité du Seigneur   *4 'Le Verbe'*

the same sort of irregularity at a slow speed, coupled with repeated returns over the same melodic ground, conveys an impression of ideas being weighed. One keeps hearing the same cadential gestures – particularly in this example the one that ends with the ubiquitous falling tritone – but the approach is always different; or one hears the same rhythmic pattern set to different notes, or the same note differently harmonized. (Messiaen remarks that there are nine different harmonizations of the final G.) And allied with this is a basic shift in harmonic technique. In such music Messiaen takes less advantage of the diatonic forces that he had twisted to his purposes in *L'Ascension*, for his modality and his rhythm are now independent enough to create their own musical world, which diatonic harmony visits as decorator: the nine different harmonizations of the final G are not meant to be understood as functionally different but instead savoured as different colourings. Harmonic, melodic and rhythmic variety all serve to give the sense that a single loop of time is rotating past the present, moving in a different way only for each circuit, and that the process could continue forever.

Similar images of the eternal glimpsed in the quotidian abound in *La Nativité*, whose ostensible subject of course is the coming of the eternal into the earthly in the Incarnation. As usual, development, with its appeal to forward-moving time, is abandoned; the only change is that it is abandoned for longer, since this is Messiaen's largest work so far, playing for nearly an hour. Decorated repetition and palindrome are the main formal principles at work, as in the *Préludes* and *L'Ascension*, and the movements Messiaen regards as developmental do not justify that term in quite the way that the music of Brahms does. He has, for instance, described the fifth piece, 'Les enfants de Dieu', as the coda of an otherwise non-existent sonata form,[11] but whatever the difficulties of making such a diagnosis, the second mode chords as usual destroy any thrust to the harmony, which could circle between seventh chords on F sharp and G sharp indefinitely, fixed on the same melodic pattern.

Another instance of heightened stasis, this time operating across the work as a whole, is provided by the handling of a five-note motif following an 'M' pattern intervallically, its only universal characteristic being a final tritone drop to the starting point. Messiaen relates this pattern to the opening of *Boris Godunov* (and thereby also to the opening of *Pelléas et Mélisande*), though his highly characteristic tritone is an expansion of what is a fourth in Mussorgsky. Nevertheless, it will be convenient to follow him in describing the pattern as 'the *Boris* motif'. In his *Technique de mon langage musical* he lists it as the first of his 'beloved melodic contours',[12] and in *La Nativité* it proves irresistible to the first piece and also to the seventh, while it can be discerned too behind much of the rest. Like the theme of *Les offrandes oubliées*, however, it is a signature much more than a source.

Of course, no reference to the operatic or real history of Boris Godunov is to be presumed from this prominence of a theme borrowed and bent from Mussorgsky, but it is a different matter when Messiaen quotes plainsong. He has himself pointed out that the organ sings the introit to the third mass of Christmas Day, *Puer natus est nobis*, in the middle of the first movement,[13] and that one theme of the finale is a 'Magnificat, alleluiatic praise in bird style';[14] Robert Sherlaw Johnson adds the suggestion that the final part of 'Le Verbe' touches on the sequence *Victimae paschali*.[15] But though the first of these is practically a quotation, albeit with an introductory flourish in mode 6, the others are so altered that the model is barely recognizable. The 'alleluiatic praise' of 'Dieu parmi nous' (see example 14) for instance, is more obviously an imitation of birdsong – its first appearance in Messiaen – than it is a transcription of any Magnificat source.

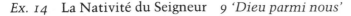

Ex. 14   La Nativité du Seigneur   9 'Dieu parmi nous'

It must be clear already that the breadth of reference in *La Nativité du Seigneur* is much wider than in *L'Ascension*, encompassing many of the things out of which Messiaen was to continue to make music in the coming decades: his own modes, major and minor tonalities, 'Hindu rhythms', plainsong, number and the songs of birds. The reason for this diversity may be found in the purpose of the work, to which again the preface gives the most important clues. For the first time Messiaen speaks of the 'theological' aspect of his music, choosing a word that he prefers to 'mystical', since he sees himself not as communicating a personal vision of the divine but rather as transmitting by the most efficacious means the truths contained in the doctrines of the Catholic Church. In the case of *La Nativité*, the central doctrine is that of the Incarnation, and Messiaen's preface outlines five 'principal ideas' that are connected with that doctrine and, in intention, expounded in the work: 'our predestination realized through the Incarnation of the Word' (No. 3, 'Desseins éternels'); 'God living among us, God suffering' (No. 9, 'Dieu parmi nous', and No. 7, 'Jésus accepte la souffrance'); 'the three births', being the eternal birth of the Word, the particular birth of Christ and the spiritual birth of Christians (No. 4, 'Le Verbe'; No. 1, 'La Vierge et l'Enfant', and No. 5, 'Les enfants de Dieu'); the 'description of various personages giving a special poetry to the festival of Christmas' (No. 6, 'Les anges'; No. 8, 'Les mages', and No. 2, 'Les bergers'); and finally the provision of 'nine pieces in all to honour the maternity of the Holy Virgin'.

The association of the number nine with motherhood and with the Virgin is of long standing, and one is bound to assume too that the pleasures of numerology played some part in Messiaen's definition of five technical and five theological interests here, for both lists appear slightly arbitrary. Number, however, is only one element of Messiaen's symbolism. Another is, quite simply, a musical depiction of the descent of God into the world by means of thunderingly falling pedal themes in the fourth and ninth pieces: this is directly comparable with the use of an eternally rising idea in the last movement of *L'Ascension*. The difference between the works – and it is a big difference considering the gap was one of only two years – is that *La Nativité* is more inclined to deliver its symbols and let them be read, without working them into any coherent musical form. In 'Le Verbe', for instance, the long slow second section can perhaps be heard as a response to the tension contained in the first part, with its 'chord on the dominant', its irregular rhythms and its powerful descent, but as a musical movement the piece remains irremediably in halves. And in 'Dieu parmi nous', even though Messiaen has analysed this movement as a development of three themes,[16] the ideas are so distinctly presented – they are more objects than themes – that they remain wholly apart from one another, and the effect is rather, as the composer largely acknowledges, of a grand toccata taking in material from a previous conversation of separate ideas. As for the significance of those ideas, it is not difficult to accept Messiaen's view of the triumphantly descendant first as illustrative of the Incarnation: he quotes the authority of Bach and Dukas for using a musical fall to picture a real one.[17] The birdsong 'Magnificat' also makes its effect without explanation. One probably needs Messiaen's prompting, however, to hear the second theme as 'expressing the love for Jesus Christ of the communicant, of the Virgin, of the entire Church'.[18] Here we have a composer himself acting like those Wagnerian cicerones who would understand every motif as indicative of a particular emotion or personality.

Messiaen's insistence on the 'theological' bearing of his work reinforces such an impression, and yet in choosing to convey his theology in music he is selecting a medium never used for that end by the fathers and doctors of the Church. To understand a work like *La Nativité* in terms of its declared theology would seem, even when the subject is so awesome, a limitation, since the theology of Messiaen's verbal comments is rudimentary, and likely to seem woefully naïve by comparison with the examinations of professional theologians. And yet because the intention of theological exposition produces such a stiff form, the music may appear similarly simple-minded if its aims are ignored. The dilemma is central to Messiaen's work: too theological to be purely musical, too musical to be theological. What cannot be denied, however, is the power and newness of imagery the music derives from its brush with the things of God, so that meditations on the supernatural similarly venture beyond the familiar natural world of diatonic harmony, stable metre and so on.

In this case, there is the repeated astonishment of new effects being discovered within the repertory of the organ: new effects, above all, of timbre and texture. And though *La Nativité* lacks the single shaping idea of *L'Ascension*, its movements belong in a community by virtue of their grouping around E major, the eventual key of 'Dieu parmi nous' and the key, too, in which *Les offrandes oubliées* had finished and *L'Ascension* been forcibly made to begin: in all three works, despite other great differences, it is a key of very present connection between earth and heaven as far as Messiaen is concerned. Besides coming to dominate 'Dieu parmi nous', E is also important in 'Les bergers' and, with its relative minor C sharp, in the symmetrically disposed movements 'Desseins éternels' and 'Jésus accepte la souffrance', while the centrepiece, 'Les enfants de Dieu', exults in the dominant, B major, the key of ecstasy in *La mort du nombre* and 'Cloches d'angoisse'. Rather as one might expect, the tritone opposites of these three key notes are also significant: B flat in the first movement, G in the fourth and F in the sixth. It should not be assumed, though, that there is anything like the enveloping continuity of *L'Ascension*, either within movements or within the work as a whole; the tonal relationships act rather to induce a sense of kinship among a collection of startling inventions sparked off by sacred texts.

The third great organ cycle of the 1930s, *Les corps glorieux*, is at once more intensively shaped and more heterodox. Its cohesion is perhaps encouraged by the subject, since Messiaen is here concerned not with the accidents of an event (however poetic may be the suggestions of shepherds, magi and the rest) but rather with a single phenomenon placed beyond the diverse matters of this earth: the work is described in its subtitle as 'seven brief visions of the life of the resurrected'. Brief the visions are only by comparison with that life, since the cycle plays for around three-quarters of an hour. In Messiaen's style, however – as in Bruckner's, for example, but not in Webern's – long duration normally goes along with concentration; indeed, a certain breadth of time is necessary for the music to exert itself as a new mode of being, as a kind of unofficial liturgy. So it is here. The contemplation of resurrected bodies gives rise to three studies of their properties, backed by scriptural references: subtlety (No. 1), power and agility (No. 5), and joy and clarity (No. 6). These are balanced by three studies of the resurrected environment; its plenitude of grace (No. 2), its angelic inhabitants (No. 3) and the presence of God (No. 7). The two triptychs are then interleaved, and placed around the massive centrepiece, which occupies about a third of the work's playing time, and which concerns itself with death and resurrection, with the temporal gateway into the eternal.

At the same time there is a large-scale harmonic scheme more purposeful than that of *La Nativité*, as may be suggested by the following outline of chief key areas:

1 'Subtilité des corps glorieux'   D mode 2
2 'Les eaux de la grâce'   G modes 2 and 3
3 'L'ange aux parfums'   C Indian mode
4 'Combat de la mort et de la vie'   C mode 2, then F sharp mode 2
5 'Force et agilité des corps glorieux'   various mode 2, ending with
   seventh chord on C sharp

6 'Joie et clarté des corps glorieux'   D flat mode 2
7 'Le mystère de la Sainte Trinité'   D mixed modes

There is a perfect symmetry here. The first three movements step down
the cycle of fifths; the middle movement effects a tritone switch; and
the last three pieces then step back up in fifths, except that the last of all
replaces A flat with its tritone opposite, the D of the first movement
(though in so slippery a chromatic context that the feeling of a tonic is
never very steady). This scheme must help bind together movements of
such wide variety, but certainly no less important is the pervasiveness
of the second mode and of chords associated with it, notably the added
sixth and the dominant seventh. Its prominent tritones, too, contribute
to the sense of austere solemnity that runs through this work, retreating
into the background only when the joy and clarity of the celestial state is
extolled in warm D flat major.

Symmetry is a feature not only of the cycle's large form but also, as in
L'Ascension and La Nativité, of its constituent movements: clearly this
reflects the changelessness of the resurrected, and musically answers
the symmetry of the basic modes. The only piece that is required to
embody an alteration is the middle one, and here Messiaen goes back to
a form he had used in the Diptyque of nine years before, bringing a
toccata movement to issue in a rapt adagio based on the same theme.
Messiaen calls this a 'development-exposition form',[19] but of course
there can be no real question of the adagio being heard as the exposition
of something already encountered in quite different terms: the feeling is
rather that the theme has been freed from a hostile, challenging environment, and that feeling accords very well with the theological intention
of the piece, so similar in this respect too to the Diptyque. At first the
theme is heard in the bass, and set about with tumultuous chases of
chords; then in the second part of the movement it floats over soft
chords in a melodic contemplation, gaining the F sharp major on which
Le banquet céleste had fixed its gaze.

The trinities of movements on either side of the 'Combat' each
begin with a monody, the first, 'Subtilité des corps glorieux', being
strictly so, while the second, 'Force et agilité des corps glorieux', has
the hands matching each other in octaves. In character, however,
these movements are utterly different. The subtlety of the resurrected
– their angelic purity, the inscription from St Matthew would have
one suppose – is conveyed by a chant in lines ending always with a
cadential formula which, like the motif adapted from Boris, squats on
the tonic from the upper tritone (see example 15(a)). Messiaen has
mentioned the importance here of the plainsong Salve Regina,[20] and
one might well point to a connection with a fragment of that plainsong he quotes in his Technique de mon langage musical (see example

Ex. 15 (a) Les corps glorieux 1 '*Subtilité des corps glorieux*'

(b) Salve Regina

15(b)).[21] It must be obvious, however, that the contour has, modally and rhythmically, been completely adapted to Messiaen's style: it does not sound like a quotation. Musically, the two are not talking about the same things, which may raise doubts about whether they are doing so on any meaningful theological level. If the insertion of a Gregorian theme carries the implication of its associated text – and Messiaen speaks of a 'homage to the Holy Virgin, queen of the bodies in glory' – then any distortion of the theme ought to imply a distortion of the message.

Elsewhere in *Les corps glorieux* the very individuality his style had by now achieved must raise similar questions. Theology is a science where exactitude and universality of terminology are crucial; Messiaen in 1939 was moving into a world of musical terms he had largely discovered for himself, or had at least newly coloured with his modes of limited transpositions. Proof of that individuality had come with his discovery of an entirely personal line in pure melody, for the first time in the 'serene alleluias' of *L'Ascension*. From that point onwards he could afford to lose major–minor harmony, though of course it is only in particular movements that this happens. Non-developmental in its nature, Messiaen's music has been non-developmental too in its largest span, so that his career from *Le banquet céleste* onwards is not one of linear progression but rather of the gradual achievement of an ever wider range of techniques, any of which, once acquired, may be used at any time.

The monodies of *Les corps glorieux* are highly individual, whether that of 'Subtilité' or that of 'Force et agilité' which, in quite opposite fashion, avoids definite cadences with its repeated-note motif adapted from a játi, but instead hops in sovereign freedom from one gravitational field to another, using the technique of interval enlargement from *La Nativité* and making much of a long–short–long pattern derived from a Greek metre variously called by Messiaen 'cretic' or 'peonic' (see example 16). This same rhythm also features importantly in 'Joie et

Ex. 16   Les corps glorieux   5 *'Force et agilité des corps glorieux'*

clarté', while 'L'ange aux parfums', which once more opens in pure monody, uses the same játi.

As it is throughout the cycle, the number three is central to 'L'ange aux parfums', there being three different interpretations of its theme: in monody, in melody with accompaniment and in toccata-style canon. There are, moreover, interludes in obstinate triple counterpoint, recalling the similar texture and tempo of the brief 'Les eaux de la grâce' and looking forward to the longest and knottiest instance of this art in the cycle, 'Le mystère de la Sainte Trinité'.

Triple counterpoint, as Bach had observed, is a fit medium in which to pay tribute to the trinity, and one that suits the organ well, with its triple control of left hand, right hand and feet. In this case, though, threeness goes much further. The middle voice is, like the monody of 'Subtilité', a plainsong-derived chant in mode 2 centred on D, even sharing similar tritone cadences but formally as well as melodically based on a kyrie. The melodic source is the plainsong *Kyrie IX*; the formal outline is more generally that of a ninefold kyrie, each word of which is allotted a musical phrase, with an extension for the final 'kyrie' and the same melody for each 'eleison'. However, this rhyming main line is set about by voices organized on quite other lines, as may appear in the opening fragment (example 17) showing the first 'Kyrie eleison'.

Ex. 17   Les corps glorieux   7 *'Le mystère de la Sainte Trinité'*

The bass line is executing a wholly independent cyclical process, running five times through a rhythmic sequence formed from three deçî-tâlas: *râgavardhana* in varied retrograde (first six elements, G–D), *candrakalâ* (next seven elements, C sharp–F sharp) and *lakskmiça* (last four elements, F–E flat), the sequence ending with a long note not included in the example. One may note here how Messiaen chooses deçî-tâlas that embody his particular rhythmic interests: taking a cell and then reducing all its values in proportion (his derivative from *râgavardhana*, splitting a long value into three crotchets) or else increasing them (*candrakalâ* and *lakskmiça*), adding a dot (*râgavardhana*) and adding a value (*candrakalâ*). Each time the sequence starts out on the notes of a chromatic descent, and each time it finishes on a low D, but there are variations along the way. The top line also has obvious recurring features, but it is much more freely composed and even more chromatic, lacking the eventual D home in which the 'tenor' and the bass, though from different standpoints, concur.

Clearly the comparison with Bach is somewhat misleading, since what confronts us here is not counterpoint but heterophony: the simultaneous presentation of lines that continue to be felt as utterly distinct. The whole effort of Western music had been to avoid heterophony, and for the good reason that heterophony conveys the experience of different understandings of time proceeding at once and therefore is incompatible with uniform progression. But for Messiaen heterophony is clearly an invaluable technique in attempting to remove a sense of time having a single speed and direction. In this case the slow cycles of the kyrie, conveyed by melodic repetition and palindromic rhythm, are present with still slower cycles in the bass and faster, erratic ones in the treble; and where in a Bach chorale prelude the differing speeds would all be geared to the same pulse and phrasing, here the wheels run free of one another. The mystery of the trinity is that of three divine persons sharing the same substance; the mystery of this movement is that of three divergent experiences of time being had at once.

'Le mystère de la Sainte Trinité', consistently quiet and marked to sound 'distant', brings *Les corps glorieux* to a conclusion far from that manoeuvred by the extrovert 'Dieu parmi nous' in *La Nativité*. Quite simply, the newer work is not concerned with the same sort of public success; it has still more the quality of a contemplation rather than that of a concert suite. Even so, one may go too far in accepting Messiaen's own valuation of the movements, as communicated in their titles and inscriptions. As has already been suggested, his bending of plainsong themes must imply at least a bending of the Church's musical truths so that they may take their place in a newly invented liturgy, and Messiaen's claim that his work is 'theological' – concerned with the explanation of universal dogma rather than with the communication of a private vision he contrasts as 'mystical'[22] – must be open to question. For one thing, his 'dazzlement' is scarcely a theological technique. Then again, his 'theological' terms are not those of ordinary discourse, for

even if the Indian influence on *La Nativité* and *Les corps glorieux*
accords with an openness to Oriental enlightenments accepted by such
contemporary Catholic writers as Thomas Merton, Messiaen's ideas are
very much his own, and become much more his own as his *oeuvre*
increases and his movements grow, in intention, ever more precise in
what they convey.

There is also the fact that the music needs a verbal clue. By contrast
with the motifs of a religious picture, those of a Messiaen composition
have to have their hoped-for connotations explained, while the more
general features that might be supposed integral to the religious effect –
the modality, the non-progressive time and the static structures – are
also the sources of musical interest. Indeed, the objects and musical
states that Messiaen offers to our inspection in *Les corps glorieux* are so
very singular that we may well be disinclined to accept them as
invitations to meditate on something else, preferring to make of them
the centre of our contemplation.

CHAPTER 4

La Jeune France

If Messiaen's achievement at La Trinité in the 1930s was very much a personal one, as represented by the musical substance and even the theological character of *Les corps glorieux* at the end of the decade, he was very far from isolating himself in his organ loft. The first performance of *Les offrandes oubliées*, when Messiaen was 22, brought his name before the public, and there it regularly remained, thanks to further orchestral premières (*Le tombeau resplendissant* in 1932, the *Hymne au Saint Sacrement* in 1933, *L'Ascension* in 1935) and to occasional performances of smaller pieces. His reputation was gaining ground, but like many French artists of his time, he felt the need to associate himself with a group, and from among composers of his generation there emerged in 1936 La Jeune France.

It was a rather motley foursome. As a creative figure Messiaen was matched only by André Jolivet (1905–1974), who in 1936 might even have appeared the more boldly adventurous composer: he had studied with Varèse and written a controversially non-tonal String Quartet (1934) as well as a set of six piano pieces, *Mana* (1935), that won Messiaen's admiration as expressed in the preface he wrote for the work. However, much of what he found to praise in Jolivet's music – the motivic conception of rhythm, the repetitive structures, the resonance effects, the melodic individuality – he had already acquired for himself, and it would be difficult to diagnose any unquestionable influence. The two composers were simply reacting to similar outer and inner circumstances, and perhaps most particularly to an intuition that the East held clues for changing Western music. One of the *Mana* pieces, all six of which were suggested by particular cult objects Varèse had given his pupil, is 'La princesse de Bali', appearing in the same year as the Indian inclinations of *La Nativité du Seigneur*.

The other members of La Jeune France were Daniel-Lesur (b. 1908) and Yves Baudrier (b. 1906). Daniel-Lesur was closest to Messiaen not only in age but also professionally, being a fellow teacher at the Schola

Cantorum (Messiaen began teaching there and at the Ecole Normale de Musique in 1936) and an organist. His music, however, has always been more conventional in style than Messiaen's or Jolivet's, its modalities coming directly out of plainchant or folksong, and its dignity out of Dukas. Baudrier was a late starter who published nothing before his first meeting with Messiaen in 1935. The association then, however, did not express itself stylistically. Baudrier had more in common with Honegger, and like Honegger he enjoyed working for the cinema: his most important piece is an imaginary film score, *Le musicien dans la cité* (1937), following its protagonist about the streets of Paris at night. In later years he was dogged by ill-health and wrote little.

Such, then, was the group of contemporaries who banded together as La Jeune France in 1936. Three of them – Messiaen, Jolivet and Daniel-Lesur – had been among the founders the previous year of La Spirale, an organization for promoting chamber concerts, the others involved in that undertaking being Georges Migot (1891–1976) and Paul Le Flem (b. 1881). Presumably those two were disqualified from the new grouping because Messiaen and his colleagues wanted to emphasize their youth. What they also insisted on was 'a living music, having the impetus of sincerity, generosity and artistic conscientiousness'.[1] By implication they were attacking the thread of frivolity always associated with Parisian neoclassicism, and advocating almost on every point a rejection of Cocteau's manifesto *Le coq et l'arlequin* of eighteen years before: music was now to be personal and manifestly serious.

The first Jeune France concert, given in the Salle Gaveau on 3 June 1936, was something of an event, Valéry leading the artistic luminaries present. Roger Desormière, though closely involved with exactly the kind of music the group was reacting against, was the conductor; even more curiously, Ricardo Viñes had been invited to play Germaine Tailleferre's Piano Concerto. Otherwise, however, the programme consisted entirely of music by the four young composers, Baudrier being represented by his symphonic poem *Raz de Sein* and *Chant de jeunesse*, Daniel-Lesur by his *Suite française* and *Interludes pour cors*, and Jolivet by his *Danse incantatoire*. These were all compositions of the last two years, but Messiaen, who had been occupied most recently with *La Nativité du Seigneur* had to look back further in his portfolio and offer repeat performances of *Les offrandes oubliées* and his *Hymne au Saint Sacrement* (1932).

Together with the intervening *Le tombeau resplendissant*, these form a trinity of different meditations on the Eucharist, the *Hymne* being the most physically joyous. Since the unpublished manuscript was lost during the Second World War and the work reconstructed for a performance under Stokowski in 1947, it is hard to be sure how much the exuberance of the *Hymne* was coloured by the nearness of the

Turangalîla-symphonie, especially when a ghost of its main theme turns up in that work's fourth movement. The *Hymne* sounds, however, generally like the work of the young Messiaen, being scored for the same normal large orchestra as *Les offrandes* and *Le tombeau*. The first gesture Messiaen aptly likens to a 'gust of wind',[2] ushering in first some impassioned melancholy neumes that dissolve into intent meditation on muted violins accompanied by the rest of the strings. This latter section gives the impression that the end of *Les offrandes* is coming first: the communion is taking place, and what follows, a marvellous bounding melody in modally shaded but still bright D major, expresses the resulting grace. The whole process is then repeated in transposition, with the dynamic music now still more brilliant in B major, the key of spiritual fulfilment also in *La mort du nombre*, 'Cloches d'angoisse' and 'Les enfants de Dieu'.

As for musical fulfilment, Messiaen was finding that very much within the two spheres considered on either side of this chapter: in the organ music he wrote for himself, and in songs he composed to celebrate his domestic life after his marriage to Claire Delbos in 1932. These two areas also served him as public musician. After the first performance of *La Nativité du Seigneur*, at La Trinité in 1935, he played pieces from the cycle at an important recital on 17 February 1938, when he shared his organ with the other two rising stars among French organists, Daniel-Lesur and Jehan Alain (1911–1940), of whom Alain was much influenced by him while developing a more consistently outgoing style. He also played two movements from *La Nativité* at the ISCM Festival in London in June 1938, which must have been one of the first occasions when he performed, or when his music was heard, outside France. Also in 1938, his song-cycle addressed to his wife under a pet name, *Poèmes pour Mi* (1936), was twice performed at Jeune France concerts, on one occasion in the company of Jolivet's *Poèmes pour l'enfant* for mezzo-soprano and eleven players (1937), written on the birth of that composer's son, and on the other with settings by Delbos from *L'âme en bourgeon*. Daniel-Lesur also contributed to this intercourse of family and group with a set of *Trois poèmes de Cécile Sauvage* for voice and piano (1939).

The outbreak of the war in that year naturally brought an end to the activities of La Jeune France, which in any event seems not to have been maintaining the éclat of the opening concert and pronouncements three years before. As far as Messiaen is concerned, the episode is of interest only in as much as it helps one to understand the background against which music so extraordinary appeared. Undoubtedly there was a general wish to compose works unfiltered by the irony and polish of someone like Poulenc. Messiaen found himself of that party because his theological intentions permitted no ambiguity (though, as we have seen, there is a profound ambiguity between the personal and the universal in his work), and also because elegance would seem too trivial an aim to one seeking a musical measure of divine facts. However, not all the members of La Jeune France took at all the same line. Jolivet wrote some Catholic works but in the 1930s was much more impressed by the magical power attributed to music in certain Eastern and primitive religions: hence his *Mana*, or *Cinq incantations* for solo flute (1935), or *Danse incantatoire*, or *Cinq danses rituelles* for piano or orchestra (1939). Messiaen, who has always preferred to approach very particular myths through very particular symbols, is appreciative but guarded in his one reference to this face of Jolivet's art: 'This incantatory aspect is certainly not to be dismissed: no one yet understands the psychic, physiological and perhaps therapeutic action of a work like the *Danses rituelles*: it is perhaps an unknown force. . . .'[3] Where the two composers were certainly together was in their enthusiasm for Oriental music, which Jolivet naturally saw as occupied with similar aims to his own, and which Messiaen too may have regarded not only as a source of new modes and time-scales but also as a model for the embodiment of sacred knowledge.

If they shared as well a search for 'sincerity, generosity and artistic conscientiousness' (these were apparently Jolivet's words), they were part of a movement in Parisian music wider than La Jeune France. Honegger, indeed, might well have subscribed to their manifesto, as might his compatriot Conrad Beck (b. 1901), whose music Messiaen came to value during the time he was resident in Paris, from 1923 to 1932. Another composer who impressed Messiaen at this time was Pierre Octave Ferroud (1900–1936), a French Bartókian who was also active as a critic and concert organizer.

And yet among all these friends and contemporaries, Messiaen alone had found in Christian theology a body of thought containing powerful stimuli to composition, richly endowed with imagery but hardened by two millenniums of disputation, and demanding the seriousness they all wanted. His musical imagination became so fixed on theology that, almost immediately, it was impossible for him to compose for any other reason, and when his colleagues reproached him with an inability to write light-hearted music, he produced in his virtuoso *Fantaisie burlesque* for piano (1932) one of his least successful works, a stiffly sectioned verse–refrain form in F that misses a scherzando character the more decisively for attempting it so deliberately.

Very much more important is the other separate piano piece of this period, the *Pièce pour le tombeau de Paul Dukas* (1935) that Messiaen contributed to a wreath of musical tributes published in the *Revue musicale*. Short, and accommodatingly marked 'Très lent et solennel', this is one of the few Messiaen pieces to lie within the compass of the modest amateur, but it has values beyond that merely practical one. It is, in Messiaen's words, 'static, solemn and unadorned, like an enormous block of stone',[4] the effect achieved by chords in mode 3, clamorous with tritones, marching down repeatedly to low octave Bs. This is not the brilliant B major of the *Hymne* and other works, that B major seen from below as a lofty vault; it is, rather, approached always from above, and appears as the first expression of an image that was to be developed in later works, that of the abyss. Here, despite the small dimensions of the piece, there is an imposing monumentality which does honour to Dukas that he could elicit it.

As a figure of increasing prominence in French musical life, Messiaen gained other commissions too. With the *Vocalise-étude* (1935) he provided the 151st in a series of studies for singers edited by A. L. Hettich, a professor at the Conservatoire. The piece is a simple one in A major warmed by mode 3, marked 'Lent, avec charme', and in simple ternary form with a little brilliant cadenza in the last part. Much more substantial in duration is *Fête des belles eaux* for a sextet of ondes martenot, written to accompany a display of illuminated fountains and fireworks on the Seine during the Exposition of 1937.

This is the hardest of Messiaen's works to admire. The substance is thin, and the ethereal vibrato of the ondes martenot reduces some cherished ideas, including the '*Boris* motif' and a whole section later incorporated in the *Quatuor pour la fin du temps*, almost to self-parody. The remarkableness of the scoring, though, has to be conceded. Messiaen must have been aware of Maurice Martenot's efforts from the time of his first demonstration, at the Opéra in May 1928. He could well have heard of Varèse's use of a pair of electronic instruments in his *Ecuatorial* (1933–4); nearer at hand there was the example of Jolivet, who had included two ondes martenot in his score for the Jeune France début concert, the *Danse incantatoire*. Like Jolivet, and indeed like Varèse, Messiaen seems to have heard the wail of the ondes martenot as that of a disembodied human agency, a voice of the spirit, but it was a voice he was to realize more surely and positively in subsequent works from the *Trois petites liturgies* to *Saint François d'Assise* (a pair of monodies for ondes martenot of 1938 remains unpublished).

Unremarkable music for ondes martenot, two piano works and a vocalise, a couple of essays, some teaching and membership in a group: it is not much to represent Messiaen's non-religious activity in the 1930s, but in its meagreness it is typical. Nearly all his music, as has been made clear, is concerned with personal responses to the divine, to the growing exclusion of other subject matter. One may wonder whether his works actually convey more about God than is contained in his increasingly elaborate verbal commentaries on them, but his success in creating a religious aura around his style – or in establishing a style with musical means already having a religious connotation (modality and plainsong, for example) – seems clear: it even restrospectively affects such early secular works as the *Préludes*, which, simply because they are musically so typical of Messiaen, sound to be speaking of God. And religious art is not a medium for coteries. Indeed, in demanding 'sincerity, generosity and artistic conscientiousness' La Jeune France were creating conditions under which they as a group could not exist, for to be sincere and conscientious is to be individual. Messiaen's works of the Jeune France period, *Les corps glorieux* and the two song-cycles to be considered in the next chapter, were triumphantly individual; their world was one that the other members of the group could enter only by trespassing; their time was not that of any contemporary.

The end of this tangent to Messiaen's career can be marked by his brief essay on Stravinsky's rhythm for the *Revue musicale* of 1939. Here, drawing a parallel with his favoured Indian formulae, he applauds Stravinsky's conscious manipulation of rhythmic figures, changing one element while another remains constant. He writes of this, however, as something belonging to Stravinsky's past, a technique emerging in *Petrushka*, reaching its climax in 'his two masterpieces, *The Rite* and *The Wedding*', diminishing in *Histoire du soldat* and becoming 'completely extinguished by the return to Bach in the *Symphony of Psalms*.'[5] The harsh judgement on neoclassical aesthetics could have come from any of the members of La Jeune France. For Messiaen, however, this was not only his first but also his last engagement in polemics. His half-hearted career as a public musician – writing essays, backing manifestos, accepting commissions, composing for the conventional concert world – was at an end.

CHAPTER 5

The Holy Family

Messiaen's marriage in 1932 to Claire Delbos naturally changed the private circumstances of his composing; more unusually, it gave him a new subject. His appointments in 1936 at the Schola Cantorum and the Ecole Normale de Musique gave him financial security, and in 1936 too he established a regular summer base at Petichet in the département of Isère, not far from his childhood home of Grenoble, and a place where he could compose in the neighbourhood of his beloved mountains. *La Nativité du Seigneur* and the Dukas memorial had been composed in Grenoble in 1935; the *Poèmes pour Mi* followed at Petichet in 1936, and then, also at Petichet, another song-cycle, the *Chants de terre et de ciel* in 1938 and *Les corps glorieux* in 1939.

Like the *Poèmes pour Mi*, the *Chants de terre et de ciel* were composed as a marital offering, but there had been another, more modest homage, perhaps an unofficial wedding present, in the *Thème et variations* for violin and piano of 1932, for Delbos was a violinist as well as a fellow composer (another work written for the two of them to play, the *Fantaisie* of 1933, has not been published). The *Thème et variations* is a quite straightforward piece, though entirely characteristic in its third mode harmony and units of seven rather than eight bars. Equally characteristic is the lack of any development within the variation form: the first four variations are, rather, increasingly fast decorations of the theme, which returns plain in octave-transposed apotheosis in the fifth and last variation. The solo instrument was not, of course, specifically Messiaen's choice, but the work belongs with such immediate predecessors as *Les offrandes oubliées* and *La mort du nombre* in projecting the violin as a spiritualized human voice. Only the genre is unusual. Messiaen's published output of what can be considered chamber music is limited to just three works: these variations, the *Quatuor pour la fin du temps* and a test piece for flautists at the Conservatoire, *Le merle noir* (1951). Only very special circumstances, it would seem, can lure him into a medium essentially concerned with dialogue, a medium therefore resistant to his non-developing art and his singleness of vision. No doubt the breach in this first instance was made by love, but in later expressions of that love Messiaen turned to the medium of song, where, setting his own texts, he could again operate from a single vantage point.

Although that vantage point would seem to be one he deeply felt to be his own – the 'sincerity' of La Jeune France is here paraded as in no other work – both the *Poèmes pour Mi* and the *Chants de terre et de ciel* were conceived for the soprano voice. There is, however, no paradox in this. A male singer would tend inevitably to appropriate the husbandly feelings Messiaen expresses, whereas a female interpreter can leave them intact as the composer's. Moreover, the soprano voice has access to a physical warmth and ecstatic brilliance uniquely its own, and Messiaen had already shown his partiality to those qualities in his *Trois mélodies*, in his vocalise study and in his arrangement of his motet *O sacrum convivium!* as a solo for soprano and organ.

Like *La Nativité du Seigneur*, the *Poèmes pour Mi* are a novenary. The difference is that the element of symmetry is much heightened. The first and last songs both contain long jubilant melismas imitated from plainsong; the second and penultimate are both simple love songs, ignorant of the theological implications brought out in all the other numbers. Relatively simple and gently addressed, too, are the third and sixth songs, each followed by an aggressive contrast: 'Epouvante', the fourth song, is a rare expression in Messiaen of spiritual mistrust, fiercely chromatic and couched for the singer mostly in formalized demonic laughter, while the seventh song, 'Les deux guerriers', is more optimistically combative, portraying husband and wife as soldiers of Christ on their way to the celestial city. The middle song, 'L'épouse', contains the nub of the work. Like many of the others, it borrows words and images from the Bible, in this case going to St Paul for the view that: 'The husband is the head of the wife, even as Christ is the head of the church.' And indeed *Poèmes pour Mi* is not just a document of marital affection but a tract, as heady as the Song of Songs, on human love as parabolic to divine.

It is, therefore, not the normal stuff of song recitals, but rather, quite as much as *La Nativité du Seigneur* or *Les corps glorieux*, a concert liturgy; and this is emphasized by such borrowings from plainsong as the frequent use of a reciting tone, or the long embellishments of phrases, or the sevenfold alleluia of the first song. Necessarily, a change in attitude is required from both singer and audience when this, Messiaen's first important vocal work, is performed. The fact that the singer is not expected to identify with the emotions presented has already been mentioned: the songs have to be delivered, not interpreted, sung with the sweetness they demand but not made to seem confessional. Lise Arséguest, in a recording accompanied by Messiaen, well shows the sort of priestly objectivity required, which can then accommodate a pressingly enthusiastic rendering of psalmody and vocalise. The problem is largely one of overcoming embarrassment, as Messiaen did in bringing his theological love songs into the public domain, and as his listeners must do if they are to accept so fierce a swerve from good taste.

It may be possible to enjoy the organ cycles in total ignorance of their purported subjects, but the *Poèmes pour Mi*, having words, resist any such understanding. And Messiaen ensures that his words are heard: something which is not so hard to achieve in a style generally lacking in counterpoint. Often the voice is heard over some neutral background: a sustained chord, a characteristic ostinato of chiming chords, even silence. At other times the sung note is doubled by the piano, usually with added harmony: practically the whole of the middle song is contained in the piano in this way. Moreover, the songs are all short and in most cases their language is highly repetitive, according with the repetitive musical structures and also facilitating aural comprehension of the words.

Since the musical language of the *Poèmes pour Mi* is in every way typical of Messiaen's work in the 1930s, the words of the songs can provide clues not only to the intended significance of this cycle – which is fairly straightforwardly that of comparing God's love, as expressed in his establishment of the Church and the Eucharist, with man's, as expressed in marriage – but also to the meaning of Messiaen's imagery more generally. In many respects his approach is conventional. Ideas of forward or upward motion are conveyed by rising phrases; anxiety is chromatic and joy diatonic: this is all part of his immediate and whole-hearted manner of musical expression. However, there are points where the music makes original and important points at a level of closeness not available to an instrumental work. One such is in the third song, 'La maison'.

The basic object of contemplation here (see example 18), as so often in Messiaen, is the diminished-seventh chord. One could describe the first bar as being in mode 2, but one could also say that Messiaen harmonizes the notes of a diminished-seventh chord with sixth and seventh chords on those same notes. The second bar is unusual in Messiaen's music of this period in containing all twelve notes, but again the basic units are simpler: the melody is diatonic, or could even be construed as pentatonic, while the first three chords are again based on notes from the diminished-seventh chord C–D sharp–F sharp–A. Yet despite what is conventionally a more normal melodic profile, 'the truth' enjoys a more uncertain setting than does Messiaen's contemplation of himself contemplating. The harmony moves outwards in growing diffuseness, but always in mode 2, until it reaches the final D minor diminished-seventh

chord, and the square 4/4 metre is gradually extruded. The effect of this
is curious. It is as if 'the truth' is being presented as something
profounder than the music's contemplation of it, and yet that presentation is itself part of the music, even though, by virtue of its chromaticism, it is an irregular part. Perhaps the passage can be understood as
suggesting that the truth is more complex, and less personal (less
attached to Messiaen's particular modality, returning to universally
basic pentatony), than the instances of it contained in the rest of the
work.

Ex. 18   Poèmes pour Mi   3 'La maison'

What is certain is that it is the first bar of example 18, rather than the
second, that best represents the melodic and harmonic quality of the
Poèmes pour Mi. And, by virtue of its medium, this is a work in which
melody and harmony are unusually distinct, by contrast with the piano,
organ and orchestral compositions, where ideas are very often presented
in harmonies of ambiguous root, so that the identification of a principal
melodic voice is partly foxed. Here in many cases the melody turns out
to be fixated on a diminished-seventh chord: to the example from the
third song could be added others from the fourth, fifth, seventh, eighth
and ninth. The alternative frame is that provided by a 'truncated' whole-
tone scale, omitting one note in the tritone between the pitches that
function as tonic and dominant. (The tritone dominant is of course a
link with the diminished-seventh model, and a feature of Messiaen's
harmony very generally.) An instance of this is the opening of the second
song, 'Paysage' (example 19). This is pure whole-tone melody, though
the very first two notes have established A sharp/B flat as the tonic and E
as the dominant; thereafter the range is extended symmetrically
upwards and downwards, to F sharp and A flat, and D is introduced as a
dissonance to this perfectly equilibrated scheme, preparing the final
resolution on to B flat. As in examples already discussed from *L'Ascension*, Messiaen uses diatonic chords to underline functions ascribed
within a non-diatonic system. Thus the dominant quality of the intial E
is enhanced by a dominant-seventh chord, with a fiercely dissonant C

that allows the fall to A sharp to be felt as an alleviation of tension. In a similar way, the dissonance of the D is underlined by the combination of an augmented triad (F sharp–B flat–D) with a diminished-seventh chord (C–E flat–F sharp), and the final superimposition of 6–4 chords of G minor and E major is scarcely a conventional consonance: what it really provides is a return to the opening harmony with the addition of a G to lend support to the B flat as its flattened mediant.

Ex. 19   Poèmes pour Mi   2 'Paysage'

Where the combination of triadic harmonies and diminished-seventh melody produces mode 2, their interaction with whole-tone melody results in mode 3, but, as in other cases mentioned, the modes of limited transpositions are resultants, not determinants of the harmony. The underlying forces are diatonic, operating on ideas developed from symmetrical divisions of the octave. Such a use of diatonic harmony may appear factitious, and certainly it would seem incapable of any long-term momentum: example 19 could as well be the end of a song as the beginning, and in fact it is. (It is also in the middle.) One could go further and suggest that the whole refrain is simply a statement and prolonged repetition of a tritone fall, a dwelling on a single interval. But that accords with Messiaen's objectives in stopping time, and the compression of harmony to short-term objectives leaves it free to be opulently alluring, as here, and to match in colourfulness the colours of which the words speak: Messiaen's view of harmonic colour as something more than a metaphor will have to be considered later. The relative separation of melody and harmony also makes it possible for the same melodic motif to be harmonized in different ways very quickly with no loss of coherence.

This Messiaen does in the parts of the song interleaved between repetitions of example 19, parts where the tonality switches to the diminished-seventh variety. The joins, naturally, are of special interest. The chain of chords at the end of example 19, which might have been expected to land next on another B flat atop a chord of G minor, instead leads to emphatic octave As, rudely introducing a pitch that has not so far occurred in the piece. This becomes the starting point for the 'Boris motif', and hence for a diminished-seventh expression that, towards the end of this first interruption, is quickened by dynamic and harmonic forces until it leads by semitonal displacement into the first chord of the refrain (see example 20).

Ex. 20   Poèmes pour Mi   2 'Paysage'

The change in musical construction is very clearly explained by the text, for an image of rest, the lake, is replaced by an image of travail, the road. The second interruption begins like the first, but now the beloved is seen in the landscape, and the harmonic dichotomy is resolved by figures that include both whole-tone and diminished-seventh elements, so leading unproblematically to the concluding appearance of the refrain.

'Paysage' is one of the simpler songs of the *Poèmes pour Mi*, but none the less typical for that. The adjustment of rhythmic values in example 20, producing variations of an underlying 4/8, is very much characteristic of Messiaen's style at this time, and feels to be at one with his harmonic adjustment of melodic symmetries. Above all, the tonal structure of 'Paysage' is that of the cycle in microcosm. The great alleluia at the end of the first song, for instance, is again based on a whole-tone mode centred on A sharp, though while the right hand of the piano ripples in mode 2, the left hand insists on diatonic F sharp with added sixth as the guiding harmony (see example 21). The presence of the second mode here draws attention to the fact that the mode of two–four–two–four semitones (here A sharp–B sharp–E–F sharp) can exist within both the second and the third modes. Its importance to Messiaen's harmony is such that it can, in this same transposition, underpin almost the whole of the cycle, whose principal tonal centres are as follows:

1	F sharp	4	C	7	C
2	A sharp	5	A sharp	8	B sharp
3	E	6	F sharp	9	A

The only exception to the whole-tone rule is the last song, for a very good reason: it is here that Messiaen glimpses the possibility of separation from the beloved, through death, and that possibility coincides with an anchoring to the pitch that, in 'Paysage' and again in 'Epouvante', had been associated with anxiety. Moreover, A combines with the B sharp and F sharp of the two–four–two–four structure to make a diminished-seventh harmony, so that the choice of tonality for the three songs before the last can hardly have been accidental.

Ex. 21   Poèmes pour Mi   1 'Action de grâces'

The *Poèmes pour Mi* are not only Messiaen's first important vocal work but also his first large-scale composition involving the piano since the *Préludes*. They are simpler to play, possibly because Messiaen was here writing for himself and not for a colleague intending to make a career as a pianist. Nevertheless, the treatment of the piano is more personal, less Debussyan. Nearly always the textures are chordal, to the extent that the exceptions stand out, and no doubt are meant to; the main ones are the toccata under the final alleluia of the first song, the weird artificial birdsong in the sixth (presage of so much) and the doubling of the voice in octaves for a vocalise in the last. The individuality, however, comes not just from the chordal textures but from the frequent suggestion of resonance effects, often because the suggestion of a fundamental is ambiguous, as it may well be with bell sounds: the first chord of example 19, for instance, might be a collection of harmonics from a low E or a low B, and the inharmonic quality of piano tone makes such ambiguities the stronger. Coupled with the decisive pulsation of so much of the *Poèmes pour Mi*, despite the rhythmic interventions, this clangorous sound-world recalls nothing so much as the Balinese gamelan to which Messiaen had been introduced five years before.

One might have thought this would tie the music to its medium indissolubly, and yet in 1937, the year after the composition of the cycle, Messiaen orchestrated it. Moreover, the result is a genuine alternative to the original and not an inferior copy as was the case with the second version of *L'Ascension* and, still more so, *Les offrandes oubliées*. Using an ensemble similar to that of those and his other orchestral scores of the 1930s, Messiaen disposes timbres as judiciously and colourfully as he does harmonies. The substance of the music remains very much the same, though with necessary alteration to some peculiarly pianistic passages and with the occasional addition of extra décor, such as a discreet halo of violin harmonics for the voice in the first song's alleluia. Since there would not seem to have been any outer compulsion for this arrangement, which had no performance until 1946, one must assume it was motivated internally: perhaps by a love for the music that another love had inspired. It remained a single experience. Messiaen has customarily separated the task of orchestration from that of composition (we are informed, for example, that *Saint François d'Assise* was entirely 'composed', though apparently composed in short score, before it was orchestrated), but *Poèmes pour Mi* is his only piece that, like so much of Ravel, has two distinct and equally valid identities.

It is not difficult to see why this did not happen in the case of the *Chants de terre et de ciel*. The accompaniment now is much more demanding, and much more specific to the piano, including such things as scintillating quick figures in the high treble, chords left to resonate, and forceful low bass notes designed to set off sympathetic vibration higher up the instrument. Even more than in the *Poèmes pour Mi*, the piano is a source of resonances, and Messiaen's interest in these phenomena, already noted in the *Préludes*, comes right to the fore. One result of this is to open out the harmonic world of the work towards concerns other than the diatonic embrace of whole-tone and diminished-seventh chords, or at least to do so nominally. An example is the 'chord of resonance'. Messiaen introduces this term in *Technique de mon langage musical*[1] and gives an example (see my example 22) from *Chants de terre et de ciel*, from the song 'Arc-en-ciel d'innocence'.

His explanation of this chord, presented first in 'second inversion', is that it contains in tempered fashion, 'nearly all the notes perceptible, to an extremely fine ear, in the resonance' of a low fundamental. (This would seem to include everything up to and including the fifteenth harmonic.) But of course the process of tempering, particularly for the higher harmonics, obscures any such origin, if it were not already thoroughly obscured by the dynamic levelling out and the compression of register. Moreover, since both chords in the quotation are founded on dominant sevenths, one is more likely to hear them as complex

Ex. 22   Chants de terre et de ciel   4 'Arc-en-ciel d'innocence'

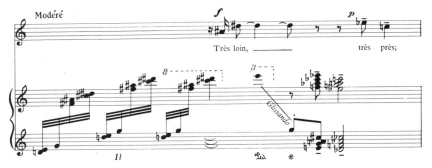

dominants, with no more relationship to resonance, and no less, than is held by much of Messiaen's harmonic repertory.

Much closer to natural resonance is another extract quoted in *Technique de mon langage musical*, this time from the final song, 'Résurrection' (see my example 23). Here Messiaen speaks of the low G–D–A as an 'inferior resonance'[2] to the decisive dominant chord on C sharp – and the tritone clash is eminently characteristic, without destroying the effect of resonances produced by the fifths in the bass, by the octave doublings in the dominant chord, by the registral layout and by the dynamic level. The ensuing flurry is described by Messiaen as being in 'bird style', though it can equally be understood as a shimmer of upper harmonics.

There is evidence here, implicit and explicit, of a choice of notes dictated by particular effects of timbre rather than by harmonic function and connection: in other words, instead of occupying itself with phrase structure, Messiaen's harmony is tending to narrow its focus to the

Ex. 23   Chants de terre et de ciel   6 'Résurrection'

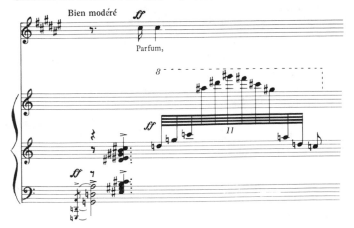

individual sonority. This is, however, only a tendency. There are many passages that would be at home in the *Poèmes pour Mi*, most of them melodically centred on the C–E flat–F sharp–A diminished-seventh chord. (The third and fourth songs are rich in examples.) But the new cycle is harmonically as well as texturally more complex, and it is also, inevitably, more complex in expression, being related to the *Poèmes pour Mi* rather as *Les corps glorieux* is related to *La Nativité du Seigneur*.

As in that parallel case, the individual members of the cycle are longer: there are six songs, lasting as long as the nine of the earlier group. They can be regarded as forming a triptych of diptychs, each pair being devoted to a member of the young Messiaen family. The first song, 'Bail avec Mi', is another offering from the composer to his wife, and it is followed by an 'Antienne du silence' in which an angel replaces the woman as object of meditation: the two are quite literally songs of heaven and earth.

The third and fourth songs, 'Danse du bébé-Pilule' and 'Arc-en-ciel d'innocence', are both dedicated to the composer's only child, Pascal, born on 14 July 1937. Pascal's dance has a charmingly simple refrain built around the diminished-seventh chord – Messiaen uses it in *Technique de mon langage musical* to exemplify the possibility of 'false folk songs'[3] – and there are also passages of unclouded melodic pentatony. Both these songs have an atmosphere of bright *naïveté* within a thoroughly aware context that suggests the music for Yniold in *Pelléas et Mélisande*: Pascal is promised 'rainbows of innocence' instead of the arrows Golaud uses to bribe his son.

Then finally Messiaen turns to himself. The fifth song, 'Minuit pile et face', is a vision of death much more violently enacted than in the corresponding 'Epouvante' of the *Poèmes pour Mi*. It is violent, too, in the range of its imagery. The poetic voice sees its sins dancing to a quasi-fugue in Bartókian Bulgarian rhythm, for all the world as if no progress had been made since the middle part of *Les offrandes oubliées*. (There may be some significance in the fact that Messiaen finds it hard to develop as a composer in contemplation of the negative.) More persuasive is the variety of usage given to pairs of clashing fifths, which, besides other appearances, evoke tolling and then high alarm bells. Another nice point is the gradual dissolving of the 'Boris motif': this brings the central prayer to a firm close, but in four repetitions it is slowly stretched, melodically, harmonically and rhythmically, preparing for a return of the music of death and damnation. The song then finds its proper resolution in a lullaby, a Christian advance into the childlike. After that the final song can speak of resurrection, as it does in jubilant Easter alleluias, accompanied by strident bell sounds from which quotation has already been made.

The alleluias of 'Résurrection' are unusual for Messiaen in remaining so much within modalities of a conventional kind, Dorian and Mixolydian. By contrast, the 'Antienne du silence' – which also has its alleluias, in the middle and at the end in the manner of Easter antiphons – looks to a new way of creating modes. This is the only other piece of the 1930s to bear comparison with Messiaen's more speculative organ movements, such as 'Le mystère de la Sainte Trinité'. The piano plays a three-part heterophony crammed into a space of around three octaves in the middle to treble register, the central voice being modal and melodic while the others are chromatic and more ornamental. The soprano's part is modally akin to the piano's melody, but rhythmically they are independent, taking different paths among the stepping stones of even semiquavers provided by the top line (see example 24).

Ex. 24   Chants de terre et de ciel   2 'Antienne du silence'

The governing mode here is not one of the modes of limited transpositions; instead it consists of one five-note set, F–G flat–A–B–D flat, coupled to its transposition up a fifth, C–C sharp–E–F sharp–G sharp.

The notation invites the singer to treat D flat and C sharp as different notes, the first occurring within the lower set and therefore always dropping to B, the second coming from the higher set and so nearly always rising to E. This is just one example of how the mode has become more than a collection of notes and some more or less defined hierarchies: it is, rather, a repertory of melodic possibilities, and so more like an Indian rāga or other Oriental tonal system. The lack of octaves (there is just a single enharmonic one, G flat–F sharp, and that is not available to the soprano, who omits the G flat until the close of her line) helps Messiaen to establish his own tendencies, which include his highly characteristic tritone cadence but otherwise a preference for small intervals. Meanwhile the lowest piano part mixes fragments from different transpositions of the mode, emphasizing instead the larger leaps of fourths.

Where Messiaen's modes had been most usually concerned with bringing diatonic harmony to bear on non-diatonic melody, in the 'Antienne du silence', as in 'Le mystère de la Sainte Trinité', their business is with maintaining some survival in atonal heterophony: the mode itself is based on that primary diatonic interval the fifth, and the melodic phrases of both voice and piano end always on one of the notes of the F major triad. (The voice chooses only F or C.) Atonality is for Messiaen a medium of mystery, as the title and nature of the movement from *Les corps glorieux* make clear. To discover within that medium some familiar signposts is to find amiableness even in the most inscrutable doctrines of Christianity.

There is a link too with Messiaen's poems for the *Chants de terre et de ciel*, for just as modern atonality is made to coexist with ageless pitch centrality in the 'Antienne du silence', so the texts of the songs, including those of the *Poèmes pour Mi*, find the imagery of surrealism suitable for the expression of religious truth. Fright, inevitably, brings the connection out most clearly. 'Bleeding shreds will follow you into darkness', sings the soprano in 'Epouvante', 'Like a triangular vomiting,/And the clamorous shock of rings on the irreparable door,/Will give a rhythm to your despair.' But the quieter moments of both cycles, too, have their oddities of diction: indeed, it is by such means that the homely is made holy, set in a cosmic context of angels and stars, birds and colours. Messiaen has recalled that while writing the *Poèmes pour Mi* he was influenced by his reading of Pierre Reverdy,[4] and certainly there is something of the same blend of intimate piety with vast metaphor in his own poems. Reverdy, and other poets connected with the surrealist movement, gave Messiaen the freedom to range as far as his imagination could travel in search of imagery, and gave him the verbal means thereby to suggest a different level of experience: the spiritual for him, the unconscious for most of them. He has, however, insisted that his poems have no literary merit, and finally it must be the music of the *Poèmes pour Mi* and the *Chants de terre et de ciel* that opens new areas of response by presenting familiar objects and tensions in quite unfamiliar surroundings, and by placing the recitalist in front of new and strange antiphoners.

CHAPTER 6

Technique for the End of Time

The completion of *Les corps glorieux* on 25 August 1939 was followed a week later by the outbreak of the Second World War. Messiaen was called up, but by reason of his poor eyesight was found unfit for active service. He was at Verdun, a medical auxiliary, in May 1940, when the German invasion took place, and then in the company of three other musicians he made his way on foot to Nancy. There he and his colleagues were captured. He was taken to a prison camp at Görlitz in Silesia (now in Poland), Stalag VIIIA, where he fiercely guarded 'a haversack containing all my treasures, i.e., a little library of scores . . . going from the Brandenburg Concertos of Bach to the Lyric Suite of Berg'.[1]

Another would soon be added. With him in the camp he found a violinist, a clarinettist and a cellist, for whom he wrote a short trio that they performed in the washrooms. Then, out of this humble beginning, came a full-scale chamber work with the addition of himself as pianist, a *Quatuor pour la fin du temps*. The first performance of this work at the Stalag in January 1941 has, together with the première of *The Rite of Spring*, become one of the great stories of twentieth-century music. With the composer playing at a run-down upright piano, the performance was given before an audience of 5,000 prisoners, sitting in the depths of winter at the blackest point in a world war. 'Never', Messiaen has recalled, 'have I been heard with as much attention and understanding.'[2]

The title of the 'quartet for the end of time' might suggest that it was written in response to imprisonment, but Messiaen has resisted any such interpretation and emphasized rather its dependence on the imagery of the apocalypse contained in the Revelation of St John the Divine. The score is inscribed 'in homage to the Angel of the Apocalypse, who raises his hand heavenwards saying: "There will be no more Time."' And the three most vigorous of its eight movements all declare this homage in their titles: they are the second, 'Vocalise, pour l'ange qui annonce la fin du temps,' the sixth, 'Danse de la fureur, pour les sept trompettes', and the seventh, 'Fouillis d'arcs-en-ciel, pour l'ange qui annonce la fin du temps'. Of course, imprisonment may have played its part in directing Messiaen's thoughts towards the eschatological, but the subject matter (like the musical style) was already implicit in *Les corps glorieux* and some of the songs from the mid-1930s.

What was new was the instrumentation. Previously Messiaen's only ventures near chamber music had been in the two works for violin and piano and in *Fête des belles eaux*: it was not much of a preparation for a work occupying four players for nearly an hour, especially one from a composer whose only important instrumental works for several years had been organ cycles. Messiaen answered the challenge, however, entirely on his own terms. Like the organ cycles, the *Quatuor* is a sequence of related meditations; like *Les corps glorieux* in particular, it mixes purely monodic sections with others that are chordally conceived and still others that are heterophonic. The difference is that the four dissimilar instruments can, when conjoined, make the monodies more incisive, or alternatively, when separated, render the heterophonies more distinct. There is also the difference that the quartet, whatever the singularities of its première, was written for the concert room and not for the church: it was going to have to face an audience not necessarily sympathetic to its theology, which may have influenced Messiaen towards making it a show-piece of his musical techniques at their present zenith.

Such it certainly is. Not surprisingly, when Messiaen soon afterwards wrote his *Technique de mon langage musical* he chose more examples from the *Quatuor* than from any other work. There is therefore some justification for considering the treatise and the chamber piece together, particularly when the latter carries a preface that is a diminutive pre-echo of the theoretical work, following the other pre-echo contained in the preface to *La Nativité du Seigneur*.

The first movement of the quartet, 'Liturgie de cristal', is considered at comparative length in *Technique de mon langage musical* as an instance of 'rhythmic pedal', a synonym for ostinato already encountered in *La Nativité*. Here, though, the repeating patterns are more complex, and they help to create textures in which the piano and the cello, both playing through ostinato cycles, are very much separated from each other and from the violin and the clarinet that figure the background circulations with imitated birdsong. The work thus opens at an extreme of heterophony (see example 25). The piano, throughout the movement, keeps repeating the 'tala' of seventeen values that has already appeared in 'Le mystère de la Sainte Trinité' from *Les corps glorieux* (see example 17) and in 'Arc-en-ciel d'innocence' from the *Chants de terre et de ciel*, and Messiaen in *Technique de mon langage*

musical makes it clear that its attraction lies in the apparently conscious manipulation of basic cells mentioned with reference to the
Corps glorieux movement. However, the presentation of the tala in
'Liturgie de cristal' is unlikely to make much rhythmic impression; it
serves rather to provide an irregular framework on which to drape a
sequence of chords, a quite distinct repeating cycle consisting not of
seventeen but of twenty-nine elements.

Ex. 25   Quatuor pour la fin du temps   *i 'Liturgie de cristal'*

There is an obvious parallel here with medieval isorhythm, though
Messiaen has implied he was unaware of such predecessors at the time.[3]
In any event, his 'color' is decidedly more complicated. Twenty-nine is
the number of four-note pitch sets that remain separate however
transposed or inverted, but Messiaen would appear to have chosen it
from his taste for prime numbers (another source of allure for the tala,
which has a length of thirteen crotchets). His explanation of it in
Technique de mon langage musical distinguishes three fragments as
coming from the 'chord on the dominant', from mode 3 and from mode
2, and certainly the modal derivations at least are connected with the
flavouring of chords on the augmented triad G flat–B flat–D and then on
the diminished-seventh chord B flat–C sharp–E. The 'chord on the
dominant', however, is a more problematic creature, lacking here the
clear dominant function it had on its first appearance in *La Nativité du
Seigneur*. According to Messiaen's prescriptions in *Technique de mon
langage musical*,[4] the second, fourth, sixth and eighth chords in the
piano are inversions of dominant chords on F, C, E flat and G respectively, each preceded by a version of itself with the top two notes both
raised by a major second to become 'appoggiaturas'. The implication is
that each pair of chords is a resolution, but one must doubt that they are

heard in that way, or that the 'chord on the dominant', a widespread harmonic and arpeggiated unit in the *Quatuor*, is other than a complex sonority allowing Messiaen to bring out or obscure tonalities: for example, the first and third chords are theoretically transpositions of one another, but the latter, since F remains in the bass, conveys a sense of D minor while the corresponding E minor of the former is a good deal more muted, if it is felt at all.

It is of the nature of *Technique de mon langage musical* that it is very much more concerned with how the music is put together than with how it sounds and is heard. Right at the outset Messiaen insists that his work is 'not a treatise on composition', but neither is it an analysis, nor could it be when the creator is his own commentator. It is, rather, an attempt to establish general rules from particular instances of creative process, and as such it carries no special authority: it cannot tell us how Messiaen's music works, but only how in the early 1940s he thought it had been composed. Yet sometimes this has not been understood. Messiaen's music has been investigated as if his *Technique de mon langage musical* provided the only avenues of approach, whereas its explanations are often only partial and occasionally downright questionable. The nature of the modes of limited transpositions, for example, is only very incompletely indicated, as has already been suggested: Messiaen says nothing of how they might have arisen from a wish to bring diatonic force to bear on non-diatonic phenomena, nor even of how they might be useful in that regard, despite his plain use of dominant chords to give dominant quality to the tritone. To take another example, the melodic turn that has here in deference been called the '*Boris* motif' arguably has much less to do with Mussorgsky (whose theme is contained within a perfect fourth) than with Messiaen's own liking for the tritone and for its division into intervals of a major third and a major second (the whole-tone and mode 3 model) or else two minor thirds (the diminished seventh and mode 2 model).

Where *Technique de mon langage musical* does have value is in helping us to understand the quality of Messiaen's musical mind. It reads a little like a recipe book. Messiaen's method is to give attention successively to matters of rhythm, melody, form and harmony, and to delimit categories and subcategories within each domain, always with reference to his own usage in works from *Le banquet céleste* to the immediate successor of the *Quatuor*, the *Visions de l'Amen* for two pianos (1943). The discussion of 'Liturgie de cristal', for instance, comes in a chapter on 'Polyrhythm and Rhythmic Pedals' where Messiaen discusses the superimposition of different rhythmic successions, with examples of simultaneous ostinatos of different lengths from *La Nativité du Seigneur*, of durational sequences placed over their retrogrades in *Les corps glorieux*, of rhythmic canon in the *Poèmes pour*

Mi and of rhythmic pedal in 'Liturgie de cristal'. The impression – rather dangerously for analysts and perhaps also for composers – is that the diverse techniques described can be freely combined in any way.

Such an impression is not, however, entirely misguided. There is an element of composition by rule in Messiaen's music, and the 'Liturgie de cristal' provides a classic instance of it. Having set up the system of twenty-nine chords rotating on a rotating rhythm, Messiaen allows it to go its own way until, after just under ten patterings of the tala, it stops. If the intention is to produce an image of eternity (Messiaen's preface speaks of 'the harmonious silence of heaven'), the movement is highly successful, for the repeating cycles appear to the ear unmotivated by any human agency, while the analytical brain may calculate that it will take twenty-nine repetitions of the tala, or seven minutes, for the original coincidence with the chord sequence to be regained, and nearly two hours (29 × 16½ repetitions of the tala) for the cello too to be brought back into line as at the beginning. What we hear in the three minutes of the actual movement is only a fragment of an enormous process.

But though it takes an objective process to execute what seems to be Messiaen's expressive intention here, the scope of his intention on the smaller scale is obviously much reduced. It is simply a matter of selecting sufficiently long sequences of chords and durational values; exactly how they marry is taken care of by the system, and one can scarcely feel secure in saying that Messiaen intended particular interactions of harmony and rhythm at particular points. (In *Technique de mon langage musical*, still with reference to this movement, Messiaen recalls Dukas's injunction to his students 'Rhythmicize your harmonies!', but the composer of *L'apprenti sorcier* can surely not have had anything like this in mind.) Of course, music is always a dialogue between a composer's taste and his system: one can argue about what we mean in saying that Beethoven 'intended' the E flat major chord at the start of the 'Eroica' Symphony, since he could not have opened the work with one of Messiaen's chords from the 'Liturgie de cristal', or if in some extraordinary way he had, it would of necessity have become a very different work. But music of the great Western tradition is normally expected to show the given and the conventional being grasped by the composer's intending mind: the means then become inseparable from the substance, the basic elements of pitch, rhythm and so on contained within larger continuities so that they no longer strike us as elements at all but are subsumed within original thoughts. The rupture of this organic wholeness is possibly the central characteristic of music in the twentieth century, and Messiaen's 'Liturgie de cristal' documents that rupture with what is, for its period, unusual clarity. Perhaps only the contemporary works of John Cage show so deep a penetration of mechanical process into musical intention.

It cannot be without significance that both Cage and Messiaen had learned much from Eastern music, and especially from Eastern rhythm. At the same time, Cage's cultivation of non-intention may have had a parallel in Messiaen's thinking if he had been aware of, and troubled by, the constraints of the personal on his theological expression. In this light 'Liturgie de cristal' could be understood as an attempt to dilute personal intention in the hope that the universal symbol of 'harmonious silence' might be the stronger. Although the techniques are inevitably different, there is a link too with the surrealist poets, who hoped through automatic writing to bypass the control of consciousness, rather as Messiaen might have hoped through automatic composition to express a vastness with no human inhabitants. Indeed, the only creatures present are birds, in stylized representations from the clarinet and the violin. In striking contrast with his later practice of indicating species' origins precisely, Messiaen's preface to the *Quatuor* remarks casually on 'a blackbird or a nightingale' as singing its solo as day breaks, though comparison with birdsong notations in *Technique de mon langage musical*[5] would suggest that the clarinet at least is a blackbird.

The systematic repetitions of the piano and cello music are not to be found in the two bird parts. Unsystematic repetitions, though, they have in plenty: the clarinet has a typical figure of a triplet followed by a large interval leap on to a staccato bounce (see bars 2 and 4 of example 25), while the violin has a number of tics including as cadence a C sharp–G–E motif. In neither case is there any apparent framework of rotation, the clarinet, in particular, being free to unloose long and varied phrases against the quietly revolving ostinatos and the violin's imitation of a more distant bird. What binds it to the rest, if exceedingly lightly, is the key of B flat. Although at times the existence of this is no more than notional (and notational), the cello is forever dropping to B flat as its lowest note; the clarinet often ends its phrases on notes of the B flat minor triad; the violin's cadential figure wants only B flat to make a diminished-seventh chord, and the B flat below middle C keeps tolling away in the changing chords of the piano's color. There is thus a heterophony of harmonic relationships to the vestigial tonic among the four voices of this extreme heterophony, preparing for the heterophony of styles among the seven movements that follow.

The complete scheme of the work, indicating instrumentation and principal tonal centres, is this:

1 'Liturgie de cristal' quartet B flat
2 'Vocalise pour l'ange qui annonce la fin du temps' quartet D
3 'Abîme des oiseaux' clarinet E
4 'Intermède' violin, clarinet, cello E
5 'Louange à l'éternité de Jésus' cello, piano E

6   'Danse de la fureur, pour les sept trompettes'   quartet   F sharp
7   'Fouillis d'arcs-en-ciel, pour l'ange qui annonce la fin du temps'
    quartet   C
8   'Louange à l'immortalité de Jésus'   violin, piano   E

Thus pinned to the notes of a whole-tone scale omitting one member,
the work displays on the largest scale a unit that is also important at a
more local level. One example has already been quoted in the cello
music from the first movement (example 25), where the five pitches are
even the same: Messiaen's comment on this comparatively rare usage of
mode I over a long period is that it 'can be tolerated when it is thus
mixed with harmonic combinations foreign to it',[6] though the high
register, marginal sonority and quiet dynamic surely help as well in
making this part only a fugitive contributor to the texture and not a
harmonic determinant.

   A distinctly more startling use of the whole-tone scale comes at the
start of the 'Danse de la fureur', aggressively scored for the quartet in
loud, bare octaves. (Example 26 shows only the upper part.) Like the

Ex. 26   Quatuor pour la fin du temps   6 'Danse de la fureur, pour les
         sept trompettes'

opening of 'Liturgie de cristal', this is lengthily quoted in *Technique de
mon langage musical*, but Messiaen's discussion of it there is limited
largely to its instancing of the rhythmic 'added value'; of its pitch
qualities he remarks only that it is 'written entirely in the *sixth mode of
limited transpositions*' (his italics).[7]

This is at once more and less than the truth. One could argue that the notes of the sixth mode F sharp–A flat–A–B flat–C–D–E flat–E have a particular force, but the 'entirely' seems hard to justify in the light of such more developmental passages as the last bar in example 26. On the other hand, there are different modalities that appear to describe the music more exactly: outstandingly the whole-tone scale in the piece's principal theme or refrain (bars 1–4, 7–8, etc.). Once more we are concerned with a five-note segment of the scale (D is omitted), and though there is one stranger to the scale (B), this is of reduced significance: it appears only twice, in unaccented positions and in what are chromatic diversions from the main continuity. The elements of that continuity are unusually clear. They are two: a whole-tone descent followed by a tritone jump (F sharp–E–B flat) and then, after a whole-tone rise, a tritone fall that can be stepped (C–A flat–F sharp) or at cadences immediate (C–F sharp). We are at some distance from Debussy's whole-tone practice. Indeed, we are very much within Messiaen's territory in that the tritone is treated as dominant. (The B in bar 2, a 'real' dominant for the E, in fact sounds a melodic dissonance and has to fall back to B flat.)

But if there are dominants in this music, which is the tonic? As usual, a symmetrical division of the octave produces an ambiguity. (Or alternatively an ambiguity calls forth a symmetrical division of the octave.) Normally Messiaen directs his ambiguities into flickering sensations of tonality (he writes of a 'stained-glass window' effect brought about by the 'chords on the dominant' of 'Liturgie de cristal'), or else uses uncertainty as a means to substantiate his own harmonic claims (for the dominant quality of the tritone in so many instances). In this case, however, the ambiguity is open conflict between E, from which the refrain always gains its power, and F sharp, on which it falls to rest. Quite possibly this sort of cleft tonality was suggested by the discussion in the Lavignac encyclopedia of Indian játis and their variegated distribution of harmonic functions among different notes.

The same source is even more likely to have provided impetus for the strongly pulsed motivic rhythm of the 'Danse de la fureur', which follows on directly from the játi-based movements of Les corps glorieux. Messiaen has often written as if his rhythmic quirks were introduced independently of any melodic or harmonic considerations, and his treatment of this movement in Technique de mon langage musical points out only how the 'added dots', as in the fourth bar of example 26, 'slacken the descents by elongating their penultimate note'.[8] Even this is doubtful as a statement of their action, which is essentially to accentuate the resolution – on to a questionable tonic – by delaying it. (Bars 1–3 have taught us to expect a fall from C.) The 'added values', too, are much more than decorative. That in the first bar, for example, gives added emphasis to the first B flat and so strengthens the first upward tritone push, since one feels not that a semiquaver has been inserted into a pair of quavers but rather that the first value in a semiquaver–semiquaver–quaver pattern has been lengthened. Messiaen has often written and spoken as if the first aim of his rhythmic innovations were that of avoiding regular metre, and certainly the effect here is to upset an underlying 2/4. The moments of upset, however, are far from arbitrary.

It would be revealing to examine every bar of the 'Danse de la fureur' for its close interaction of rhythmic and harmonic irregularities, but a broad outline of the movement must suffice. The first 'couplet' (bars 5–6) begins by covering as soon as possible a range greater than that occupied throughout the refrain: a major sixth, C–A, compared with a minor sixth, E–C. The tonic is now quite definitely C, and so this couplet could be interpreted as making a move to the modal dominant. There is, though, a change of mode. The whole-tone scale is replaced by mode 2, with particular weight thrown on to the diminished-seventh chord C–E flat–F sharp–A, and again there are preferred tendencies in the melody, even if these neumes are by no means as pronounced as those of the refrain (or to take another example, those of the central slow melody in mode 3 centred on D in 'Vocalise').

The second couplet (bars 9ff.) begins as a variation of the first, but then there is a semitone rise to C sharp for a new flight, which shows how the music has by this stage gained enough rhythmic momentum to carry it from one harmonic area to another (or to look at it another way, how the harmonic instability here achieved serves to increase tension and therefore dynamism). There are at first arpeggios of A major, C sharp major (enharmonically spelled) and E, and hence a 'super-arpeggio' of A major, out of which the melody turns into one transposition of the pentatonic scale (C–D–E–G–A) and then into another of totally different make-up (D flat–E flat–F–A flat–B flat). A sequence derived from diminished-seventh chords leads finally to an old acquaintance, the 'Boris motif', used here, perhaps, to secure the cadence after so wide-ranging a phrase. One wonders if Messiaen took the Lyric Suite out of his haversack when contemplating music where diatonic and pentatonic features are maintained in twelve-note melody.

There is more of this second couplet, followed by a reprise that mounts in excitement until halted for something new. (Again, in example 27, only the upper octave is shown.) Even more clearly than in the last bar of the previous example, there is here a swinging from one arpeggio to another: the D major triad, the pentatonic scale on F sharp, the B major triad, the C major triad and then more fleeting intimations of F major and B flat major leading back to D major. Morover, the connections are classical, and contribute, with the different pacing and dynamic, to the smoother, airier feel. Nothing could be more contrived, though, than the rhythm, which is non-retrogradable in each bar, rather as the melody is more lengthily circular. However, as in the piano part of 'Liturgie de cristal', there is the appearance of accident in the combination of pitch and rhythm, since the same sequence of sixteen notes is rotated over a tala of fifty-seven values in seven palindromic successions. This is a more mundane conundrum than that of 'Liturgie de cristal': it would take just under eight minutes for the original coincidences of pitch and rhythm to be restored. Messiaen, however, stops it when the seventh repetition of the melody has run its course. One is thus tempted to understand this pasage as belonging to the seven trumpets of the title, the seven trumpets blown by seven angels in Revelation 9–10 to signal the end of the world: the clear D major, after all, does begin the melody as a fanfare, and Messiaen's preface speaks of imitations of trumpet sound.

Ex. 27   Quatuor pour la fin du temps   6 *'Danse de la fureur, pour les sept trompettes'*

It speaks too of gongs, which cannot be mistaken in the second half of the piece, suggested there by fortissimo low piano octaves doubled by the clarinet. (The marking is 'bronze-like, brassy'.) What has happened is the accomplishment of the 'mystery of God', as promised by St John in a verse inscribed at the head of the preface. The dance of the first part of the movement is flattened out into an exotic toccata of racing semiquavers, urged on by the gong sounds that cover an augmented triad in Messiaen's favoured cretic rhythm. This last gives the opportunity for him to display a third cherished rhythmic technique, after the 'added values' of the dance and the palindromes of the presumed trumpet calls: it is the regular augmentation and diminution of a rhythmic cell, changing the values here from an initial minim–crotchet–minim to, for example, quaver–semiquaver–quaver. The climax of this alarming section is a grotesque wide-flung parody of the first theme, made the more grotesque by the strain to which it puts the players (see example 28). And in this case Messiaen has cited Berg's *Lyric Suite* as his authority.[9]

Other Viennese liaisons are tantalizing. It can hardly have escaped Messiaen's notice that the ensemble he found in the Stalag included all but the flautist of *Pierrot lunaire*, a work he had known since his student days.[10] There is, however, no parallel of texture, style or sonority sufficiently provoking to make one want to pursue the comparison. More suggestive is the correspondence between serialism and

Ex. 28   Quatuor pour la fin du temps   6 *'Danse de la fureur, pour les sept trompettes'*

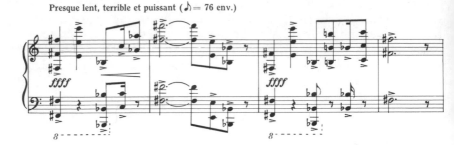

Messiaen's handling of durational successions as abstractable entities. Even if the *Lyric Suite* was the only piece of serial music that he had contact with (and it is not clear that it was), he could not have lived through the 1930s in total ignorance of serialism, and Schoenberg's method could have played some part in encouraging the view of rhythm as an independent commodity that comes out progressively in works from *La Nativité* to the *Quatuor*. The basic impulse, though, would seem to lie deeper, in Messiaen's sense of time.

There is the further possibility that the six-movement form of Berg's *Lyric Suite* had a part in facilitating the eight-movement form of the *Quatuor*. Anything other than the classical pattern of movements was then extremely unusual in a chamber work, and the *Quatuor*, like the *Lyric Suite*, begins at a moderate pace and then moves out to extremes in both directions. The important difference is that the *Quatuor* has absolutely nothing of the symphonic about it. There is, in other words, no thrust from one movement into the next: like the whole-tone steps on which they are placed, the movements are comparatively indifferent as to order, and this helps to make the large form ambiguous. There are elements of symmetry. For instance, 'Fouillis d'arcs-en-ciel' develops the framing music from 'Vocalise', and the central 'Intermède', said to be identical with the trio piece Messiaen wrote before embarking on the *Quatuor*, includes quotations from the 'Vocalise' and from the 'Danse de la fureur' – or perhaps they should be considered premonitions if they were there before the movements later to contain them.

Symmetry is one means at music's disposal of creating images of the end of time, since symmetry makes the last moment identical with the first; it denies the sort of progress by which most Western music proclaims itself at one with a notion of events changing through time, and it was something that, as we have seen, Messiaen had found natural right from his earliest published works. Of course, Stravinsky, Bartók and Webern, among others, had been exploring this area for a full generation before the *Quatuor*, but Messiaen's work is in some parts more blatantly symmetrical than anything outside his own output. In 'Fouillis d'arcs-en-ciel', for example, the symmetry is again seven-fold (like the colouring of the rainbow itself), and the music even drama-tizes the gap between the changing and the changeless, in that three sections developing ideas from the 'Vocalise' are interleaved among four repetitions of a melody close to that of the middle song from the *Poèmes pour Mi.*

It is rather the same in the *Quatuor* as a whole. While there are strong indications of a palindrome, at the same time there is a powerful finality to the last movement. The situation is, however, slightly complicated by the fact that there are two finales. The two 'Paeans', 'to Jesus's Eternity', and 'to Jesus's Immortality', are both slow solos for string instrument with piano accompaniment, both with the key signature of E major, both formally in two parts (Messiaen reasonably distinguishes them as ABA and ABAB forms,[11] but in both the main discontinuity comes with the reawakening of the first theme) and both with origins in earlier pieces, the cello movement coming from *Fête des belles eaux* and the violin one from the *Diptyque.* Once one knows how the work is going to end in fact, the cello movement comes to seem like a finale, with all the rest taking place after the work is over. Alternatively, the potential remains for more movements and more finales, since the work has demonstrated that an apparent conclusion need not in fact be the end.

This is just one of the larger ways in which the *Quatuor* is an image of the end of time, the end of any logic to temporal succession. Another is in the origins of these twin adagios, both with their roots in earlier works and now made to coexist with music that Messiaen could not possibly have composed in 1930 and might not have imagined even in 1937. There is a discontinuity of taste as well as of period. Along with the abstruse compilations of pattern and birdsong in 'Liturgie de cristal' and 'Abîme des oiseaux' (a mirror canyon this, full of topsy-turvy inversions and reversals), there comes a little tune of banal perkiness in the 'Intermède', and in the two 'Louanges' music that many of Mes-siaen's stoutest adherents have found regrettable or else passed over in silence. For not only do the added-sixth and diminished-seventh chords appear at crucial moments and in profusion, but the atmosphere is that of the sentimental piety exuding from such similarly scored movements in the French repertory as the 'Méditation' from *Thaïs.*

These movements refuse, however, to be ignored. Nor need they be. On the one hand, judgements of taste are based on experience and therefore on time: a work situating itself at the end of time may well demonstrate its special position by ignoring them. This is not to say that Messiaen consciously wrote vulgar music for his two adagios. On the contrary, he has maintained with some fierceness that they are not vulgar at all, notably in a remark to Antoine Goléa, where he insists, presumably referring above all to these movements, that 'they are not at all luscious nor sweet; they are simply noble, bare, austere'.[12] However, a musical sensibility that can form such an opinion is awesome indeed: it takes a sublime, even saintly *naïvité* to accept materials from Massenet and Glenn Miller, then use them to praise Christ as if they had never been employed for any baser purpose. But this is Messiaen's way, and though the two 'Louanges' offer the greatest stumbling block to the sophisticated, in doing so they only exemplify in extreme fashion a refusal of discrimination typical of Messiaen's art. The challenge to the religious artist is to make all things sacred, and to deny the self that would discriminate.

Yet though special pleading of this kind may be helpful to an appreciation of the *Quatuor*, it is not essential. For besides permitting the synchrony of alarmingly divergent tastes, the subject of the work, which has general musical and philosophical implications beyond its religious origin, also encourages images of eternity such as these movements contain. Where the 'Liturgie de cristal' is a similar image that leaves observers outside, the two 'Louanges' invite an active participation in the experience of eternity, since the string melody, unbroken in both movements, provides a comfortable vehicle for the listening mind, which in the first movement had been faced by the unaccommodating milieu of ostinatos and bird calls. Naturally the very slow speed of the 'Louanges', as of *Le banquet céleste* or the endings of *Les offrandes oubliées* and *L'Ascension*, assists the impression of everlastingness, but that is not all. Making a convincing image of eternity is not so easy. One might have thought it could be done merely by holding a sound for a very long time, as in certain pieces by LaMonte Young, but so literal an image gives the mind no foothold: it remains an objective phenomenon, and one of considerably lesser interest than the 'Liturgie de cristal'. The problem is to give the impression of changelessness while all the time there is change, to make an image of blessed eternity that is still intelligible to minds existing in the present world.

Messiaen bases his solution on a long-established connection in Western music between speed and harmonic complexity. From at least the time of Monteverdi, quicker speeds have been associated with straightforward harmony, slower ones with more chromaticism and dissonance. (Much of Schoenberg's difficulty comes, perhaps, from his music being the highly accelerated version of something that 'ought' to be exceedingly slow.) Messiaen's 'Louanges' have the harmonic substance of quickness, since in essence the themes are pentatonic; but at the same time there are chromatic complications that lend a reasonableness to the long delay. For example, the theme of the 'Louange à l'immortalité de Jésus', played entirely over a 6–4 chord with added sixth, is based on the pentatonic scale E–F sharp–G sharp–B–C sharp (see example 29).

Ex. 29   Quatuor pour la fin du temps   8 *'Louange à l'immortalité de Jésus'*

The additional features here are those that more frequently in Messiaen's harmony become centres of stability, the tritone and the diminished-seventh chord, for the first two bars add to the pentatonic set the pitches A sharp and F ('exchange notes' removed by a tritone from the tonic E and its fifth B), while the third bar begins with a diminished-seventh arpeggio that leads to an expectation of continuation. It does this so well, indeed, that it becomes the main motif in the unstable rise that follows a repetition of the theme down a whole tone, a drop that preserves three of the original pentatonic notes, including E and B. The main business of the movement is with the removal of the non-pentatonic elements, until finally the piano can return to a 6–4 chord of E major with added sixth to support a pure harmonic E in the violin. There is no real development, only the gradual emergence of an immediate, simple idea (the pentatonic scale) from chromatic hesitations that had made it drag through time. And one may interpret Messiaen's treasuring of the added-sixth chord elsewhere as due not only to its combination of a root-position triad (e.g. C–E–G) with an inversion (e.g. C–E–A) but also to its hint (as in jazz) of pentatonic simplicity, the pentatonic being the most ancient musical system known to us and therefore arguably, on a human time-scale, eternal.

In most respects, the 'Louange à l'éternité de Jésus' differs from the 'Louange à l'immortalité de Jésus' only to the extent that eternity differs from immortality: Messiaen's preface discloses that the first homage is to Christ as 'the Word', the second to him as 'the Word made flesh'. However, the tempo markings are fascinatingly different. Whereas the eighth movement asks only to be played 'Extremely slowly', the marking for the fifth is 'Infinitely slow'. Of course, this instruction is not going to be fulfilled in performances on this earth: if and wherever it is fulfilled, it must make everything after the opening B of this movement redundant, or place the rest after the end of time.

Here, then, is yet another way in which the work aspires to its title, in addition to the dislocations of pulse brought about by Messiaen's rhythmic techniques, the achievement of symmetry (and there is now another symmetry between the objective eternity of 'Liturgie de cristal' and the subjective eternity of 'Louange à l'immortalité de Jésus'), the confusion of tastes, the compression of history ranging at least from thirteenth-century India to twentieth-century Europe, the setting up of long-term process and the involvement of the listener in the paradoxical pleasure of observing eternity as it happens. In all these ways the *Quatuor pour la fin du temps* is more than a metaphor. To be sure, Messiaen's allusions to the Book of Revelation provide stimulating food for the imagination even of the non-believer: the inscription at the head of his preface refers to the great angel of the Apocalypse as clothed in a cloud, having a rainbow on his head, a face like the sun and two pillars of fire for feet.

The preface can also be rather illuminating as to Messiaen's intentions. 'In my dreams', he writes of the seventh movement,

> I hear and see classified chords and melodies, known colours and forms; then, after this transitional stage, I pass into the unreal and submit in ecstasy to a wheeling, a girating interpenetration of superhuman colours. These swords of fire, these blue and orange lava flows, these sudden stars: here is the jumble, here the rainbows!

What is interesting here is not just the language familiar from mystical writing, and not just the description of sound in terms of colour (a commonplace with Messiaen, as has already been observed), but the presentation of the movement as a vision. This may be no more than a pleasing literary conceit, but it does show Messiaen prepared to countenance his works as documents of personal experience and not, as he has more usually insisted, as theological exegesis. One may even be reminded of Berlioz's programme for his *Symphonie fantastique*, and indeed, seen in this light, the *Quatuor* is a fantastic symphony of images a hugely imaginative composer might conceive on studying the text of St John.

In any event, the re-use of passages from earlier works must cast doubt on the value of any explanation in terms of movement titles or prefaces, for although it may be no great distance from the 'blessed eternity' of the *Diptyque* to the 'Immortality of Jesus' here, or from seeing water as a 'symbol of Grace and Eternity'[13] in *Fête des belles eaux* to conceiving the same music as illustrative of the 'Eternity of Jesus', the introduction of the Word can scarcely be dismissed as insignificant. Here again one encounters the problems, faced by both Berlioz and Messiaen in peculiarly acute fashion, of discovering and comprehending verbal clues to musical expression. We can go only so far with any certainty. For instance, it would not be reasonable to doubt that the two 'Louanges' are effective images of eternity, on both intrinsic and extrinsic counts. The nature of the material, as has been suggested, prepares for the prolongation of simple elements through time, and Messiaen is in line with predecessors as diverse as, say, Fauré ('In paradisum') and Berg (*Wozzeck*) in associating the infinite with music of high pitch, clear scoring, bright harmony and long duration. On the other hand, it is difficult to find any reason of musical substance or historical convention to justify the differences between Messiaen's statements of these movements' meanings. Nor is there any need to give any great authority even to an author's preface. Messiaen the annotator is not Messiaen the composer, and there may be respects in which the comments misrepresent the music as much as, perhaps, the music misrepresents the vision: Messiaen has described the hesitation he feels in speaking of his work,[14] and very possibly he was more realistic in his first version of the *Quatuor* preface when he wrote of 'the author' and not of 'me'.

To emphasize the musical values of such a work as the *Quatuor* is not to seek to deny its spiritual values, but rather to look for what is explicable. And already we have found a great many ways in which the 'end of time' is conveyed through music and through music's direct associations (with a rainbow of historical periods). There is one more. Western music had mastered time through its development of the major–minor system, giving it a variety of long-term and intermediate goals that appear to justify the flow of time: in listening to a Haydn quartet, for example, one has the impression that the music is at one with its element, that it shares the qualities of tempered, forward movement we have learned from the clock. Messiaen's quartet is different. The interval most inimical to the major–minor system has now gained a position of dominance (often literally so), and the complex hierarchy of the diatonic scale has given way to the much simpler harmonic functions of the tritone, the augmented triad or the pentatonic mode. The result of this is that a rich labyrinth of potential pathways to the tonic has been replaced by a straightforward dominant–tonic relationship, except in those cases, such as 'Liturgie de cristal' and 'Abîme des oiseaux', where the tonic has all but disappeared. The music is not fixed to time so securely: it can very easily go too slowly, as in the 'Louanges', or too fast, as in the semiquaver movement in the latter part of the 'Danse de la fureur' and elsewhere; it can also move irregularly. This dislocation between music and time is something that Messiaen had discovered in Stravinsky, as he affirmed sketchily in his 1939 essay and more fully in *Technique de mon langage musical*, where, indeed, the very first example comes from *The Rite of Spring*. In the *Quatuor* he had already gone further, and though the effect may not be to bring time to a halt, it is at least to hint that time is more unruly and uncomprehended than earlier music had assumed.

CHAPTER 7

Arrows and Amens

In the spring of 1941, after the winter première of the *Quatuor pour la fin du temps*, Messiaen was released from prison camp and went first to Neussargues in the département of Cantal, where he had worked on *L'Ascension* in 1932 and 1933, and also written his unpublished mass for sopranos and violins in the latter year. Now he wrote there a pair of *Choeurs pour une Jeanne d'Arc* before in May 1941 he was appointed to a harmony class at the Conservatoire, where he was to remain as a teacher for almost forty years. Paris was, of course, still under German occupation, which may partly explain why 1942 was again creatively blank: only some incidental music for an *Oedipus*, scored for ondes martenot, is dated to this year. At Neussargues in the summer, however, *Technique de mon langage musical* was set in train, perhaps stimulated by the curiosity of his students, who were so soon to stimulate him.

For his joining the Conservatoire staff proved most propitious. Among his first students were some highly gifted young men and women, including the composers Pierre Boulez, Serge Nigg, Jean-Louis Martinet and Maurice Le Roux, and the pianists Yvonne Loriod and Yvette Grimaud. Messiaen himself was still only in his early thirties and, with youth and independence on his side, he was naturally a focus for the formation of a student cadre, known as 'les flèches' ('the Arrows'). He seems also, quite simply, to have been an outstanding teacher, not only in the official harmony class but also in private composition classes he gave for the 'Arrows' at the house of a musical Egyptologist, Guy-Bernard Delapierre, who he had met during his wartime confinement at Nancy, and to whom he dedicated *Technique de mon langage musical*.

Boulez has eloquently described the atmosphere of the time:

In the desert, the solitude of the Conservatoire, one man seemed to us the only sheet-anchor. He was just a teacher of harmony, but his reputation was rather notorious. To choose to study with him already meant a great deal: it was as if one were withdrawing oneself from the

mass and electing for obstinacy. . . . It was truly an epoch of exploring
and freedom – fresh air and openness amid the stupidity which
surrounded us. Secretly, or almost so, we grew to a total admiration
for unwhispered names, unknown works which aroused our attention; meanwhile we moved forward together. And our investigation
was not confined to Europe: acquaintance with Asia and Africa taught
us that we were not alone in having the privilege of 'tradition'. They
brought us to a stage at which music was not just an art object but
truly a way of life, an indelible branding.[1]

Surrounded by this band of enthusiasts, Messiaen embarked on a
decade of rapid growth in his art, a creative burst associated very much
with the musicianship, and one may guess also with the person, of
Yvonne Loriod, who in 1962 became his second wife. (Claire Delbos had
died in 1959, after an illness that had kept her an invalid since the war
years.) In 1943 Messiaen wrote a *Rondeau* (in fact a compartmented
ABABA form in B major) for the Conservatoire's piano competition, but
this was the last of his minor pieces, and in the same year he wrote a
much bigger work destined not for students but for Loriod and himself:
the *Visions de l'Amen*, of which they gave the first performance in Paris
on 10 May 1943.

As Messiaen notes in the score, the first piano has 'the rhythmic
difficulties, the bunches of chords, everything concerned with speed,
allure and quality of sound'. Evidently he had already remarked, and
well understood, what he has called Loriod's 'transcendant virtuosity',[2]
while to himself, at the second piano, he allotted 'the principal melody,
the thematic elements, everything demanding emotion and power'. It is
a division of labour that suits the heterophonies of entirely different
musical styles and speeds that he had brought forward in the *Quatuor
pour la fin du temps*; indeed, he need only have looked to Stravinsky's
recent concerto to find proof of the two-piano medium's accommoda-
tion of clangorous heterophony, though the evidence suggests that his
own precedents were closest to his mind. Like the *Préludes*, his last
major work, the *Visions de l'Amen* are centred on A major, that
luminous key that Messiaen so often finds resonating in the piano. And
like *Les corps glorieux*, whose dimensions they share, the *Visions* are a
set of seven diverse contemplations grouped three and three around a
centrepiece. Here the middle movement is the 'Amen du désir', and the
flanking triptychs consist each of a movement based on the work's main
theme (No. 1, 'Amen de la création', and No. 7, 'Amen de la consommation'), one illustrating the adoration of cosmic and celestial creatures
(No. 2, 'Amen des étoiles, de la planète à l'anneau', and No. 5, 'Amen des
anges, des saints, du chant des oiseaux') and one about suffering (No. 3,
'Amen de l'agonie de Jésus', and No. 6, 'Amen du jugement').

In subject matter the *Visions de l'Amen* mark a departure, since instead of looking directly to scriptural sources, as he had in *L'Ascension*, *La Nativité du Seigneur*, *Les corps glorieux* and the *Quatuor pour la fin du temps* Messiaen discovers his theme in a mystical writer, Ernest Hello,[3] from whom he derives four meanings of the word 'amen', expressions of the creative act, of obedient acceptance, of spiritual desire and of eternal consummation. These meanings can be associated one by one with the first, third, fourth and seventh movements, but the fundamental sense of 'amen', as a gesture of assent, can be felt throughout the work, and not just metaphorically. The obvious musical image of assent is the cadence, and the whole work is founded on a 'theme of creation' which is simply an enlargement of a pentatonic cadence.

Example 30 is the theme as it appears at the start in the second piano, heard against pianissimo bell-sounds in the first. The opening phrase introduces a tritone dissonance; the second then cadences on D from the minor third below (a typical Messiaen pentatonic cadence to be found also, for example, in the 'Vocalise' from the *Quatuor*), and the third repeats the cadence from this point, twisting it down a semitone so that it can end on B, from which note the fourth phrase can cadence back on to A. All that happens in the first movement is that the entire theme is

Ex. 30 Visions de l'Amen *1 'Amen de la création'*

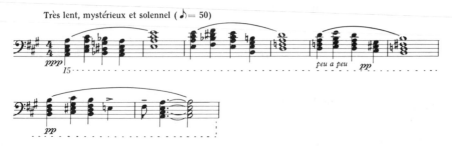

played over four times, rising in register, volume and bigness of sonority, while the bell-sounds remain in the same place though matching the theme's crescendo. The effect is of a gradual arrival, as in the *Apparition de l'église éternelle*, and since the movement does not end but is just abruptly cut off, one may imagine the arrival continuing underneath the remainder of the work, to become explicit again in the finale, where the abstruse change-ringing of the first movement's bells on palindromic rhythms is replaced by exultant peals that greet the theme's homecoming.

Sometimes the theme is glimpsed in the interim. It appears in the coda of the third movement, where it may suggest a divine acceptance of

Jesus's agony, and its cadential formula becomes in the fourth movement something to be stretched and manipulated as the music moves
through ever splashier paroxysms of cheapened harmony: this movement marks a further stage in Messiaen's abjuring of a sophisticated
response to what is musically embarrassing. Then in the fifth movement the theme provides one subject. It may even be understood as
supporting the whole structure, since the key centres of the movements
are pentatonically related, belonging all to an added-sixth chord on C: A
major (first, fifth and seventh), E minor (second), C minor (third) and G
major (fourth).

As in Messiaen's preceding three large-scale works, the *Chants de
terre et de ciel, Les corps glorieux* and the *Quatuor*, pentatonic are
combined with other modal features. For instance, the amens of the
stars and the angels both begin with melodies devolving játi-style on
repeated notes, what Messiaen calls the 'austere, very pure song of the
angels and saints' being in Phrygian E without a fourth while Saturn and
the stars have a resolute dance introduced by the second piano as a solo
in octaves. In example 31 only the upper part is shown. Style and
presentation here suggest a comparison with the 'Danse de la fureur'
from the *Quatuor*, and again the mode is a source not just of notes but of
motifs. Also characteristic is the way that pitch-centredness is held firm
against a tonally unstable structure, in this case the diminished-seventh
chord C sharp–E–G–B flat. More than in any earlier work, though, and
largely perhaps because of the principal theme that is signed across five
of the movements, one has the impression that pentatonic features are
fundamental, and that other modalities are the harmonics, sometimes
vibrating strongly, but not comprehending the complete work in the
way that the pentatonic mode does.

Ex. 31   Visions de l'Amen   2 '*Amen des étoiles, de la planète à
l'anneau*'

Its dominance goes along with other aspects of primitiveness. There
are no speculative movements here to compare with the 'Liturgie de
cristal' or 'Le mystère de la Sainte Trinité'. Complexity of harmony is,
rather, given a tonal bearing and a definite expressive function in the
amens addressed to Christ's agony and to judgement, while the struc-

tures are all based on very broad elements of repetition and symmetry. Similarly, the heterophony is always biased so that a main voice, often one that has in any event been heard before alone, is joined by what is plainly intended as merely decorative material: an example has already been indicated in the first movement, and of course this sort of texture springs naturally from Messiaen's partitioning of responsibilities between the players. It also very often brings a suggestion of the percussion ensemble to further enhance the sense of primitiveness.

In example 32 the second piano plays the fifth movement's version of the 'theme of creation' while the first executes what Messiaen calls a 'rhythmic canon' in three voices at semiquaver intervals, each voice having the same tala in palindromic durations: 3–5–8–5–3, 4–3–7–3–4 and 2–2–3–4 demisemiquavers (compare example 27). Other non-retrogradable rhythms occur quite frequently in the Visions de l'Amen, sometimes so powerfully set forth that their symmetry is unmistakable to the ear (see, for example, bars 19–21 of this same movement). In example 32, however, the effect is more likely to be of an uneven pattering of percussion instruments – perhaps a dull drum, a gong and a high bell or cymbal – the noise character of the sound being increased, as so often in this work, by sevenths and seconds.

Ex. 32   Visions de l'Amen   5 'Amen des anges, des saints, du chant des oiseaux'

But however primitive its world, the piece is decidedly also Messiaen's, and a part of its exuberance is the exuberance of a composer who has gained sufficient mastery of his technique to make anything his own. As he proudly declares in Technique,

We shall see some shadows of former times float by, we shall salute some great names of modern times; but all these borrowings . . . will be passed through the deforming prism of our language, will receive from our style a different blood, an unexpected melodic and rhythmic colour in which fantasy and research will be united to destroy the least resemblance to the model.[4]

There have already been instances of this 'different blood' in the 'Boris motif' and in adaptations of plainsong and Indian játis. Now Messiaen reveals that the dance of example 31 is a rigaudon after Rameau (there are indeed some metrical similarities) and that one of the bird themes from the forest in the middle of the fifth movement 'unites Béla Bartók and André Jolivet'. It is hard to imagine, however, that these connections could have been drawn by anyone but the composer. The most Bartókian moment – a birdsong in the fifth movement that stabs a repeated note before slipping up and down a minor third – turns out to be a premonition of a work as yet unwritten, the Concerto for Orchestra, and example 31 has much less in common with Rameau than it has with its companions in Messiaen's output, such as the 'Danse de la fureur' and 'Force et agilité des corps glorieux'. And unlike even the rudest eighteenth-century dance, it bends regular pulsation with its metrical upsets and with the favoured note-patterns that pull the melody out of the unknown into familiar contours, so that the fabric of time is now stretched, now tugged close.

There are many links between the Visions de l'Amen and Messiaen's next work, the Trois petites liturgies de la Présence Divine (1943–4), for again Yvonne Loriod is starred, again the music is centred in what is for Messiaen the joyous key of A major, and again there are prominent pentatonic features. The main difference is that the 'little liturgies' were written for the large concert audience Messiaen had not approached since L'Ascension of a decade before: the work is scored for thirty-six female voices with solo piano and ondes martenot, celesta and vibraphone, three percussionists and a moderately sized string orchestra. And though it has been suggested here that Messiaen's instrumental meditations are all liturgical in intention and time sense, in the case of the Trois petites liturgies, with their 'modern psalms' by the composer himself, this is something more than a metaphor. Messiaen has said how he wanted 'to achieve a liturgical act, that is to transport a sort of office, a sort of organized praise into the concert hall'.[5]

That was not, however, universally understood when the work had its first performance in liberated Paris, conducted by Roger Désormière on 21 April 1945. The 'Arrows' were out in full support, and apparently the new work went down well with the audience, but it became the occasion of hot dispute in the press and appears to have fostered an

international climate of opinion antipathetic to Messiaen. Such dis-
putes are scarcely to be disparaged when art generally provokes so little
remark; what calls for comment is rather the fact that the 'cas Messiaen'
was engaged so late in his career, since all the features to which his
detractors objected – the cheap harmony, the repetitiveness, the exotic
sensuality of music that purports to be divine praise – had long been
present in his work. But several reasons can be advanced. The public
character of the *Trois petites liturgies* naturally brought them more
attention, and a remarkable concatenation of premières put Messiaen
very much in the eye of the press: *Les corps glorieux* had been heard for
the first time only six days before, the piano cycle *Vingt regards sur
·l'Enfant-Jésus* three weeks before that. Moreover, the *Trois petites
liturgies* do represent Messiaen at an extreme. No other work so
abounds in repetition, brought about here by a use of liturgical verse–
refrain forms; and, perhaps because he was writing for a chorus,
Messiaen keeps his melody revolving around its very simplest features.

What is most new about the work is its instrumentation, and the
implied idea, so vital to later music, that a composer could choose his
forces freely (though this had already been part of Stravinsky's lesson to
the future). Messiaen's choice is influenced partly by trinitarian symbolism: there are three large groups (percussion, voices and strings, with
the ondes martenot joining any of the parties), three tuned percussion
instruments (piano, celesta and vibraphone), three noise instruments
(maracas and two tam-tams) and three times twelve voices. But more
particularly the selection accentuates the character of the music Messiaen writes for it. The pseudo-gamelan of tuned percussion is a natural
extension from his piano writing in the *Visions de l'Amen* and *Chants
de terre et de ciel*; violins and ondes martenot contribute spiritualized
voices as they had in various earlier works; and the whole string
ensemble is a firm support to the voices in loud, dynamic music (where
wind instruments might well be overpowering), besides being able to
surround the chant with a harmonic aureole. (One wonders if this had
been the case too in the unpublished mass for sopranos and violins,
which was perhaps a sacred adumbration of these concert liturgies.)

An instance of this is the pentatonic refrain of the last liturgy,
'Psalmodie de l'ubiquité par amour' (see example 33). Given all the
threeness about, it is unlikely to be fortuitous that here we have nine
words sung to a phrase of twenty-one quavers, but those are not the only
niceties of verbal and musical construction. The phrase 'Posez-vous
comme' is, pentatonically, inverted for 'comme un sceau': the image is
the inversion of the original (and both 'vous' and 'sceau' are sung on the
fifth degree). Meanwhile, as in an example from *Poèmes pour Mi* already
considered, the harmonization, which uses all twelve notes, propels the
melody with its dosage of tension, but not in a diatonic way: important

here are the usual tritone liaisons, the equally typical dominant sevenths and 6–4 chords whose forces are always redirected (exactly as in 'Paysage', for instance, the dominant seventh on E moves to A sharp) and the reservation of the added-sixth chord, Messiaen's equivalent to the major triad, for the end. If all this has the effect of putting chords in the 'wrong' places and yet making them sound right, it parallels the translocations of the surrealist poets and painters.

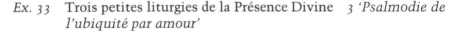

Ex. 33   Trois petites liturgies de la Présence Divine   3 'Psalmodie de l'ubiquité par amour'

Certainly the text is surrealist, on Messiaen's own admission,[6] and much more rampantly so than those of the song-cycles. The fundamental theme of the divine presence brings an invitation as challenging as anything in André Breton or Max Ernst to see the world with new eyes, to find, as the third liturgy has it, God ubiquitous in all his creatures: in the stars and the planets as in the cells of the human body. Often where the language is most startling, however, it comes directly from the Bible, or from St Thomas Aquinas or On the Imitation of Christ: 'The mountain leaps like a ewe and becomes a great ocean', declares the second stanza, to words that echo Psalm 114. But there are other places where the ideas are more personal to Messiaen, including a fourth stanza concerned with God's presence in the Eucharist and a fifth on celestial existence. This latter passage is set as an enormous toccata whose speed of almost ten chords per second must test even the fingers of a Loriod, besides coming near the limits of the ear's ability to distinguish. It brings this longest of the liturgies to a climax, and since the entire first five stanzas are repeated, it does so twice, each time issuing in an extreme adagio.

Because there is so much repetition in the work – the first four stanzas of the 'Psalmodie' have basically the same music – it may well appear that the words are very much secondary, being borne along on currents of pre-existing rhythm or draped on pre-existing harmonic progressions. And this is so even when the music seems to mesh perfectly with the text, as in example 33, or when it offers an equivalent of a verbal image, as when the choir sings 'The successive is simultaneous to you' and the orchestra revolves in a ten-note ostinato, for in both these cases the same music can appear just as well with other words in other stanzas. Nor should it be otherwise. The essence of the work is to celebrate the presence of an eternal spirit in all the accidents of the universe. It is therefore wholly appropriate that repetition should show the same musical and verbal ideas being differently handled in different stanzas, while the same principle, operating at all levels from the tiniest ostinato to the reprise of giant formal blocks, makes the work once more an image of time standing still.

Although just as repetitive, the first two liturgies are formally simpler than the last, and shorter. The first, 'Antienne de la conversation intérieure', speaks of God's presence in his people, and consists simply of a 'psalm' in four stanzas held between statements of an 'antiphon'. The second, 'Séquence du Verbe, cantique divin', returns to the theme of the Ascension in order to consider God's presence in himself. It is the work's delirious scherzo, with a dancing refrain in pentatonic A major interleaved among five verses.

However one responds to the exoticism of the pentatony, the ostinatos, the repetitions and the jangling gamelan ensemble – or indeed to the eroticism that many have found in the treatment of the female chorus, despite the composer's denials[7] – the *Trois petites liturgies* belong right at the centre of Messiaen's work in their disruption of a conventional time sense. For the divine presence is the existence of the eternal at this moment; it is the denial of history, and it is fittingly contemplated in a work that remains for well over half an hour in the region of A major or its dominant, having even its fastest movements appear to race on the spot. Fixity of tonality is not a technique Messiaen has used elsewhere over so long a stretch, but it serves well to stop development, and it serves too to anchor the work's sometimes bewildering heterophonies, providing a single clear light that makes chaos sound like hectic joy, and that offers another example of the ubiquity of the eternal.

A segment from the first movement's 'psalm' (example 34) instances this. The mode 6 of the chimes in the right hand of the piano and the vibraphone is derived from the mode 5 of the second vocal phrase with the addition of just two notes, and though the violin and ondes martenot solos would seem to be just birdsong impressions, they have initial and cadential formulae respectively that refer to this same element in the chant (see the violin line in the third bar and the ondes martenot in the fourth). There is thus a bristling of diagonal correspondences working through the music, holding the heterophony loosely in place and again working against linear consequence.

Other aspects of this passage may indicate Messiaen's constructive technique even in a work of such natural exuberance. Most of the vocal line is obviously built from interlocking tritones, in ways that Messiaen might rationalize as expressing truncated mode 2 and mode 5; the exception is the cadence, which borrows its weight from a dominant-seventh chord, E–D–B–G sharp–E. The phrase lengths, meanwhile, are measured in prime numbers, being eleven, eleven again and twenty-nine semiquavers, while prime numbers are also important in the piano part. The right hand has a tala of nine elements lasting for thirteen quavers, over which it plays a sequence of thirteen chords; the left hand has the same tala in values augmented by a half, but its chord sequence has nine units, so that the same chord always appears with the same duration. As ever, the paradox is that conscious construction is necessary to the effect of freedom conveyed by Messiaen's main melodic lines, as much as it is to the sense of obscure calculation that comes from his 'rhythmic canons'. As in The Wedding, whose voice–percussion sound-world the Trois petites liturgies partly share, there is no attempt to disguise the fact that music counts out time, but in both works the counting is so far dislocated from normal musical motion as to measure only an eternal ceremonial.

The next step was a return inwards. Writing again for Loriod, Messiaen composed a book of piano music that is at the same time a compendium of his musical, philosophical and religious concerns: the Vingt regards sur l'Enfant-Jésus, begun only eight days after the Trois petites liturgies were finished, and completed in under six months. Evidently the creative exhilaration of the Visions de l'Amen and the choral liturgies was continuing, and one might even consider the three works as forming a triptych, with the A major of the first two now replaced by its favoured sixth, F sharp major. However, the musical style of the Vingt regards is notably more various, and fittingly so for a work that plays for over two hours at Messiaen's often slow tempos. Of course, the volume can be used in the manner of a Couperin ordre, as a collection of character pieces to be played singly or in groups, but, for all its diversity, there are good reasons for regarding it more importantly as an integral work, a recital programme reviewing Messiaen's music of the last sixteen years and pointing forward into the next decade.

In the first place there is the work's cyclic thematicism, involving not just one idea as in the Visions de l'Amen but four, according to Messiaen's reckoning. One of them, however, has no thematic shape but is just a sequence of four four-note chords, which can be collapsed into two eight-note chords (No. 13) or partly stretched out as a melody (No. 14). The other three are true themes: a chromatically creeping 'theme of the star and of the cross' (these two phenomena marking the beginning and the end of Christ's earthly existence, which is the work's abiding subject), a leaping 'theme of joy' and, most importantly, a 'theme of God' which looms prominently in seven of the pieces (Nos. 1, 5, 6, 10, 11, 15 and 20) and which, appearing as it does at the start, can be understood as responsible for the centrality of the F sharp major triad in its second inversion (see example 35).

Ex. 35   Vingt regards sur l'Enfant-Jésus   *1 'Regard du Père'*

A fundamental mode 2 concept, this is essentially a chromatic slippage within the A sharp octave followed by a cadence back on to the second-inversion chord: God is fundamentally unchanging, and, not for the first time in Messiaen's music, it is the capturing of the eternal within the temporal that provides the work with its overriding challenge.

The variety of Messiaen's answers to that challenge provides a second justification for considering the *Vingt regards* as a whole, and perhaps also a third, if the many musical ways of evoking eternity are understood as representing many ways of responding to the Incarnation. In his preface Messiaen acknowledges that he took some ideas for these mystic 'gazes' from two devotional books, *Le Christ dans ses mystères* by Dom Columba Marmion and *Les douze regards* by Maurice Toesca, though his own *Visions de l'Amen* had already brought into existence a similar image of sentient and non-sentient creation joined in contemplation. Now in twenty movements he projects the meditations of God the Father, of the beings already present at *La Nativité* (the Virgin, angels, shepherds and magi), of objects associated with the Incarnation (the star, the Cross and the 'awesome unction' of human flesh taken on by God) and of musical concepts (time, silence and 'hauteurs' in the sense of both 'heights' and 'pitches'), besides pieces that are not attributed to some other party, but appear to speak for the composer himself in his wonder (No. 6, 'Par lui tout a été fait') and his attempt to measure (No. 3, 'L'échange').

Messiaen's means of conveying the interruption of time by timeless-ness include all those encountered hitherto. Formal patterns of sym-metry and repetition are ubiquitous, even in the two large movements that purport to exemplify historical structural types. Messiaen des-cribes 'Par lui tout a été fait' as a fugue, but it is possibly better understood as an anti-fugue, with its clear partitioning into sections (many of them admittedly canonic), its tendency more to destroy its subject and countersubject by interval displacement than to work them towards some apotheosis, and its subsuming of itself into ecstatic insistence on the themes of God and of joy, the latter now marked in the score as the 'theme of love'. Messiaen's explanation of this turn of events, also marked in the score, is that 'creation sings the theme of God', but musically it is a removal from fugue into exultant toccata-style ostinato, and the movement has less in common with Bach, or even with Franck or Dukas, then with the anti-fugue that was to conclude Boulez's Second Sonata four years later. It is the same with the other nominally archetypal form, the sonata of the final 'Regard de l'église d'amour'. Messiaen's preface would see this as another example, following 'Combat de la mort et de la vie' from *Les corps glorieux*, of sonata form in which the development precedes the exposition, but the 'development' is really a development of much that has happened during the course of the preceding nineteen movements, and the 'exposition' serves as a triumphant recapitulation of the themes of God and of joy or love.

At a level lower than the generally formal, too, Messiaen uses by now familiar techniques for making time appear stationary or circular. Many of the movements reside steadfastly in a particular tonality, and the *Vingt regards* even include the most extreme instance of this in No. 19, 'Je dors, mais mon coeur veille', whose first seven bars, playing for more than a minute at the extraordinarily slow tempo of this movement (where 'movement' itself seems a misnomer), are entirely bathed in the second inversion of the F sharp major triad and use only the notes of that triad; there is a similar, and still longer balancing section at the end. Moreover, where the rate of harmonic change is somewhat faster, its steps are marked out as so often by equal divisions of the octave: the augmented triad and the diminished-seventh chord. A prime example is No. 10, 'Regard de l'Esprit de joie', a piece whose rousing virtuosity suggests Messiaen's practicality in providing for an interval in complete performances. As Robert Sherlaw Johnson's table[8] plainly shows, the movement begins by falling through a diminished-seventh chord (F sharp–E flat–C–A), then rises through an augmented triad (A–D flat–F), rises again through a diminished-seventh chord (F–A flat–B–D) and finally falls through an augmented triad to regain its starting point (D–B flat–F sharp). On the level of phrase and motif, too, these same symmetrical entities are omnipresent, mediated into a diatonic environment by the modes of limited transpositions in the normal way.

The printed music is liberally annotated with indications of mode, of appearances of the cyclic themes, of rhythmic procedures and of techniques of intervallic change, almost to the extent of making any analysis of its construction redundant, especially when one takes into account also Messiaen's preface and his substantial programme notes.[9] He has also drawn attention to how much the tumultuous virtuosity of the *Vingt regards* owes to Loriod, and suggested how much its variety owes to a personal pantheon of keyboard composers that includes Rameau, Scarlatti, Chopin, Debussy, Ravel and Albéniz.[10] But despite these debts to the past, there is much in the *Vingt regards* that is quite new, and it is perhaps the newest strain that, understandably, Messiaen at the time was least able to codify in his marginalia.

He says little, for example, about the bird songs of the 'Regard des hauteurs', except to make it clear that these have reached a new point of definition after the progressively less generalized similar voices in *La Nativité*, the *Quatuor* and the *Visions de l'Amen*. Two large sections of the piece are sung by a lark and by a chorus led by a thrush: heraldic emblems have been replaced by real attempts at portraiture. Messiaen remarks how the lark's song 'revolves between two poles: a long low note heard during those brief moments of hovering flight, and a dominant high-pitched note which accompanies the beating of the wings', though it would seem that these alternatives have become heterophonic parallels in a typical collapse of the successive into the simultaneous (see example 36).

Ex. 36   Vingt regards sur l'Enfant-Jésus   *8 'Regard des hauteurs'*

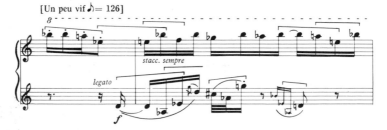

However well observed and studied this may be as birdsong transcription (and the subject will need further consideration later), it is certainly no stranger to the harmony, rhythm and sonority of the *Vingt regards* in general and of this piece in particular. The use of the keyboard's top two octaves, as also of its furthest bass, is entirely typical; so too is the staccato pitch repetition and the rebounding within narrow repertories of notes. Above all, example 36 includes numerous instances of a three-note cell prominent throughout the work, one formed most characteristically from a fourth or fifth plus a tritone, and hence basic to Messiaen's harmony, in combining a diatonic dominant–tonic with a tritone. (Its appearances here, usually in more compressed forms, are bracketed.) Since this is also true of the movement's second birdsong cadenza, the question must arise whether Messiaen's avian notations are stylistically his own, or whether all the *Vingt regards* are swung into the stylistic atmosphere of their bird soloists. For a variety of reasons one is bound to accept the former explanation, not least because the *Vingt regards* belong much more to the composer of the *Chants de terre et de ciel* and the *Visions de l'Amen* than they do to their non-human musicians, and because the fourth/fifth–tritone cell had featured in those very two works already.

Indeed, its origin would seem to be not in birdsong but in attempts to evoke bell-sounds, in which the *Vingt regards*, like the *Chants de terre et de ciel* and the *Visions de l'Amen*, are exceedingly rich. As Bartók had known, this cell provides in compact form a combination of natural resonance with inharmonic partials, and Messiaen uses it awaredly to produce bell-sounds here in No. 13, 'Noël', or tam-tam crashes in No. 16, 'Regard des prophètes, des bergers et des mages', besides seeming to profit from its summons of bells elsewhere. For though he has said that in playing the piano he makes of it 'an imitation orchestra with a wide scale of timbres and attacks',[11] and though his marginal inscriptions give a name to effects of trombones (No. 14, 'Regard des anges') and oboes (No. 16 again), the sound-world of the *Vingt regards*, like that of the *Visions de l'Amen*, is that of the percussion ensemble, and most particularly that of the gamelan.

Somewhat indirectly Messiaen has admitted this influence in pointing out how his superimposition of acceleration and deceleration at each end of No. 18, 'Regard de l'onction terrible', is a technique unknown in the West but perfectly normal to Balinese musicians.[12] What this passage also serves to exemplify is the return to Messiaen's music of speculative processes of the kind found in the 'Antienne du silence', 'Le mystère de la Sainte Trinité' and the 'Liturgie de cristal'. The *Vingt regards* are full of them, and in this lies their great difference from the *Visions de l'Amen*, their aloof remove from the innocent world of the *Trois petites liturgies*.

In some cases the process is much more patently set forth than ever before: No. 3, 'L'échange', is a striking example. The 'exchange' here is between humanity and divinity, for as Messiaen has explained,[13] he was thinking of an antiphon in which the Incarnation of God as man is celebrated as a means for men to share in his divinity. The musical image of this is simply a sequence of balancing interval changes worked on a two-bar statement, shown in example 37 in its original and first altered form. The first idea (bar 1, upper two staves) like God is changeless, and throws a beam of E flat minor through the whole piece. The second widens away by a semitone each time around its E axis, and the process is completed when after a dozen changes the original pitch classes have been restored. Meanwhile the nonuplets simply move down a semitone each time and the following figure in the left hand slips in the opposite direction, while its right-hand counterpart flattens and partly inverts itself by curious manoeuvres: its first and third notes move progressively down a semitone and its last two notes progressively up, the second remaining stable.

Ex. 37   Vingt regards sur l'Enfant-Jésus   *3 'L'échange'*

Contortions of this kind are obviously not conducive to harmonic significance, and it is noteworthy that Messiaen's attempts to bring diatonic weight to bear on non-diatonic material are, except in such movements as 'Regard de l'Esprit de joie', rather reduced. Instead he welcomes motionlessness, or else achieves motion by means of process, paralleling in this again the contemporary work of John Cage but aligning himself with few others in the Western tradition. For while a gradual process such as that of 'L'échange' depends absolutely on temporal progress, it obviously provides a very different experience of time from that offered by a Beethoven sonata movement: in marking its steps so precisely and so openly, the music does not merely concur with the clock but actually becomes a clock itself.

As one might expect, a similar sort of process takes place in the 'Regard du temps', here operating on chordal 'verses' and on 'refrains' of bell chords in three-part rhythmic canon on palindromic rhythms. (Compare example 32, p. 111: as there, canons in the *Vingt regards* tend to be in three voices, for obvious theological reasons and also because a four-part canon of this kind might tax even a Loriod's prestidigitation.) The basic rhythmic palindrome here is a quaver–semiquaver–quaver unit, which the canons expand to three, four and five times its normal duration. The sensation this produces is odd. Because the music has established itself as a clock, one's feeling that the musical pace is changing may be tinged with an alternative explanation that the pace of time itself is flexible, the thread of events passing irregularly through the observed present.

There is a similar effect when the temporal adjustment commands a wider compass, as it does in the endpapers to the 'Regard de l'onction terrible', where one hand accelerates by running through an arithmetical series of durations from dotted minim to semiquaver while the other takes the reverse route, so presenting two streams of time of which one races towards the other's past. The same sixteenfold change of pace is found also in No. 16, where it may represent the gradual approach and withdrawal of the 'prophets, shepherds and magi', and again in the finale, where it prepares the slow glorification of the theme of God. Here in particular it can be understood as scanning the whole tempo field of the work, from the semiquavers racing at 320 per minute in the 'Regard de l'Esprit de joie' to the sixteen times slower chords of the theme of God in nearly all its manifestations. On a more pictorial level, progressively measured rallentando in No. 11, 'Première communion de la Vierge', seems to be a stilling so that we may hear the heartbeat of the yet unborn infant in low repeating Fs going at the surely pathological rate of 240 per minute. Nor is it at all out of character for this monumental volume that it should use a single technique both for challenging assertions about the nature of time and for pious picturings of the Christian story in the most naïve terms.

CHAPTER 8

The Tristan Trilogy

Messiaen has consistently maintained that the love celebrated in the *Vingt regards*, especially in the tenth and twentieth, is devotional and not erotic,[1] while insisting that his next three works, beginning with the song-cycle *Harawi* he composed once more at Petichet the next summer, form a trilogy on the theme of human love, an imaginary three-act opera on the legend of Tristan and Isolde.[2] However, the distinction is not so easily made. Messiaen himself had shown in the *Poèmes pour Mi* how human love can be an image of divine, and there seems no reason therefore why a musical image of one should not be mistaken for a musical image of the other. The problem is again that of the expression of intention, and it naturally becomes most acute when *Harawi* starts to enter the world of the *Vingt regards* and to suggest an entirely secular interpretation of motifs previously given a sacred meaning.

One instance of this is provided by the tenth song of the cycle, 'Amour oiseau d'étoile' (see example 38). With its different harmonizations of a repeated note and its soft cadence into F sharp major, this is cousin to the theme of God from the *Vingt regards*, and arguably its expressive aura is similarly one of enfolding warmth and tranquillity. Nor is it shocking that Messiaen should be moved to similar inventions in his contemplation of God and of sexual love, the two commonest experiences of timelessness available to human beings. But however that may be, the musical details of example 38 have their own interest. For instance, the harmonies of the first bar are denser than was customary in the earlier song-cycles, and they do not serve in the same way to establish a progression. Of course, in this case there is no melodic progression to be given harmonic support, but it happens elsewhere in the cycle too that harmonic variation serves to colour melodic notes rather than to order them: the emphasis is increasingly on the present moment or else, in the ostinato-based dances and incantations, on whirling circulation. What example 38 also shows is the use of birdsong motifs to pick out upper partials in a sustained resonance, usually avoiding banal repetitions at the octave or the fifth. Birds become bells. And *Harawi* joins the line of works going back to the *Préludes* (compare example 3, p. 34), in which natural resonance is a model of sound.

Ex. 38 Harawi 10 'Amour oiseau d'étoile'

Here, as in the *Chants*, Messiaen was writing for himself to play in accompaniment to his favoured singer of the period, Marcelle Bunlet: the work is now explicitly intended for a 'grand soprano dramatique', and Messiaen has not demurred at the suggestion that a Brünnhilde voice is required.[3] Nor has he appeared to resist interpretation of *Harawi* in crudely personal terms.[4] By now his wife was permanently in a sanatorium, having lost all her faculties but not her bond to him of marriage, celebrated only nine years before in the *Poèmes pour Mi*. At the same time Yvonne Loriod's importance to him was obviously immense: in his own words, she 'transformed not only the composer's piano writing but also his style, his vision of the world and his ways of thinking',[5] and the *Visions de l'Amen* and *Vingt regards* would stand as monuments to his feelings for her even without casting *Harawi* in the same light.

But if the cycle is autobiographical – and clearly an analogy with its two predecessors must suggest that it is – it places the doomed ecstatic lovers among the Incas of Peru. In doing so it makes an identification with the primitive and the sensual that had been a strong current in French culture since Gauguin, perhaps since Rameau: nearer to Messiaen one thinks of Breton in Martinique or Ravel in Madagascar, the latter particularly close in his turning of art song towards ritual incantation. However, Messiaen goes further than Ravel in basing his work poetically and musically on indigenous material. The 'harawi' is a genus of Indian love song, usually, as is often the way with love songs, having a tone of lament. Messiaen takes this as his cue for a Peruvian adaptation of the Tristan legend, evoked with a couple of textual allusions to Wagner, though the language of his poetry still owes a great deal to his reading among the surrealists: the texts now have the cosmic exaltation of the *Trois petites liturgies* rather than the cosiness of the earlier song-cycles.

In the first song, 'La ville qui dormait, toi', the beloved is discovered as a sleeping city; the second, 'Bonjour toi, colombe verte', is a morning greeting to her. 'Montagnes' then symbolizes terror, by implication the terror of love, and 'Doundou tchil' provides the beloved with a dance song. 'L'amour de Piroutcha' is a dialogue song of love and death for the young couple; 'Répétition planétaire' an incantatory lament in which their story is written across the universe. 'Adieu' brings a reprise of the second song, now in farewell to the beloved, and 'Syllabes' is a reminiscence of her that passes into drumming, repetitive incantation. The ninth song, 'L'escalier redit, gestes du soleil', would seem to be a song of the beloved released from earthly ties, while the tenth is a vision of her, the 'Amour oiseau d'étoile' quoted in example 38, which is based on a painting by Sir Roland Penrose, *Seeing is Believing*: in Messiaen's words, this depicts 'two male hands reaching out, then a woman's head upside down, and continuing upwards her hair spreading out, her brow, her eyes, her face, her neck, but then the rest of her body is missing, or rather it is continued in the sky and the stars'.[6] This celestial vision, already announced in the sixth and ninth songs, then carries over into the penultimate 'Katchikatchi les étoiles', a dance for the lovers with the stars and the atoms. The final 'Dans le noir' is a second reprise of the second song, recalling also the first and the eighth in a tranquil acceptance of aloneness. It thus brings together the two principal tonal centres of the work, separated by the major third so important to its harmony: E flat, the key of the cyclically repeating song (Nos. 2, 7 and 12) and of other songs alluding to it (Nos. 4 and 7), and G, the key of Nos. 1, 5 and 8.

The importance of the third, major or minor, is one feature that Messiaen took from his source, the d'Harcourts' *La musique des Incas*, which he read with enthusiasm, becoming convinced that 'Peruvian music contains . . . the most beautiful folk melodies of the world.'[7] In *Harawi* he set about using them, though transferring them out of their original, fundamentally pentatonic modalities into his own modes of limited transposition. For example, the d'Harcourts' 'Delirio'[8] (see example 39) is very obviously the origin for the cycle's theme song, transcribed in example 40 purely as a melody from the second number. Simply by sharpening the second and sometimes the sixth, Messiaen takes the tune into a defective version of his second mode; the only other melodic adjustments are to raise by a fourth the first note of the folk song's fifth phrase and to leave the melody resting on its third (though decisively anchored in the piano by chords of E flat major). Even in rhythm the two songs show many points of correspondence.

It would be wrong to suggest, however, that *Harawi* is anything like a

Ex. 39 '*Delirio*' *(Peruvian song)*

Ex. 40 Harawi   2 '*Bonjour toi, colombe verte*'

set of folk-song arrangements. No other melody is so plainly adapted, and Messiaen's more normal practice would seem to have been to choose turns of phrase from throughout the d'Harcourts' collection in forming his own lines, just as he worked images and words from the folk songs into his poems. The likening of the beloved to a dove – common enough, in all conscience, and already implicit in the first of the *Préludes* – is sanctioned by a great many of the Indian love songs, and Messiaen's 'green dove' is simply a combination of this image with the 'colour of my hopes' from No. 38 in the d'Harcourt volume; it is not quite enough to establish much fellow feeling with that other great Tristanesque song-cycle, Schoenberg's *Gurrelieder*. Messiaen also takes over the apparently meaningless 'doundou tchil' from No. 150 for incantatory repetitions in his own fourth song and elsewhere, while he sometimes uses meaningful Quechua words purely for their sound: an example is the 'kahpipas, mahpipas' of his fourth and eighth songs, taken from the d'Harcourts' No. 172. Among other borrowings, the idea for the dialogue song could well have come from their No. 37, and certainly the name 'Piroutcha' is abstracted from their No. 31: its literal meaning is 'spinning-top', the suggestion being of a fantastic dancer.

Interspersing more conventional songs among primitive dances, forest calls and rosaries of incantation, *Harawi* is considerably further from the normal repertory of the song recital even than the *Poèmes pour Mi* and the *Chants de terre et de ciel*. Indeed, its disruption of the normal concert proprieties is hardly less violent than that of the *Trois petites liturgies*, except that its effort is not to transplant a sacred office into secular surroundings but rather to make of the recital hall what Antonin Artaud wanted to make of the theatre, a place where minds could radically be changed by exposure to what is unmediated by good taste. And it is this refusal of good taste, rather than the dream or nightmare poetic imagery of the work, that makes *Harawi* one of the few surrealist masterpieces in music.

The *Turangalîla-symphonie* must be counted another. According to Messiaen's own account, the commission came from Serge Koussevitzky without any qualifications as to size or medium;[9] his response was a symphony in ten movements, calling for an orchestra of over a hundred players, and needing from its composer well over two years of creative work. Indeed, the period of composition might well be extended back before the official starting date of 17 July 1946, printed in the score, for Messiaen has recalled that he had been considering the work for a long time,[10] and it does serve as a climactic résumé of the first half of his *oeuvre*. Quite apart from direct reminiscences of other works – *Les offrandes oubliées* in the second movement and the *Hymne* in the fourth – the symphony employs all the estranging (and thereby surreal) techniques to be found throughout Messiaen's music from *Le banquet céleste* onwards: cyclical repetition and patent symmetry, manipulation of the time sense by gradual change of rhythmic unit, or the application of diatonic harmony to non-diatonic subject matter, here more than ever providing a parallel with Ernst's or Salvador Dali's use of conventional means to represent highly unconventional images.

There is a straightforward instance of this in the most opulent moment of the fourth movement, often repeated, which bears comparison with example 19, p. 81, from the *Poèmes pour Mi*. Melodically example 41 can be regarded as a simple cadence from a whole-tone chord, E–F sharp–B flat, on to the dominant seventh of B major. (One sees here very clearly how the dominant seventh is particularly useful in offering a diatonic explanation of a tritone.) Typically, though, the dominant-seventh arpeggio comes to rest not on F sharp but on E, and

Ex. 41   Turangalîla-symphonie   4 'Chant d'amour II'

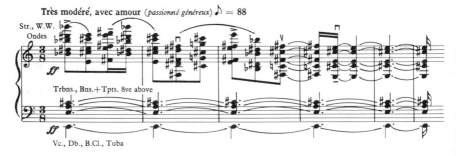

though the passage can be understood as operating in pure mode 2, one perhaps comes nearer the nature of Messiaen's modality in seeing it as an interpretation of E as both dominant of A major and flattened seventh in F sharp major, and at rest in both capacities. (The double fall from the upper tritone helps to establish this 'tonicity' of E.) A major and F sharp major are both keys of central importance to the work as a whole; moreover the dual harmonic perspective and the gravitation towards some note other than the natural tonic are highly characteristic of Messiaen's harmony.

They are not, of course, varieties of harmonic thought that lend themselves particularly well to symphonic writing, and it need be no surprise that the *Turangalîla* is a symphony of a rather special kind. If the prime feature of a symphony has to be development, then it is scarcely a symphony at all, since each of the movements proceeds in the usual patterns of symmetry and repetition, with the only difference that large orchestral forces give Messiaen the means to make accumulation another structural type. For instance, the fourth movement, already quoted, can be regarded as a scherzo with two trios, but it is also a structure of small musical blocks that can be played in alternation or piled on top of one another to a depth of at least eight discernible layers. Ideas that first are heard quite separately – a scherzo theme in piccolo and bassoon, a chordal chant for double wind quintet, a pentatonic melody for high cello chromatically harmonized by a small group of other strings, and an emphatic idea on trombones and tuba – are by the end brought all together and overlaid with further decoration in the orchestra's full percussion section.

Such processes of development by accumulation are by no means confined to the fourth movement, nor is the resulting heterophony rare. As in the *Trois petites liturgies*, it can often give a rather Balinese impression, enhanced as in that work by frequent ostinatos, by motion in even semiquavers and by a gamelan within the orchestra. Once more there is a piano soloist, and though there are important cadenzas along the way, her more common function is to lead an athletic chiming ensemble that also includes glockenspiel, celesta and vibraphone. Often, as in the passage mentioned from the fourth movement, the other orchestral sections are similarly used as distinctive ensembles and separately, the strings often with their top line doubled by the symphony's other soloist on another instrument brought back from the *Trois petites liturgies*, the ondes martenot.

Example 41 may give some indication of the effect of excess when an already fulsome melodic expression on the strings is played too by the electronic instrument in its most vox humana mood, and though the ondes martenot is used also in quite different ways – to rip glissandos across the orchestral texture or to produce a metallic timbre that allies it with the gamelan – one of the most characteristic sounds of the symphony, as of the liturgies, is of this electronic voice joining the chorus of violins in sumptuous melody. Perhaps vulgarity in music is a quality not easy to define, but it does seem reasonable to call these rapturous, overloaded dominant sevenths and 6–4 chords vulgar, and not just vulgar but stupefyingly vulgar. The work thus poses problems of appreciation similar to those of the *Trois petites liturgies* and *Vingt regards*, except that here the embarrassment has its origins not in the transfer of religious meditation into the concert hall but in the inrush of eroticism, now quite denuded of the Christian dress with which it was presented in the *Poèmes pour Mi*. But the resulting vulgarity is itself proof of Messiaen's innocence, for there is absolutely no irony to it, no sense of posturing. Nor is there any guilt. Like the temple sculptors of India, Messiaen celebrates the erotic not as an obverse to the spiritual but as a companion in the shedding of the ego.

Parallels with Hindu art and architecture seem thus to extend beyond the use of Śarṅgadeva rhythmic formulae, even though these have become more prominent in the surface of the music: the change is marked in the 'Répétition planétaire' from *Harawi*, where the tala from 'Le mystère de la Sainte Trinité' and other works is reproduced as a monotone chant, and this same tala is, for example, executed by a wood block under the scherzo material of the fourth movement of the symphony. Curiously, one Śarṅgadeva motif that is not prominently displayed is *turangalîla* itself, consisting of a pair of dotted values followed by a pair of the same values undotted, unless its three–three–two–two pattern can be seen as underpinning the entire ten-movement structure: there is even a strong implication of that in the work's latter part, where the last two movements repeat the characters of the two that had gone before. However, other groupings of the movements are no less persuasive, and the symphony has to be considered as being not about *turangalîla* the rhythm but about *turangalîla* the word. As Messiaen has put it, *turanga* 'has a meaning analogous to that of "tempo"', though a literal translation would be 'the speed of a horse', while *lîla* 'means at once the force of life, the game of creation, rhythm and movement'.[11] Hence a work that unites all the secular aspects of Messiaen's musical personality: the exuberance, the joy, the excess, and also the measurement, the exalting and the negation of time.

Naturally the interplay of these things is different in each of the ten movements, which are as follows:

1 'Introduction'. This begins by setting out, in sympathetic musical environments of implacable tritones and then gentle undulations, the work's two principal themes, which might be described as 'masculine' and 'feminine', or in Messiaen's terms as 'statue' and

'flower', the former marching always in thirds while the latter opens out gradually from a minor second to a minor third (see example 42). A piano cadenza then leads to a complex construct of simultaneous rhythmic processes, all revolving in repetition: it is a typical, though unusually dense, image of constant uniformity and constant change, and as a collage of different rotations it serves to gear up the orchestra for the remainder of the work.

Ex. 42   Turangalîla-symphonie   I '*Introduction*'

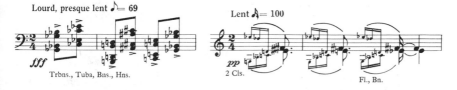

2   'Chant d'amour I'. Fast verse–refrain form, where the refrain is a 'love theme' in F sharp, the movement's principal key.

3   'Turangalîla I'. ABABA form with accumulation of material as it proceeds, and accumulation too of instruments: the first section is scored only for a clarinet and the ondes martenot in dialogue, supported and punctuated by bells, vibraphone and pizzicato double-bass. As in the other two movements borrowing the symphony's title, the tempo is slow and the harmony much less diatonic, the emphasis being on the contemplation of time as it is conducted through different successive and then simultaneous processes.

4   'Chant d'amour II'. Moderately paced scherzo with two trios, or alternatively again verse–refrain structure, the second interpretation strengthened by much repetition within sections, with gradual accumulation. The principal key is A major.

5   'Joie du sang des étoiles'. The real scherzo of the symphony: an 'African dance', as Messiaen has called it, in driving 3/16 and pentatonic D flat, the same tonality that had conveyed the joy of the resurrected existence in *Les corps glorieux*. There is a middle section in which Messiaen works with three 'rhythmic characters' ('personnages rythmiques'), as he calls them,[12] these being elements whose durations all regularly expand (4–1–4, 5–2–5, etc.), or contract (8–4–8, 7–3–7, etc.) or stay the same (1–1–1–1–1–2–1–2). The technique has its acknowledged origins in the 'Sacrificial Dance' from *The Rite of Spring*,[13] but here the characters are much less forwardly presented, and the passage retains the racing semiquavers of the outer sections: the effect is therefore one of simple dynamism entering a zone of confusion created by the

rhythmic characters (and redoubled when the processes with them come to be superimposed on the same processes in retrograde motion), but then emerging with its original rush.

6　'Jardin du sommeil d'amour'. The work's slow movement, a ternary piece in F sharp major.

7　'Turangalîla II'. By contrast with the preceding, a short movement in short sections, chromatic and introducing a 'chromatic scale' of durations.

8　'Développement de l'amour'. Less a development than a cross-cutting of different products of the earlier love music: a hectic toccata that keeps spinning free on a three-chord ostinato and that issues in a ripe cadence, and an ecstatic melody heard successively in C major, D major and F sharp major. These two sorts of music are interleaved in an ABABAB pattern contained within an introduction and a coda, of which the coda ends with the first type's cadence but substitutes a tam-tam crash for the final concord, leaving room for further developments, or rather altered states, in the finale.

9　'Turangalîla III'. Like the first 'Turangalîla', this is an accumulating set of choruses on a theme announced by clarinet and ondes martenot, and like the second it uses 'chromatic' durations in a rhythmic process initiated by the untuned percussion. The thematic choruses and the rhythmic process go on in tandem, the former drawing in the tuned percussion and the wind, the latter picked out in subtle colours by thirteen solo strings.

10　'Final'. A hugely exuberant but compact sonata form, if one where the sounding of themes in different keys is more important than development, and where the impetus comes, as in the fifth movement, from regular and irregular groupings of fast 3/16 bars of semiquavers. Both principal ideas belong to the symphony's family of love themes, but the first, with its pentatonic substructure and its leaping alternation of iambs and trochees, looks back also to the fifth movement, while the second speeds up and rhythmically flattens out the melody of the sixth, which comes at the end to crown the work in something much nearer its original form, and in its original key of F sharp major, in which the symphony duly ends.

Earlier frenzied excitement in this key has sometimes suggested Skryabin's *Prometheus*, but Messiaen's programme is very much his own, and so too is the sheer sound of the main love theme in its apotheosis. To quote his own description: 'The three groups, woodwind, brass and string, support each other mutually, and the power of the brass gains in feeling from the supraterrestrial voice of the ondes in a high register, communicating to the whole orchestra its light and its tears of joy. The melody remains in suspense, in a state of luminous waiting –

and this great gesture towards an end which does not exist (Glory and Joy are without end) draws on and provokes the coda.'[14]

If the ending on an F sharp major triad is thus unreal (the tuned percussion decline to take part), then so too is the symphony's notion of development, and hence its very status as a symphony. Even the titles of the movements invite one to consider it piecemeal: as a triptych of rhythmic mechanisms (the 'Turangalîlas') and a quartet of love songs contained within the beginning, middle and end of introduction, scherzo and finale, or perhaps as a normal four-movement symphony (1, 5, 6, 10) interrupted by alternating subsidiary facets of its opulent melodiousness and constructive severity. Moreover, Messiaen himself, while holding that complete performance is the ideal, has allowed the possibility of giving only extracts, suggesting a representative selection from the first half (3, 4, 5), an ascetic concentration on the 'Turangalîlas' (in the order 7, 9, 3) or a more hedonist trio (in the order 6, 2, 4) to be framed by the outermost movements.

It would be absurd, nevertheless, to dismiss the symphony's claims to be an integral conception. The point is simply that it willingly abandons the unidirectional movement through time that had given the symphony the imperative to remove itself from the suite in the middle of the eighteenth century, the continuity of idea that had developed until it became continuity of substance in Schoenberg's Chamber Symphony, Op. 9. Messiaen's extreme discontinuity of substance is an outward expression of discontinuity of idea. Instead of developing his themes so that one form grows from another, he presents the altered form as a *fait accompli*, and so in this way too the music releases itself from embodying a forward progression through time. Rather it appeals to another time outside itself, to the time of composition, where the processes may be imagined as having taken place that led to the leaps of change appearing in the music.

This can be seen most clearly in the love music, as its basic components are turned in a kaleidoscope to produce different configurations in each of the even-numbered movements (see example 43 (a) to (d)). Although this is only a selection from the symphony's store of leitmotifs, it may serve to illustrate the principles. The two, differently paced sections of the main theme from 'Chant d'amour I' open themselves to interpretation again as masculine and feminine, and can arguably be regarded as derivatives from the 'statue' and 'flower' themes: there is something like the zigzag outline of the former in the masculine half's concluding phrase, while the feminine part opens from a chromatic cell rather as the 'flower' theme starts by closing into one. Less equivocal, though, are the relationships with themes from the other movements treating aspects of love, all of them combining the two parts of the second movement's song just as love combines two

Ex. 43   Turangalîla-symphonie   *Love Themes*
(a) 2 'Chant d'amour I'

(b) 6 'Jardin du sommeil d'amour'

(c) 8 'Développement de l'amour'

(d) 10 'Final'

creatures: taking up a central idea from Wagner's second act, Messiaen speaks of the ecstatic climaxes of the eighth movement as symbolizing 'Tristan and Isolde transcended by Tristan-Isolde'.

The union has already taken shape in the sixth movement, which abstracts from the masculine part of 'Chant d'amour I' its crucial major sixth and its key of F sharp major with a melodic rest on the dominant, and from the feminine part its close chromatic weave and its arpeggiated 6–4 chord. (See the start of the third phrase on a high C sharp.) The fragment shown from the eighth movement adapts the cadence of the same phrase, and prepares the tonality that the whole melody will have when rushed to make the finale's second subject. Such techniques of thematic transformation can be traced to Liszt and Bartók, and as in those composers they express a conception of time which is other than symphonically continuous and progressive, which has more to do with sudden jumps and returns. And if Berlioz is perhaps Messiaen's authority for a symphony so immense and so individual, Liszt's *Faust* and Bartók's *Music for Strings, Percussion and Celesta* may also be among the antecedents crowding behind this score, along with ancient Indian music, birdsong and the whole corpus of music Messiaen himself had achieved.

What is most new about the work, apart from its size, is its devotion to process along lines more frankly exposed than in earlier compositions like the *Quatuor pour la fin du temps*. This side of it comes to the fore in the 'Turangalîla' movements, but is by no means exclusively a feature of them: 'Chant d'amour I', for instance, opens with a construction of three different orchestral groups on separate rhythmic tracks, implacably machine-like. But indeed the most determined artifices of this kind are to be found in the 'Turangalîla' movements, and most especially in the second of them, which divides very clearly into sections as follows:

i   Piano cadenza in insistent high octaves, flurrying around chromatic and diminished-seventh motifs.

ii The ondes martenot marches down a chromatic scale in even crotchets while trombones and tuba march up, and the rest of the orchestra erupts in what must be the first 'pointillist' texture: a sequence of semiquavers, seemingly related to the work's 'chord theme', is fractured by the colorations of tuned percussion plus piccolo, oboe, clarinet, horn, trumpet or tutti violins pizzicato.

iii Noise percussion in six-part counterpoint patter out streams of chromatic durations.

iv Chromatic durations are again employed in a process of expansion and contraction in the cymbals and vibraphone, forming one line in a busy heterophony that also features brilliant high figuration in the piano, woodwind phrases and a low cello solo bouncing on repeated notes.

v   Section ii is turned backwards, and because the basic image is so simple, its reversal is a potent symbol of time turning back on itself, as in the 'Regard de l'onction terrible'.

vi The first thing we encounter in this backwards time is a dense trellis of processes, giving the symphony its most complicated texture.

vii The piano emerges with fragments of its opening cadenza that summon the 'statue' theme and lead finally to a gallop in clusters down the keyboard.

viii Section ii returns again, back in its original form to set time moving forwards once more and bring the work to an abrupt end on a short sharp drumbeat.

The first, fourth and seventh of these concise sections are the freest in effect – and significantly they are all dominated by bird-style high piano music – but the others are all severely guided by process, whether that process is quite evident, as in the chromatic fanwise movements of ii, v and viii, or hermetic and audibly interpreted as a process only because there is no other reason for the music to behave as it does (iii), or compounded of apparent and hidden elements (vi). There is thus a threefold pattern of relatively free music followed by a raising or lowering of the scalar curtain and then by a passage of process, the pattern broken off in its third cycle.

As an instance of musical mechanism, the sixth section contains in its complexity most of the ways in which Messiaen's music of this period tends at times to freeze itself into the artificial, and indeed had been doing so since *La Nativité*. One of those ways reintroduces an old acquaintance, the tala of three Śarṅgadeva motifs, noted in 'Le mystère de la Sainte Trinité' and other movements, which now provides the rhythm for a two-part canon in the piano, where each part is simply a sequence of three chords, the right hand falling as the left hand rises. But there are several other layers of process, many of them based on the same principle of contrary motion. For instance, the criss-cross of durational scales returns from 'Regard de l'onction terrible', the parts now taken by a triangle and by a bass drum with pizzicato double-basses moving up the pitch scale in chromatic steps too. Similarly, temple blocks and cymbals plus maracas execute a cross pattern in larger durations, the former reducing their intervals of entry from nineteen to eleven semiquavers, the latter increasing them from seventeen to twenty-three. (The end points, then, are all chosen from Messiaen's beloved prime numbers.) On other levels there is no mirroring of change – the vibraphone and the glockenspiel give out in canon the vibraphone–cymbals rhythm of the fourth section – or else the change is cyclical: there is a twenty-three quaver ostinato of Śarṅgadeva motifs in the side-drum, and a repeating five-bar flurry of semiquavers played by a flute and the celesta.

In all this activity, however, the most prominent processes are the strongest and simplest, involving a pattern of four chords, Messiaen's 'chord theme', interpreted by large orchestral masses (see example 44). The third and fourth of these chords are stamped out regularly every two bars, but the first and second move through time, approaching their companions by a semiquaver in each cycle. As the chords become crushed up against one another, so it becomes evident that the first of them is, in the everyday sense, dominant, for in the seventh cycle it swallows the second chord and in the eighth it similarly eliminates the third, operating like some aggressive motif in a computer game. It is just about to erase the great crash of brass and tam-tam in the ninth cycle when the section stops, and we hear instead the solo piano, drawing a line out of the preceding music as it continues the double-basses' chromatic rise.

Ex. 44 Turangalîla-symphonie 7 'Turangalîla II'

This nifty dovetailing of sections is unusual, but the attacca follow-up is not, and the succession of disparate images without interruption or explanation contributes something to the movement's dream character, as does Messiaen's literary gloss on this sixth section. Like many another French symbolist he works with an imagination stocked as much by Edgar Allan Poe as by Wagner, and the processes of enclosure here he has connected with 'The Pit and the Pendulum' as picturing 'the double horror of the pendulum knife gradually approaching the prisoner's heart while the wall of red-hot iron closes in, and the indescribable, inexpressible depth of the torture pit'.[15] The passage is, however, quite strange and disturbing enough without such interpretation, for quite apart from its mighty sonorities, it embodies a wholesale commitment to process unparalleled except, as has already been suggested, in works by Cage that Messiaen at this date is most unlikely to have known, since he crossed the Atlantic for the first time only in 1947, when Koussevitzky conducted *L'Ascension* at Tanglewood, and Cage did not visit Europe until 1949.

The movement of greatest contrast with 'Turangalîla II' might seem to be its predecessor, 'Jardin du sommeil d'amour', which prefers continuity to disintegration, euphonious harmony to heterophony, slowness to hectic change, and constancy of colour to shattering diversity. But though the main substance of the movement consists of a simple ternary presentation of the love theme at an indulgently slow tempo as a song for ondes martenot and strings, there are other features as redolent of calculation as the processes of 'Turangalîla II' – and as redolent for Messiaen of Poe, since he has referred to the latter's Ligeia in speaking of the combination of forwards and backwards time in the movement's second half, where one stream of increasing chromatic durations in the untuned percussion is heard against another of similarly decreasing values. This is, however, quite unlike the case of 'Regard de l'onction terrible', as the crossover structure is very much in the background, and the obliteration of past and future, the sense of an enduring present, results much more from the character of the main

music, and in particular from its immense deceleration and its cyclical
re-enactment of a straightforward perfect cadence from a dominant-
seventh chord on C sharp to an added sixth on F sharp. As in other slow
movements, an obvious gambit becomes quite odd when it is abnor-
mally slow and often repeated, as if caught in a loop of film running at
slow motion.

But a sensation of removal from ordinary conceptions of time comes
too from the decoration provided by piano, vibraphone, flute and
clarinet. The woodwind instruments serve to emphasize the slowness
by taking languid curves down into agreement with the string harmony,
while the vibraphone, heard only in the outer sections, plays a phrase in
palindromic durations adding up to forty-nine semiquavers (in the first
part; at the reappearance values start to be augmented or diminished in
regular fashion). The piano, which is the subsidiary instrument heard
most clearly, quite properly sounds the most definite alternative to the
strings and ondes, in that the latter's hugely extended phrases are in
extreme contrast with its biting little motifs and note repetitions, its
imitations by these means of the nightingale, blackbird and garden
warbler.[16] Nor is it only by evocation that the piano seems airborne, for
its birdsong flurries are usually centred on the anti-gravitational modes
of limited transpositions, as in the simple case shown in example 45,
where the mode is the sixth.

Ex. 45   Turangalîla-symphonie   6 'Jardin du sommeil d'amour'

Nevertheless, the piano figurations need the smooth flow of the
strings. For one thing, as in the example quoted from 'Amour oiseau
d'étoile' in *Harawi*, the darting high treble ejaculations can seem to be
adding a sprinkling of upper partials that belong to the underlying
harmony even when they are in conflict with it. Also, it is the contrast
between the continuous and the fragmented that makes each most fully
itself. This interdependence Messiaen interprets in poetic terms, not
attempting to disguise his own dependence on Wagner:

> The two lovers are immersed in the sleep of love. A landscape has
> emanated from them. The garden which surrounds them is called
> 'Tristan'; the garden which surrounds them is called 'Isolde'. This
> garden is full of light and shade, of plants and new flowers, of brightly
> coloured and melodious birds. . . . Time flows on, forgotten, the
> lovers are outside time.[17]

The sleep of love is the sleep of reason, and the *Turangalîla-symphonie* is nothing if it is not grossly irrational on every front. The rational musical phraseology made possible by classical diatonic harmony is either wholly ignored or made strange by deceleration; simple ideas are colossally inflated (see example 41) while highly complex patterns are tucked away at a level below perceptibility. Ultimately, therefore, the work is not made to be understood, but made rather to draw its listeners through mind-defying complexity, alterations of time sense and sheer brilliance into a state of amazement. Nothing in fashionable neoclassicism could help in this; Messiaen had to look to another time when diatonic harmony was stretched, bent and overcome by the incursion of modal and atonal elements. No doubt, since he has freely admitted as much, Villa-Lobos provided some help, but Messiaen's more significant masters were perhaps the European ones: the Dukas of *Ariane et Barbe-Bleue*, the Bartók of *The Miraculous Mandarin* (which might even, in its music for the two central characters, have suggested the 'statue' and 'flower' themes), the Stravinsky of *The Rite of Spring*, which offered much more than a model for rhythmic characters. Indeed, the *Turangalîla-symphonie* comes nearer than any other successor to Stravinsky's penetration to the barbaric through sophisticated means, his imagery of the machine as mediation between the modern and the archaic, the individual and the general. Like Stravinsky's, Messiaen's machines are usually rhythmic, but they can also be actual, for it is a machine instrument, the ondes martenot, that gives the work its most human voice, its most distinctive colour and the means by which it sings of the most universal human experience, that of love, in a manner all its own.

What is most remarkable about that manner, and quite outside the intellectual network of Messiaen's own time, is its freedom from the sexual guilt that Wagner had composed in *Tristan und Isolde* long before Freud gave it a scientific authority. In terms of idea, of course, this dazzling innocence is religious in its orgins, possible for Messiaen because sexuality is wholly justified when it is offered in an adoration that is both human and divine: the 'joy of the blood of the stars' is the expression of the lovers' delirium on a cosmic scale, but it is also a vision of Christ's blood streaming in the firmament, and a vision not so much of an act of redemption as of a universe in a perpetual state of salvation. Musically the absence of guilt is a function of the absence of continuity and hence the absence of memory, the conquering of historical time in a gigantic apotheosis of Messiaen's favoured techniques: the extreme slowness, the repetitions and symmetries, the images of reversal, the piling up, especially in the 'Turangalîla' movements, of so many conflicting streams of time that no single one can claim the observer's attention and the music becomes a detached object, experienced as being and not becoming, examinable whole only in the continuous present of the memory.

The third and last part of this Tristan epic followed the *Turangalîla-symphonie* very swiftly, in the following month, December 1948: it was the *Cinq rechants* for twelve solo voices, three each of sopranos, contraltos, tenors and basses. In some respects the piece is a pendant to the symphony, since it takes up a number of that work's less conspicuous themes;[18] at the same time it can be seen as a return to the world of *Harawi*, since again the human voice is involved, again in a mixture of meaningful language and sounds chosen for colour and attack, and since Messiaen has admitted the influence of Peruvian folksong,[19] which must therefore, as so much of the melodic material of the *Cinq rechants* is shared with the *Turangalîla-symphonie*, have been drawn into the orchestral work as well. *Harawi* and the *Cinq rechants* together emphasize how distant Messiaen's use of the voice is from the civilized norms of the Western tradition, since both are filled with incantations having no rational sense, with melismatic ululations, percussive patterns and other features suggestive of an Artaudesque identification with primitive song.

The *Cinq rechants*, however, also look towards much more cultivated traditions. Their very title, as Messiaen has explained,[20] is a homage to Claude Le Jeune, the most gifted as well as the most dogmatic of Jean-Antoine de Baïf's collaborators in the late sixteenth-century Académie that sought to create a rhythmically measured art of song in emulation of the ancients, as they thought. The longs and shorts of metrical feet were set as minims and crotchets, and though subdivision was sometimes permitted, in general the music adheres very closely to the poetic metre, so that de Baïf's ventures in the revival of Greek lines brought similar, musically unusual metres into Le Jeune's compositions, many of which are divided into verses and refrains, called 'chants' and 'rechants'.

Messiaen's five pieces have the same sort of verse–refrain structure, twofold or threefold, except that the verses have all the same text and change instead by increasing musical complication: new layers may be added (first, second and fifth *rechants*), or there may be extension and variation (third) or simply changes in the pseudo-instrumental hummed accompaniment (fourth). The Hellenizing influence of Le Jeune, though, is limited. Messiaen had known of Greek metre since his studies with Emmanuel twenty years earlier, and could be expected to be attracted to its musical potential by his very evident conception of rhythm in terms of single quantities. However, the only demonstrable use of Greek metre in the *Cinq rechants* comes right at the beginning, in the setting of 'les amoureux s'envolent' as an Aristophanic: — ‿ ‿ — ‿ — — (the prime-number total of eleven units may partly explain

Messiaen's favouring this line). More commonly the metres set in motion in the *Cinq rechants* are derived from the Śārṅgadeva collection,[21] and more commonly still they are invented by the composer in the spirit of Indian or Greek pattern, as in the extract (example 46) from the second *rechant*, illustrating the contrast of relatively free solo vocalises with music measured in irregular quantities. (Time signatures have been omitted for the sake of clarity.)

Ex. 46   Cinq rechants   2

Also typical is the rhythmic advantage Messiaen draws from his meaningless Quechua–Sanskrit constructions, and the higher degree of chromaticism than in any earlier work. The melodies appear to be guided less by the reach towards a modal final than by motivic answers, especially concerning motifs with a tritone: one may note, for instance, how falling tritones are answered by rising ones in the French lines and in what follows, and how the firm arrival on A flat in the former is achieved more by the rallentando and decrescendo than by any modal character, the sixteen notes of the phrase including all the chromatic degrees except D flat. Quite unusually, too, there are scarcely any triadic harmonies except in the lush third *rechant*; most often the chant is monodic or else sustained by fierce discords strident with tritones.

The French text is all, as here, in isolated fragments which the verse–refrain forms cause to appear two or three times – and more often in the case of the couplet from the first *rechant*, which is another crystal liturgy of superimposed ostinatos in differing lengths, cut off arbitrarily while the second soprano is in the middle of a word and barely beyond the start of a process whose completion would require her to repeat her part 31,080 times. This powerful current of the cyclical in the *Cinq rechants*, along with the regular abandonment to meaninglessness, effectively obscures any narrative line even more than in *Harawi*, and though the work can be regarded as moving towards and then away from the ecstatic consummation of its middle movement, its character is more that of a liturgy, perhaps a mass of love, with its five movements, its central 'Credo' of *Turangalîla* love music transposed into glowing E major and its final 'Agnus Dei' that comes to rest on a soft, bare tritone.

But equally it belongs with a class of songs to warn lovers of the approach of day: there is an appeal to Brangäne early on (Tristan and Isolde themselves at last enter their trilogy in the centrepiece) and Messiaen has acknowledged too the influence of a troubadour genre of this type, the alba.[22] Like a troubadour he makes free allusion to prototypes of love from the classics and romances – Orpheus, Bluebeard (Dukas's), Viviane, Yseult – adding to these some images from paintings: the flying lovers of the opening he identifies as Chagall's, and the 'crystal bubble' from the same movement is Bosch's prison for lovers.[23] The musical influence of troubadour song would seem to be equally vague, more a matter of analogy than of imitation in the manner of the Peruvian borrowings of *Harawi*. Of the three troubadours whom Messiaen has cited as important to the work,[24] Giraut de Bornelh was the author of a celebrated alba, 'Reis glorios', Jaufre Rudel offered examples of measured rhythm and the appearance of a refrain in his 'Lanquam li jorn', and Folquet de Marseille is known for another alba as well as for his unusually clear setting out from melodic formulae that recur from song to song, just as they do in Messiaen's own music. (The *'Boris* motif' is an obvious example from earlier works, replaced now by ideas associated with the *Turangalîla-symphonie*.)

There is another sense in which the *Cinq rechants* relate to troubadour song not as a derivative but as a symmetrical closure, for if the troubadours stand at the beginning of a tradition of song as art, Messiaen's work makes the attempt to return human vocalization to more primitive functions; to the expression of emotions from a time before words (as in the soprano solo from example 46) or to the rhythmic binding of individuals in a corporate ceremonial. And it does so by looking not only to the troubadours but also to the rhythmic practices of the musicians who were their contemporaries in India.

CHAPTER 9

New Modes of Thought

The period of Messiaen's engagement on his Tristan project was also one of spectacular advance in other areas of French music. Some of his early pupils, having gone on from him to study with the Schoenberg disciple René Leibowitz, had started on the adventure of serialism: Boulez had done so in his piano *Notations* of 1944 dedicated to Serge Nigg, who had quickly taken the same path himself. Then in May 1948, while the *Turangalîla-symphonie* was nearing completion, Pierre Schaeffer created his first study made from recorded sounds and so initiated *musique concrète*. Both these developments, but particularly the serial interests of his pupils, excited Messiaen's attention and had an enormous effect on his music, so that the master–student relationship began to reverse itself. However, one may wonder whether Boulez and Nigg would have taken to serialism so readily if the way had not been pointed by their teacher in the first place, for Messiaen has recalled how in 1944 he showed his class scores of *Pierrot lunaire* and the *Lyric Suite*, and expressed his regret that Schoenberg and Berg had not worked with series of timbres, intensities and durations as well as pitches.[1] The 'chromatic' rhythms of 'Regard de l'onction terrible' were perhaps a first tentative towards restoring the balance, a step taken much further in 'Turangalîla II' and 'Turangalîla III'; Boulez was moving in the same direction at the same time in his Second Piano Sonata, but the initiative would appear to have been Messiaen's.

By the summer of 1949, though, the dialogue had been well established, and Messiaen had all but released himself from the triad in favour of twelve-note entities (if not series) such as Boulez was working with. He had also put into effect the serialization of other pitch parameters adumbrated five years before, for it was during that summer, spent teaching at Tanglewood and Darmstadt, that he conceived three decisive piano works: *Cantéyodjayâ, Neumes rythmiques* and *Mode de valeurs et d'intensités*, of which the last two were later grouped in the *Quatre études de rythme*.

Cantéyodjayâ, which looks forward to the other two pieces as well as backward to *Turangalîla*, is generally reckoned for that reason a transitional work, though one might equally describe it as his most radical composition in being open to so many disparate objects. Not for the first time, the structure is basically one of verses and refrains, but complicated to a degree without parallel in Messiaen's output. At the start it is quite clear that the music alternates refrains (labelled 'Cantéyodjayâ' in allusion, it is said,[2] to Carnatic rhythmic theory) with verses (labelled 'djayâ'), but after these have been heard in an ABACA pattern there is a widening to receive more disparate and larger excursions, introduced each time by some or all of the 'Cantéyodjayâ'. First comes a little set of variations on a rhythmic pattern, headed 'râgarhanakî' perhaps to supply a name for a motif not mentioned by Śarṅgadeva. The next episode is an 'alba' in ABABA' form, played as a monody over deep, close bass chords making a percussive effect as they execute repetitions and subtle variations on the Śarṅgadeva rhythm *lakskmiça*, named thus in the score. Messiaen's dawn song has wide chromatic intervals quite unlike any troubadour melody, and a suppleness of rhythm carried over from the unaccompanied solos of the *Cinq rechants*, but D is very distinctly the final, approached in characteristic fashion either from the tritone dominant or from the leading note C.

Of course, the opening (shown in example 47) could hardly be more modal, being restricted to a single pattern formed by three notes, but the same modal characteristics of moving towards a final and working through variations of melodic formulae are present even in the chromatic line that follows. There is, for instance, a recurrent B–A flat(G sharp)–B configuration, and the minor-ninth span of the first motif is recalled in the leaps or in the extremities of several of the later cells, or 'neumes' as Messiaen would call them: one obvious neume is the falling tritone in bars 2 and 6, which retains the same rhythm and accentuation. There are also, as in the *Cinq rechants*, larger melodic traits that recur from other works: one of them (see example 48) comes just before the 'alba' and has a history going back through the choral piece to a pair

Ex. 47 Cantéyodjayâ

Modéré, avec une nostalgie passionnée

of woodwind phrases from the 'Jardin du sommeil d'amour'. Possibly one should understand this *Turangalîla* figure as coming with the text it had acquired in the *Cinq rechants*, since it issues in the violent cut-off of two fortissimo treble chords, followed immediately by the 'alba', whose falling tritones and gruff accompaniment could well make it a death song for Orpheus as much as an aubade. However that may be, *Cantéyodjayâ* is so filled with references to earlier works (though not the *Vingt regards*, whose piano style has been drastically pared down) that it is almost a private introspection.

Ex. 48   (a) Turangalîla-symphonie   6 'Jardin du sommeil d'amour'

(b) Cinq rechants   1

(c) Cantéyodjayâ

Its other face, though, is that of fresh speculation, represented most obviously by the episode that follows the 'alba'. Messiaen heads this 'mode de durées, de hauteurs et d'intensités', and like the most abstract constructions of earlier works from 'Le mystère de la Sainte Trinité' onwards, it is a three-part heterophony, implicitly a meditation on the most abstract construction of Christianity (the Trinity), though quite new in the manner suggested by the title: each voice has its own mode of eight pitches, eight durations and two or three dynamic levels, and every note is a conjunction of these three parameters at the same magnitudes, so that, for instance, a D in the top line is always a demisemiquaver marked *pp*. The durations are chromatic, on a scale chosen to suit the register: demisemiquaver to crotchet in the top part, the lower 'octave' of semiquaver to minim in the middle line, and the 'octave' lower still of quaver to semibreve in the bass. Within lines too the general principle is that higher pitches are assigned shorter durations, though there are numerous exceptions, even within the opening bars, shown in example 49.

Ex. 49   Cantéyodjayâ

Another general principle is that the note successions are inscrutable, though again there are exceptions. For example, the top line starts with a parade of its notes in rank order of duration, and the middle line does the same after a single-note false start, while the bottom part waits till near the end of the section before embarking on the same course; there is also a retrograde of the durational scale later in the top part. On a smaller level of correspondence, there are some groupings that are preferred, providing islands of motivic repetition in a texture that otherwise appears random: one such is the collection F–E–B–B flat associated with the first four rhythmic values in the middle part, a motif that stands out the more because F and B are not represented in either of the other two lines. [The only other pitch class present singly is G, in the bass; E flat, A flat, and B flat are all included in each part, and the other pitch classes appear twice each.]

The motivic islands are the main evidence of an ordering agency in music largely determined automatically or else by chance, and perhaps they indicate also how Messiaen, even when working with modes so far from tonal gravitation, still has a tendency to think in 'neumes'. Just as significantly, the passage indicates how far his notion of mode had developed in the few years since the publication of *Technique de mon langage musical*. The middle part could be described as an expression in mode 4, but neither of the others has anything to do with the modes of limited transpositions or with modes of any other previously described kind, and the use here of mode 4, avoiding triadic formations and locking each note into its own registral, rhythmic and dynamic corner, has very little in common with Messiaen's practice in earlier works.

1. *Messiaen with his wife, the pianist Yvonne Loriod, and his pupil, the composer George Benjamin, notating bird-song in a wood near Paris in early 1984 during the filming of a programme for London Weekend Television's South Bank Show.*

2. *Messiaen in the Church of La Trinité, Paris, 1984.*

3. *A page from the autograph score of the 'Combat de la vie et de la mort'*
section from Les corps glorieux *for organ, 1939.*

4. *From the autograph score of* Sept haïkaï *for orchestra, 1962.*

5. *The composer at a rehearsal for the première of his opera* Saint François d'Assise *at the Paris Opéra, November 1983.*

6. *St Francis (José van Dam) preaching to Brother Leo (Philippe Duminy) in the first scene of* Saint François.

Nor is there any evidence of a structuring of modes from smaller units (as has been detected in the 'Antienne du silence'), either here or in, for example, the 'alba' already considered. Instead such passages are definable as modal because they work with limited repertories of objects (whether pitches, rhythmic values or dynamic levels) and because they ascribe certain functions to particular objects: finality to D and dominance to A flat in the 'alba', or adhesiveness to some groups of notes in the 'mode de durées'.

On this description the whole of *Cantéyodjayâ* can be considered a composition with a mode of musical types, and like the 'alba' it starts by forming patterns with just a few of them before going on to engulf more, its range becoming particularly broad after the 'mode de durées' has been broken off. At this point the 'Cantéyodjayâ' music returns, and restores the 'alba', but only for a single bar before new material enters. This proves to be the start of a big new verse–refrain structure, where the verses and refrains are themselves mosaics of fragments. The music erupts in diversity, and erupts too in fake Sanskrit headings, where Messiaen usually draws on some character in a fragment to give it a name: 'doubléafloréalîla' for a passage whose chromatic clusters might justify a connection with the 'flower' theme from the *Turangalîla-symphonie*, 'boucléadjayakî' for arch-shaped motifs in the hard bright treble (French 'bouclé' = buckled), 'linéacourbârasa' for the one warmly diatonic moment in the piece, 'statoua' for a suggestion of the *Turangalîla* 'statue' theme, and so on.

All these little titles have the suggestion of a private game, and coupled with the extreme heterogeneity of *Cantéyodjayâ* they may suggest an imagination at a crisis of control, besides offering a parallel to Messiaen's musical use of ideas to which he had himself given a meaning, the ideas perpetuated from the *Turangalîla-symphonie* and the *Cinq rechants*. Of course, he had always worked in this way: a great deal of his earlier music had been concerned with giving new meanings to the tritone, the diminished-seventh chord, the whole-tone scale or the pentatonic mode by the use of diatonic harmony. The difference now is that the scope is broadened, to the point where the composer might justifiably have felt uncertain of his power to discriminate between what belongs to a particular work and what does not.

One wonders whether such discrimination will ever be possible for the analyst. There are evident reworkings of cells in *Cantéyodjayâ* – particularly of the fifth plus tritone cell that opens the 'alba', is embedded in the recurrent motif mentioned in the 'mode of durées', sounds through 'doubléafloréalîla', becomes a subject of motivic variation in the middle part of 'colonnoulévalaghou' and is even bound into the main 'Cantéyodjayâ' theme (see example 50). Here the fifth–tritone idea crowns the descending limb of the phrase, which depends as much on piano resonance as do the more obvious vibrational effects of earlier works: for instance, each of the first two notes in the left hand enhances just one of the right hand's notes (first the D flat, then the C) before the phrase opens to a widespread major triad and then closes back via a double tritone to a chord of the same family as the first two – the fifth–tritone family, indeed. But despite the pervasive presence of this cell, which beside occurring too in numerous other works by Messiaen can be found in pupils' compositions influenced by him (Boulez's Flute Sonatina of 1945 is an example), its function is not to unify the work but rather, like the theme of *Les offrandes oubliées*, to write the same signature across disparate materials. The essence of *Cantéyodjayâ* is its variety, out of which the next two piano works were to choose very particular elements as the basis for their own fields of action.

Ex. 50   Cantéyodjayâ

The 'transitional' character of the piece is thus not just an adventitious effect of its time of composition, but rather an aspect of the balancing of different time streams Messiaen achieves by splicing together his miscellaneous fragments. For if the work looks forwards and backwards within his output, it does so also within itself, switching from one kind of music to another, and also from one conception of time to another, since in some of its strands time is quite stationary (example 50 appears nineteen times, always in exactly the same form) while in others it moves in irregular fits (the 'mode de durées') or turns back on itself either sequentially (the palindrome of 'collinâlaya') or simultaneously (the crossover of two voices in chromatic durations, now extended from the 'Regard de l'onction terrible' to run to twenty-three values). Messiaen might have taken this idea of editing different materials together from *musique concrète* or from film, though it seems more likely his models were such works of Stravinsky as the *Symphonies of Wind Instruments*, from which *Cantéyodjayâ* differs only in that its collage is more complex and its ending less monumentally conclusive. Once the patchwork of verses and refrains has been properly completed, the 'Cantéyodjayâ' returns again and begins to reintroduce the 'alba' by way of its Orphic prelude (example 48(c)), but loud staccato diminished-seventh arpeggios in contrary motion dismiss the attempt and the piece ends with the hands on solitary As seven octaves apart. An arbitrary finish is thus imposed on the piece: its process of widening spread could continue indefinitely, and in a sense does so in the works to come.

The first of these, *Neumes rythmiques*, is similarly composed of mosaics of growing diversity, but in a much more organized, monumental manner. There are very clearly three kinds of material, of which the first and the third are subject to rhythmic process: the first is a sequence of three bass chords, with treble decoration that marks out the changed durations as the original shape of one–six–eleven semiquavers becomes distended to five–ten–fifteen, and the third is a palindromic rhythm beaten out by clusters and tritone oscillations at both ends of the keyboard, similarly growing along the chain of prime numbers from forty-one semiquavers to fifty-three. As this implies, there are four appearances of this material, and four too of that based on the three-chord figure, the alternations always occupied by music constituted from the 'rhythmic neumes' themselves.

Messiaen's concern with modality, and his regular contact with plainsong as a practising musician, made it almost inevitable that he would be influenced by the neumatic notation and the associated formulaic character of medieval monophony, and indeed signs of that influence have already been detected: the '*Boris* motif' might be described as a prominent neume of his music from the second half of the 1930s, and the construction of such things as the 'alba' from *Cantéyod-jayâ* suggests neumatic thinking. But in *Neumes rythmiques* the revival is standardized. The seven 'lines' interspersed among the two sorts of refrain are made up from nineteen kinds of neume – another prime number – distinguished not only in terms of melodic contour like medieval neumes, but also in terms of rhythm, dynamics and harmonization – though this last is perhaps a misleading word when Messiaen's technique here (also foreshadowed in *Cantéyodjayâ*) is to add chords above or below melodic notes in order to colour them with resonances, using harmony as an organist uses registration. As has already been indicated, Messiaen's harmonic method on the small scale often involves adding chords to substantiate a function: this preoccupation with the single event finds an obvious parallel in his rhythmic thinking. But now that triads have suddenly become scarce in his music, the element of function has all but disappeared, and the point of interest is the resonant sympathy between the melodic note and its added chords. Where there is a simple frequency ratio (more or less, allowing for equal temperament) the added notes will tend to blend into the main note's harmonic spectrum, but where this is not the case there will be sharp conflict. Messiaen thus looks forward to Stockhausen's conception in *Mantra* of dissonance and consonance as measures of frequency ratio with a central pitch, while his working with a fixed array of sound objects suggests a parallel with the prepared piano of Cage.

The first 'line' of neumes (see example 51) may illustrate these points. The bar lines here clearly mark off the nine neumes, illustrating six different types. With the exception of the penultimate one, all these neumes focus on the same pitch, the E above middle C, but in each variety it is differently shaded by its melodic preparation and resonant aura. Thus, for instance, the inferior fourth and fifth in the first neume produce a relatively consonant support, whereas the added chord in the second, with its major seventh and its low F sharp to sound conflicting

Ex. 51   Neumes rythmiques

Bien modéré (neumes rythmiques, avec résonances, et intensités fixes)

partials, generates a gruff noise in which the E is much less surely sensed. Obviously dynamics are as important here as intervals: the first E in the last bar remains prominent despite antagonistic support because it is distinctly louder. This last neume also shows the change of perspective that Messiaen can achieve by means of his added resonances and subresonances, for where the first E is heard above a dimly perceived chasm, the second is comfortably at the bottom of a pile of overtones (this is Messiaen's 'chord of resonance'): it is as if the note were being twisted in space so that it looks upwards instead of downwards.

As the later lines add more to the repertory of neumes, so the fixation on this middle E declines, though it returns strongly in the last two lines, of which the last of all restores at the end the final neume of the first line, which, as the 'comma' at the end of each line, has been subject to change in the interim. This is unusual. Most of the neumes remain, like the 'Cantéyodjayâ' music of the previous work, unchanged from appearance to appearance. Among the exceptions are a couple of cases of systematic rhythmic expansion (in the second line, for instance, the dimensions of the fourth neume of example 51 are changed from two–three–two semiquavers to two–four–two and then three–five–two) and two dramatic turns of events in the last line. Twice the strongly arrowed fifth neume of example 51 is turned backwards, reversing time, and then one of the simplest and most easily recognized neumes, based on a falling B flat–E tritone in semiquavers, takes on the rising C sharp–D minor ninth of another neume, and with slightly increasing speed contracts this to D–D sharp followed by D sharp–C. The alarming effect is of a warp in the substance of the piece, and this, added to the temporal reversals that have gone before, brings the line and the work to a climax from which it descends in a sequence of neumes anchored once more to the central E.

The once-and-for-all interlocking of pitch, register, dynamic and colour in the neumes of *Neumes rythmiques* is an extension of the principle at work in the 'mode de durées' from *Cantéyodjayâ*, but a more direct relative of that section is the *Mode de valeurs et d'intensités*, dated 'Darmstadt 1949' but apparently realized the following winter in Paris.[3] This is again a three-part heterophony of lines moving in chromatic durations built from demisemiquavers (treble), semiquavers (middle range) and quavers (bass). Indeed, the only essential differences from the 'mode de durées' are that there are now twelve items in each voice (in pitch terms, a full chromatic scale), that each note is assigned a distinct mode of attack as well as its own duration and register, that the spread of dynamic levels is finer, and that the irregular circulations on three levels continue for much longer. As before, though, irregularity is only part of the piece. There are places in each voice where twelve-note collections are assembled into some sort of order,[4] and the work is given a large form by the three-times tolling of its lowest note, the piano's bottom C sharp, whose last sounding stops the music in its tracks. Once more, too, there are motivic islands, of which the most prominent is that formed by the first three notes of the middle part's repertory: G, C and B flat. Not only do these have the smallest durations, they are also emphasized by the choice of dynamics and attacks, the G uniquely having the most forceful attack of the twelve in play and the second loudest dynamic marking, *ff*. (The marking *fff* is applied only to the lowest two notes in the bass.) The G, C and B flat also occur more often than they should on average – of the 185 notes in the line, 34 are Gs – and they occur very often together, particularly near the end, where the circulation within a pentatonic grouping may suggest a folk song trying to make itself heard through a grid of random mechanical activity.

That was not, however, what excited the admiration of Messiaen's young colleagues. In 1951, two years after he had composed the piece there, Messiaen returned to the Darmstadt summer school with the records he had recently made of the *Quatre études de rythme*. (The only other works of his to appear on 78 rpm recordings were the *Visions de l'Amen*, the *Trois petites liturgies* and two of the *Vingt regards*.) He had been back to Darmstadt too the year before, but now he found ready ears for what he brought with him: he has recalled how Karlheinz Stockhausen and Karel Goeyvaerts were enthralled by the *Mode de valeurs et d'intensités*,[5] and Stockhausen has admitted the influence,[6] besides demonstrating it by going to Paris at the beginning of 1952 to study with Messiaen, whose pupil Goeyvaerts already was.

Messiaen's class for young composers, which since 1947 had been regularized within the Conservatoire as a class in musical analysis, thus became an international as much as a French institution, and those who passed through it include many of the outstanding creative musicians of three decades: not only Boulez (1943–4) and Stockhausen (1952) but also Jean Barraqué (1950–1) and Alexander Goehr (1955–6), besides Iannis Xenakis, who profited from informal encouragement. Such an eminent discipleship is equalled only by Schoenberg's, and like Schoenberg's teaching, Messiaen's was based on the study of music of the past, if of a much wider past, historically and geographically. In 1966, after Milhaud's retirement, Messiaen's class was given the official status of a class in composition, but this would not seem to have altered his methods. Each year, as he has explained,[7] he chose a theme, which might be piano music from Couperin to Boulez, opera (a personal repertory extending from Monteverdi's *Orfeo* via Rameau, Mozart, Wagner and Debussy to *Wozzeck*, thus skipping all the nineteenth-century Italians), or rhythm, including as one might expect 'Gregorian number or the rhythm of plainsong, accentuation in Mozart, Debussy's rhythmic undulation, the rhythmic characters in Stravinksy's *Rite of Spring* – all that completed by a thorough analysis of the ganas, of Carnatic theory, of the 120 deçi-tâlas of India, and by an initiation into Greek metre'.[8] It is unfortunate that Messiaen has not published any of his teaching material – a *Traité du rythme* has been in preparation for many years – but some windows into his classes may perhaps be provided by the publications of his pupils: by Boulez's study of *The Rite of Spring*, for example,[9] or by Stockhausen's essay on cadential rhythm in Mozart.[10] If these do indeed reflect Messiaen's thinking, then they indicate a close correspondence between his ideas about music and his ideas in music, his concern in both with categorizing different types, with looking at musical events as individual phenomena rather than as elements in a continuity, with considering music as being rather than becoming.

What is more exactly demonstrable than the influence of Messiaen's teaching, however, is the influence of his *Mode de valeurs et d'intensités* on the music of his younger colleagues. Goeyvaerts and another Messiaen pupil, Michel Fano, both wrote sonatas for two pianos in 1951,[11] adapting in part Messiaen's 'chromatic' durations to serial methods; Goeyvaerts also extended the idea of crossover form introduced in the 'Regard de l'onction terrible'. In both these respects his work had an influence on Stockhausen's *Kreuzspiel* written later in 1951, while Boulez's *Structures* for two pianos (1951–2) may owe something to the Fano sonata, though in making a series of the upper division of Messiaen's mode it acknowledges the importance of the *Mode de valeurs* as most decisive: Messiaen and Boulez together gave the first performance of the opening section of *Structures* in Paris on 4 May 1952.

But intensely though it may have excited composers then in their twenties, the *Mode de valeurs* was to remain an isolated, marginal phenomenon in Messiaen's own output. When asked a decade later about his current attitude to the study, Messiaen would reply only that 'there are various Messiaens who are dead', and certainly, apart from the obvious fact that it grew out of a section of *Cantéyodjayâ*, the piece has little connection with his other music. Indeed, it hardly sounds like Messiaen at all: it sounds, rather, only like itself, which is some measure of the extent to which its composition was automatic, entailing an abstention from creative choice much more severe than in other instances of automatic writing by Messiaen, for composition here becomes simply a matter of rotating the same twelve pitch-duration couples in each of the three voices. The experience was, like Cage's *4'33"* (1952), an extreme extrapolation of tendencies in its composer's music for some years, and it may be that Messiaen's automaton as much as Cage's silence was motivated by a wish to annihilate the expressive, ordering ambitions of the conscious mind. If that is so, the composition of the *Mode de valeurs* may have been a meditative exercise, producing music that certainly demands an intensive mental activity from the performer but that may leave the listener with the sense that infinity has been contemplated without the intervention of any human agency.

The two pieces that followed to complete the studies, *Ile de feu 1* and *Ile de feu 2* (both 1950), are once more earthbound, and vigorously so. Their dedication to Papua is obscure: Messiaen says that 'their themes have all the violence of magical organizations in that country',[12] but there is no evidence that he was influenced, as in his Peruvian, Indian and later Japanese works, by any indigenous music. Moreover, Papua is not within the belt of volcanic activity suggested by the common title and by the material of these pieces, of which the first is a virtuoso fanfare to head the set and the second a weighty finale for it: in complete performances of the *Quatre études*, the *Mode de valeurs* should come second and *Neumes rythmiques* third.

Each of the *Ile de feu* pieces is based on a stamping dance theme, and the two are related in starting with a jolt up and down a third as well as in continuing the concern with resonance effects rather than harmonic functions that had been characteristic of *Cantéyodjayâ* and *Neumes rythmiques*. An early appearance of the theme in *Ile de feu 1*, for example, has characteristic birdsong figurations whose resonant clarity is affected by their harmonic relation with the melody (see example 52).

Ex. 52   Ile de feu 1

The first figure here concentrates on pitches in a simple frequency ratio with those in the theme, but in the second figure the relationships are more complex and so the two hands do not so much enhance one another. Similar subtlety in the gauging of resonance characteristics may be demonstrated by the opening of *Ile de feu 2* (see example 53). The theme here is pentatonic, except for the addition of A sharp in a tritone E–A sharp cadence at the midpoint, but the frequent note recurrences are always differently coloured by the added resonance. Moreover, the resonance chords avoid the mode's final E, its dominant G and its intial A (except for a single A to colour the A sharp), so that there is biting conflict between the melody and its coloration, a conflict increased in many cases by the major-fifteenth or minor-seventeenth intervals between melodic notes and notes in the resonance chords.

Ex. 53   Ile de feu 2

The construction of both these pieces as verse–refrain forms provides the opportunity for the themes to be differently coloured at each appearance. For example, the three ensuing statements of the melody in *Ile de feu 2* are in sevenths, in chords of a fifth plus a tritone once more, and in octaves. In *Ile de feu 1* the episodes between soundings of the theme and fragments of it are occupied by great flurries in modes of limited transpositions or simple arpeggios that take the hands scooting to opposite ends of the keyboard, but in *Ile de feu 2* the verses are more substantial, and show Messiaen continuing his subserial manipulations. In particular, they make show of the technique of 'interversion' that had been introduced with a four-note motif in *Cantéyodjayâ* but that is now applied to twelve-note successions. The idea is that elements are taken one by one from the middle of the succession and placed at the start, so that for example the duration series marked in the score as 'interversion I', 6–7–5–8–4–9–3–10–2–11–1–12, semiquavers, yields 'interversion II' of 3–9–10–4–2–8–11–5–1–7–12–6 semiquavers. Pitches are interverted at the same time, since as in the *Mode de valeurs* there is an unchanging connection in these sections between pitch and duration. There are also fixed attacks and dynamic levels, though the celestial differentiations of the *Mode de valeurs* have been scaled down to the more humanly practical level of four sorts of attack and five intensities.

Serial interversion of note sequences in the manner described can produce a maxium of twelve different forms, though in this particular case there are only ten, since two members, those with durations of five and ten semiquavers, are so placed that they simply exchange positions at each interversion. In the musical setting the ten interversions follow in pairs, I–II, III–IV etc., played simultaneously and interleaved with the thematic refrains thus: theme – interversions I–IV – theme – interversions V–VIII – theme. At this point the alternations break off for a group of neumes and then a decorated retrograde of interversion I in even quavers, followed by a new sequence of paired interversions in semiquavers, these interversions derived in a different way: notes are selected from the original form in the order 6–11–5–8–2–9–3–10–4–12–1–7, and this time there are indeed twelve forms, of which the last is a chromatic scale. This duly introduces the final pair of interversions from the other system, and here too the last is a chromatic scale. But where previously the music had switched between its modal, rudely physical dance and its twelve-note abstractions, now the theme is heard along with the final interversions. Finally there is a determined toccata in the bass register, superimposing játis on a string of chromatic motifs undergoing gradual interval expansion and contraction.

Ile de feu 2 thus ends with its distinct tendencies of urgent modal dance and serial reordering bound fast if unwillingly together. Perhaps they seem more natural partners if one understands Messiaen's serial methods as 'magical organizations' matching the evocation of Melanesian magic in the refrains, for it cannot be that he intends his operations of interversion to be followed by his audience. Instead, like a pre-Vatican II priest with his back turned on the faithful, he is engaged on bringing about a transformation of which they can be aware only by its atmosphere and by its result: by the atmosphere of abstract manipulation and by the result of a chromatic scale produced from the initial all-interval series. The process by which that result is achieved must remain mysterious, except for those who examine the score by eye as well as by ear, and except of course for the composer. For him the process is obviously keenly meaningful. Speaking of the rhythmic interversions in one of his next works, the *Livre d'orgue*, he has said they allowed him 'like the hero of Wells's *Time Machine* to go back in time and also to chop its course, alternately following it and returning'.[13] It is certainly a fine poetic understanding of what interversion entails, but it is a view that, one suspects, has to come from outside, one that the work alone is not capable of eliciting. In thus opening itself to secret organization – which of course is very much a feature of the *Mode de valeurs* as well as of *Ile de feu 2*, Messiaen's music once more looks to a pre-Renaissance past, to the isorhythm of the fourteenth-century motet or the hermetic symbolism of the fifteenth-century mass.

And it was a mass of his own, though an organ mass, that Messiaen was writing at this same time, moving from the island of fire to the tongues of flame in his *Messe de la Pentecôte* (1949–50). He had composed nothing for the organ since *Les corps glorieux* a decade before, since when the outstanding young organist-composer he was in his twenties had become a much more challenging, less easily categorized artist. He was still, however, an organist, still playing regularly at La Trinité, and he has recalled how the *Messe de la Pentecôte* became the container for what he had discovered as an improviser,[14] while as a work destined for the liturgy, uniquely in his output except for the motet *O sacrum convivium!*, it necessarily had to adapt itself to a given form and given aims.

The organ mass as a genre was specially cultivated by French composers of the time of Louis Quatorze, when it was the practice to substitute organ versets for alternate lines of the plainsong. In 1903, however, the church had prohibited such suppression of parts of the liturgical text, and Tournemire's *L'orgue mystique*, written a generation after this ban, had offered organists a new kind of mass music in which movements treating the relevant plainsongs could be played as purely instrumental items at the entry of the priest, the offertory, the consecration, the communion and the withdrawal. Messiaen took over this five-movement form, and followed Tournemire too in working on plainsong themes (though, as usual, adapted to modalities of his own), but his appeal at the same time to worlds beyond the immediately sacred, to birdsong in particular, is in the naïve spirit of the eighteenth-century musicians who had enlivened their organ masses with hunting music, and something of the old alternatim tradition survives in his frequent interleaving of plainsong-stimulated material with other, seemingly freer music. For instance, the 'Consécration' alternates a monodic adaptation of the Pentecost alleluia *Veni Sancte Spiritus* with phrases in which a pedal figure is played in Śarṅgadeva rhythms with added resonance chords in the manuals.

It would be much too simplistic to interpret these alternations as switching between the general and the personal: after all, the chant is thoroughly individualized by its transposition into mode 4 on F. Moreover, the baldness of the verse–refrain form and the general slowness and deliberation of the music – with the notable exception of the final 'Sortie' briefly and vigorously evoking the 'rushing mighty wind' – strengthen what had always been most liturgical in Messiaen's music. Boulez, at the time of his reaction against his teacher in 1948, had remarked rather dismissively that 'Messiaen does not compose – he juxtaposes',[15] and there is no work that comes nearer justifying this criticism than the *Messe de la Pentecôte*. The 'Communion', which of the five movements is most markedly a patchwork, even draws attention to this fact in its subtitle of 'Les oiseaux et les sources', the former singing in the relatively non-gravitational air of Messiaen's bird music since the 'Liturgie de cristal' while the waters make a surprising return to the world of the *Fête des belles eaux* and to the added sixths and dominant sevenths floating in the region of E major: the two remain thoroughly and emblematically opposed at the end, just before the piece closes in extraordinary fashion on a diminished-seventh chord joined by sounds at the extremes of the organ's range, a C at thirty-two-foot pitch and an F sharp on a one-foot Piccolo stop. Perhaps, though, anything more like composition at this solemn moment in the liturgy would be an impertinence, as Messiaen's own published statements would appear to suggest is his own view,[16] whereas juxtaposition leaves the listener free to pursue his or her own line of thought, moving over the objects presented by the music but not being guided by them from moment to moment.

Of course, musical mosaics of this kind occur throughout Messiaen's music; the *Messe de la Pentecôte* is extreme only in so abandoning rhythmic dynamism (except again in the 'Sortie') or unity of colour. Instead it positively exults in new, divergent and surprising registrations, and scans almost the whole of Messiaen's previous output in search of motifs to which they may be applied: twelve-note sequences and interversions, a crossover bicinium of chromatic durations (in the

'Sortie') and resonance chords, along with the older features of Hindu rhythm, added-note harmonies and the modes of limited transpositions.

But while it reviews practically the whole of his music from the 'water drop' staccato of *Le banquet céleste* to the twelve-note magic of *Ile de feu 2*, the *Messe de la Pentecôte* is not without ideas of its own. One of these is irrational rhythm, and though it may appear odd that a composer in the twentieth century should have managed without this for twenty years, particularly when rhythm was one of his dearest concerns, Messiaen's preference for integral values is understandable as an expression of his view of rhythm as number and his consequent search for irregularity more in the grouping of units than in their subdivision: hence his attachment to Greek and Hindu formulae which supply irregular formations. In the 'Entrée' of the *Messe de la Pentecôte*, however, triplet and quintuplet divisions suddenly appear much more frequently than hitherto, although, as if giving himself some familiar template in this new universe, Messiaen chooses to understand them as belonging to Greek lines (see example 54). Here again the music offers a cross-cutting of old and new; for the pedal monody is highly character-istic of Messiaen's earlier modality in its emphasis on the tritone and the sixth, and so on the diminished-seventh chord, while the manual introduction is locked on to the fifth plus tritone chord of more recent compositions. The supposed scansion of the monody, however, is harder to hear than its modal quality. Possibly the important thing here is not the suggestion of poetic rhythm but the implication of speech, for Pentecost is the feast of speaking in tongues. Like those gathered with the Apostles at the time of the miracle, Pentecost congregations at La Trinité are provided by their organist with immediately familiar and even recognizable motifs (those derived from plainsong) along with expressions in more rebarbative languages, and if the twelve-note and rhythmic speculation of the *Messe de la Pentecôte* is as much automatic as it was in *Turangalîla*, *Cantéyodjayâ* and the *Etudes de rythme*, it has

Ex. 54   Messe de la Pentecôte   1 'Entrée'

its licence now not merely from surrealist poets but from the Disciples' glossolalia.

Nor did the evident creative enjoyment of the *Messe de la Pentecôte* stop there, for in 1951, the year after he had completed the work, Messiaen composed a new and larger volume, his *Livre d'orgue*. The choice of title may suggest something more abstract, but it is much more likely to have been another homage to the organist composers of the *grand siècle*, many of whom published *livres d'orgue* containing masses and other music, and Messiaen's score suggests liturgical occasions when five of his seven movements might suitably be used: the two 'Pièces en trio' (Nos. 2 and 5), being three-part inventions of a kind instituted by 'Le mystère de la Sainte Trinité', are prescribed for the feast of the Holy Trinity, the central 'Chants d'oiseaux' for Eastertide, and the two movements based on strong visual images, 'Les mains de l'abîme' and 'Les yeux dans les roues', for penitential seasons and for Pentecost again respectively. Even when it is most picturesque, however, the *Livre d'orgue* is indeed a work of much more purely musical speculation than the *Messe de la Pentecôte* had been, with plainsong quotations replaced by twelve-note sequences and by rhythmic systems of the kinds Messiaen had developed in the *Etudes de rythme*.

The simplest, awesomely exposed example of this sort of construction is the first movement, 'Reprises par interversion', which is entirely a monody, if of a most unusual variety. One of the most important lessons Messiaen had taken from serialism, especially from Webern's serialism, was a cherishing of each note as a separate event: this was something he was already handing on to Boulez and Stockhausen, but neither of them wrote anything so rigorously 'pointillist' as this movement. The notes are dispersed over the entire range of the instrument, and though at first they are grouped in patterns – six twelve-note sequences, each covering a group of three Śārṅgadeva rhythms which are rearranged in each sequence and treated as rhythmic characters in the manner of 'Joie du sang des étoiles' – these patterns are taken apart in the middle of the movement. The whole line of seventy-two notes is subject to interversion beginning at the outer edges, so that the first note is now followed by the last, then the second, then the seventy-first, and so on. This new line is then played backwards, and finally the original line is heard in reverse, with the rhythmic groupings now restored, though heard in retrograde. An ordered sequence in time is thus blown apart and then reassembled in backwards order, in a way that Messiaen's use of timbral and registral peculiarities helps to make plain: the first note of the Śārṅgadeva motif *gajajhampa*, for instance, is always played on a cavernous sixteen-foot Bombard stop and the middle two values are always occupied by a repeated pitch in the medium range, whereas the quick group *sârasa* has its natural home in the middle to high register. Notes belonging originally to these formulae may thus be recognized even when the rhythms themselves have been exploded.

Of course, a complete understanding of the interversion process here would require a musical memory capable of retaining seventy-two events in their correct order, while an appreciation of the mechanism by which Messiaen moves from one twelve-note sequence to another must need still more phenomenal powers of perception. The obvious answer to such points is that the composer does not intend his music to be heard in this way, but that is by no means clearly the case. Indeed, in speaking of the book's last movement, 'Soixante-quatre durées', which transfers the two-voice crossover pattern of earlier works to the near eternal regions of time opened up by a scale of values running from one demisemiquaver to sixty-four (a breve), Messiaen has said that he 'pushed human perception of very long and very short durations to its furthest limits. And, what is still more difficult, perception of the very small differences between very long durations.'[17] In the music, however, there is no evidence that he has given much thought to matters of perception. Although all the sixty-four values in question have their openings marked by chords of two or three notes, some part of the value may be filled by silence or even occasionally by other chords. Moreover, the whole structure is festooned with decoration in birdsong style, which being monodic stands off from the rest, but which is bound in its fanciful curlicues, its note repetitions and its unexpected entrances to alter the experienced sense of time on a level far cruder than that where sixty-four semiquavers are observed as different from sixty-three.

The mistake would be, however, to suppose that such arguments are arguments against the value of Messiaen's music when in fact their object is his intention. In that respect there is a close analogy with his expressive intentions as a theologian in sound, and it was perhaps inevitable that he should be drawn at one point in his life to work in musical areas where the twentieth-century split between intention and effect has opened widest: the areas of serialism. For although this was never Schoenberg's intention (again the gap), serialism, for the first time since the Renaissance, provided composers with means by which music could be structured without reference to how it would sound, and the addition of serial controls on rhythm, loudness and colour only exacerbates the dislocation. What remains eminently perceptible in 'Soixante-quatre durées' is the fact that a structure is being worked out; even if the details are impenetrable to the ear, there is the sense of an enormous monument within which fantastic birds glide and call. The intention, whether in such conundrums or more frequently in Messiaen's exegetical works, may be to make a demonstration, but the effect can only be to demonstrate that a demonstration is taking place, and this does not destroy the value of his music but rather allows one to see it as the repository of experiences that the mind struggles against all the odds to apprehend: experiences of the supernatural, or of supernatural discrimination. What this view also clarifies is the degree to which abstract compositions such as 'Reprises par interversion' and 'Soixante-quatre durées' are all of a piece with Messiaen's religious works, for not only is arithmetic an image of divine perfection but the aural understanding of arithmetic is as much a challenge to the mind as the understanding of God.

Arithmetic can also provide a route to evocative images, as the two movements of the *Livre d'orgue* with picturesque titles amply show. In the case of 'Les yeux dans les roues', indeed, one can even imagine that the music came before its descriptive title, since the piece is based on a simple structural conceit: a twelve-note succession of chromatic pitches married to 'chromatic' durations is played in the pedals and repeated in two different interversions before the whole process, as in 'Reprises par interversion', is recapitulated backwards; meanwhile the two hands jab out a toccata in semiquavers, each hand repeating its own sequence of six twelve-note groups from which pitch classes are dropped if they appear in either of the other voices. At the same time these hectic revolutions, which one may imagine continuing forever (the final marking is 'couper brusquement'), are an apt image of the wheels full of eyes seen in Ezekiel's vision as companions to the four living creatures.

No less immediate is Messiaen's response to a half-verse from Habakkuk: 'the deep uttered his voice, and lifted up his hands on high'. Once more the structure is tight, the outer sections being based, as in 'Reprises par interversion' and the second 'Pièce en trio', on interversions of three Śarṅgadeva patterns, while the central episode divides the twelve notes among its three voices, so that the bass uses the group C sharp–E–F–F sharp–G to march up and down in scales through a tritone, the treble makes neumes out of the remaining notes A–B flat–C–D–E flat–A flat–B, and the middle voice makes decorative patterns of mediation. (These, like the woodwind tendrils in 'Jardin du sommeil d'amour', become a more central feature of other music, one providing the twelve-note series for the second 'Pièce en trio'.[18] Here, though, the evocative power comes not directly from the structure itself but from the way in which it is coloured: by fortissimo tutti discords and an answering, complementary major-seventh call in the outer segments, and in the middle by a yawning gap of range and sonority between the one-foot Piccolo in the treble and the sixteen-foot Bourdon in the bass, marked in the score as 'la profondeur'.

The score also provides the information that this music was composed, or more likely conceived, before Messiaen's beloved mountains of the Dauphiné, for each piece in the *Livre d'orgue* is headed with a date and a place. It is no surprise to learn from these datelines that three of the most systematic pieces, Nos. 1, 2 and 6, were written in Paris, or that the two abounding in birdsong, Nos. 4 and 7, had their origins in a meadow at Fuligny, the forest of St Germain-en-Laye and heathland at Gardépée in the Charente (for 'Chants d'oiseaux'), Gardépée being the place where Messiaen received instruction from the ornithologist Jaques Delamain,[19] later co-dedicatee of *Réveil des oiseaux*, and among the fields at the composer's summer home of Petichet (for 'Soixante-quatre durées'). More remarkable is the fact that the mountains suggested not only the portrait of the abyss but also the long and obscure three-part invention of the second 'Pièce en trio', for this undemonstrative piece, which keeps throughout to the same moderate-loud dynamic level, sets its face, according to its heading, 'before the glaciers of Râteau, the Meije and Tabuchet'.

No doubt the listing of three glaciers was not accidental, since this is very much a trinitarian movement, occupying three voices like 'Le mystère de la Sainte Trinité', confounding them by its registrations and recycling sequences of three Śarṅgadeva formulae as rhythmic characters in the upper and middle parts. Otherwise it is not the majestic spectacle of glaciers that Messiaen interprets but rather their grandeur of design and, perhaps, the slow, steady pace of their movement.[20] Messiaen has described this piece as his 'greatest rhythmic victory',[21] drawing attention to the way in which the two manual voices pursue independent courses of organized change with their trinities of Hindu motifs, which, unlike the immediately graspable patterns of 'Reprises par interversion', are selected from among the most complex of the 120 deçi-tâlas. This certainly provides a highly unpredictable rhythmic surface, oddly patterned with the identities that come about from the failure of one shape in each voice to change at all, but it is not easy to understand how it constitutes a 'victory' since the rhythmic processes are not established to solve any particular problem but simply overlaid. The real victory of the piece, perhaps, is in the retention of modal aspects within a totally chromatic universe, showing that Messiaen's eternal musical and spiritual verities remain ponderable within a framework that might have seemed wholly inimical to them. The god in the glacier is the fifth or the tritone that retains its sense in music where all twelve notes and all possible melodic and harmonic intervals are in perpetual circulation.

That is the lesson of all Messiaen's music from this brief yet crucial twelve-note period of 1949–52, but it is the lesson most particularly of the second 'Pièce en trio' since this is the most elaborate of his twelve-note constructions and the only one in which he uses the conventional forty-eight forms of a series instead of interversions and other derivatives of his own (*Ile de feu 2, Livre d'orgue*, Nos. 1, 2, 3 and 6) or free reorderings (*Mode de valeurs et d'intensités*). In those examples the 'series' had really been no more than the chromatic scale, bodily represented in *Ile de feu 2* and close behind the movements of the *Livre d'orgue*: the initial succession of 'Reprises par interversion', for instance, takes a skipping course through the chromatic scale (B–C–B flat–D flat–A–D–A flat–E flat–G–E–F sharp–F: a transposition of the all-interval series from *Ile de feu 2*), and the first right-hand series from the swirling music in 'Les yeux dans les roues' does the same within each hexachord (C–E flat–D flat–E–D–F–B–A flat–B flat–G–A–F sharp). What matters is not the particular order of the notes and intervals, which interversion completely disrupts, but more the simple fact that all twelve pitch classes are in play, whereas the second 'Pièce en trio' is much more genuinely a serial composition, with statements of the series knitted across the three voices in concurrence with Schoenbergian rather than Webernian practice. Messiaen is only more capricious in moving from one serial form to another in the middle of the twelve-note succession, which he is free to do because his series, B–D sharp–A sharp–C sharp–C–G–A flat–D–E–F–A–F sharp, includes two each of minor thirds, major thirds and fourths, and three minor seconds.

Within the criss-crossing of serial forms, however, modal features are brought out in a way that appears more consistent and therefore more obviously conscious than is the case in the *Mode de valeurs*. Splitting the total chromatic across three voices clearly allows the possibility of concentrating particular pitch classes or particular intervals in particular voices, as Messiaen shows in extreme fashion in the middle section of 'Les mains de l'abîme'. In the second 'Pièce en trio' the division is nothing like so absolute, but there are regions where the two manual voices contain more fourths and fifths in close position than simple statistics would predict, and, much more strikingly, the pedal part, which Messiaen marks 'mélodie principale', concentrates on a modal phrase which in its first form uses only six of the twelve notes in fixed registers and centres quite plainly on F sharp (see example 55). The exact

Ex. 55 Livre d'orgue 5 'Pièce en trio II'

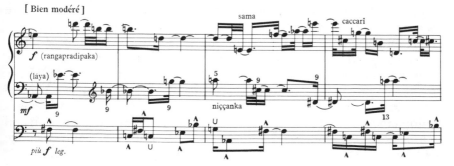

repetition of the pedal phrase here is drawn from quite different serial forms, and so the fact of repetition is disguised by the unrepeating accompaniment: the wholesale restatement later in the piece is again extracted from a new network of serial forms. The apparent serial structuring, to which one is alerted right at the start of the piece by the pure monodic statement of the series followed by its retrograde inversion, is thus merely the material out of which Messiaen can create – or perhaps reveal – other entities, phrases that pull apart and atonalize the opening melody while keeping, as a distinguishing feature, the quick oscillation of its second bar.

This way of writing non-serial music within a serial texture has much more in common with works by the young Boulez that Messiaen would by now have been familiar with – the Flute Sonatina and the Second Piano Sonata, for instance – but the Hindu-directed restriction to regular rhythmic values is wholly un-Boulezian. By contrast, the first 'Pièce en trio', in which Messiaen treats Śarṅgadeva patterns in irregular durations as he had treated Greek metres in the 'Entrée' of the Messe de la Pentecôte, has much more of Boulez's instability, of that 'rhythmic restlessness' which he has fairly attributed to his own influence on Boulez,[22] but which can certainly be seen operating here in reverse as well. Like the second 'Pièce en trio', the first is in three voices with a poetically accented melody in the bass, but this time there is no repetition of shape and no regular pulse, besides which the registration reinforces a sense of obscurity. Both trios are contemplations of the Trinity, like earlier three-part polyphonies in Messiaen's music, but where in the first his reflections are made with St Paul's as if 'in a glass darkly', the second has profited from bright mountain vision, and now the inscribed quotation from the Apostle is more definite: 'of him, and through him, and to him, are all things', even including, so it is suggested, twelve-note serialism, within which modality, that expression of the divine, can be uncovered.

The Livre d'orgue, with its perfect number of seven movements and its balance of Pauline and prophetic meditations between pillars of musical engineering, stands as a monument to the last and furthest point of Messian's twelve-note and serial speculations, though there was one unproductive offshoot the next year, 1952, in a work conceived for recorded sounds and realized in the French radio's musique concrète studio by Pierre Henry: Timbres-durées. At the time electronic music was regarded by many of the younger composers as the natural medium for serial composition, since it provided the means for a precise control of duration, timbre and volume as well as pitch. Boulez and Stockhausen completed studies at the musique concrète studio in the same year, and Timbres-durées would seem to belong to the same wave: this is to judge only from what has been published of the Messiaen[23] and Stockhausen[24] pieces, since the latter has been lost and the former, judged by its composer to be 'very bad',[25] withdrawn from circulation.

The basic materials of *Timbres-durées* were percussion and water sounds, out of which Messiaen formed a series of eleven different sounds each lasting for a different duration that was a sum of prime-number semiquavers (2, 3, 5, 7, 11, 13, 17, 19, 23, 29, 31). This constant association of sound and duration had of course been followed through earlier in instrumental works, including all the *Etudes de rythme* and many of the movements of the *Livre d'orgue*: 'Les yeux dans les roues' even introduces the term 'sons-durées' to indicate the bonding. Unlike that piece, however, the published extracts from *Timbres-durées* are severely monophonic, playing over the series in alternation with other, generally shorter sounds, and generating variety only by switching the sounds among four different stereo placements. Possibly the effect was as Messiaen describes it. In any event, he was to find his inspiration for the next few years worlds away from studios of electronic music.

CHAPTER 10
Birdsong

The first instance of a 'style oiseau' in Messiaen's music goes back to 1935, to *La Nativité du Seigneur*, but before that, at the Conservatoire, he had taken note of Dukas's injunction: 'Listen to the birds! They are great teachers.'[1] And he had done so, establishing the habit of a lifetime, which gradually bore fruit in his music. The 'Liturgie de cristal' contains the first definable attempts at rendering particular species, followed by similar efforts in most of the major works from the *Visions de l'Amen* to the *Livre d'orgue*, with the notable exception of the *Cinq rechants*, where he avoids following the gladsome imitations of a Jannequin, and with the exception too of *Cantéyodjayâ* and the *Etudes de rythme*. The songs are now more particularized than was the case in *La Nativité*, and most of them can be identified: the blackbird in the 'Liturgie de cristal' has been mentioned, and comparison with later works indicates plainly that there is a nightingale singing in the fifth of the *Visions de l'Amen*. Then in the 'Regard des hauteurs' Messiaen begins to feel confident enough in his portraits to name them, mentioning here a skylark and a blackbird again, followed in the 'Communion' from the *Messe de la Pentecôte* by a nightingale and in the middle piece from the *Livre d'orgue* by the four soloists whose parts are now quite substantial.

But though birdsong supplies nearly all the material here – as it does also in the little work he wrote the same year as a test piece for flautists at the Conservatoire and as the apotheosis of his early blackbird style, *Le merle noir* – there is little to prepare one for the chorus of thirty-eight birds who make themselves heard in *Réveil des oiseaux*, which was completed in 1953. This was Messiaen's first orchestral work since the *Turangalîla-symphonie*, whose solo piano and tuned percussion ensemble now prove themselves as apt to birdsong as they were to suggesting a gamelan: indeed, the two forms of music are not dissimilar in their quickness of figuration and their ignorance of Western human rhetoric. However, the devotion of the orchestra entirely to the production of birdsong brings a decisive move away from the lush harmonic textures of *Turangalîla*. There are a few striking places where string chords are added as resonance effects to the insistent calls of the song thrush on trumpet or the golden oriole on horns, but otherwise *Réveil des oiseaux* is a tangle of solo lines spreading around the piano.

It is formed, according to Messiaen's prefatory explanation in the score, as an image of bird songs heard in spring between midnight and noon, and though this is not explicitly stated, the songs are all those that could be heard in the gardens, fields and woods of rural France, perhaps at the composer's summer retreat of Petichet, where 'Soixante-quatre durées' had been written. (Rather unusually, the score of *Réveil des oiseaux* does not give a place, perhaps because its real location is in an aviary of the imagination.) The birds introduce themselves at different times as they do in nature. The scheme is as follows:

Piano cadenza: A lone nightingale sings at midnight, and is joined by two others.

Piano with ensemble (figure 3): Other night birds are heard – a little owl (violin), a wryneck (piano), a Cetti's warbler (E flat clarinet) and a woodlark (piccolo) – after which, at 4 in the morning, more birds begin to waken and sing, involving more instruments: blackbirds on flutes, piano and celesta; song thrush on trumpet doubled by oboes and clarinets with string resonances; chaffinches on solo violins, and robins on piano and celesta. There is a short robin cadenza on the piano to stir the rest (figure 16), and eventually the full orchestra is playing in up to twenty different parts.

Piano cadenza (figure 28): Sunrise brings a sudden silence, after which the piano performs a long blackcap solo.

Piano with ensemble (figure 29): Once more the piano's solo encourages the participation of other instruments playing other songs: blackbirds, robins and song thrushes reappear, along with the new calls of the turtle dove on trios of flutes and violins, the linnet on E flat clarinet and the blue tit on piano with woodwind and double-bass colouring.

Piano cadenza (figure 34): Another silence and then a blackbird solo.

Piano with ensemble (figure 35): A more compact tutti develops around the songs of blackbirds, robins and garden warblers.

Piano cadenza (figure 39): By contrast with earlier solos, this is a fast-changing mosaic of different songs, giving way to a long duet for robin and blackbird. At the end the midday silence is broken briefly by a grouping that returns from early in the work: two chaffinches and a blackbird on solo violins, followed by a great spotted woodpecker tapping on the wood block and a distant cuckoo on Chinese blocks.

This last gesture gives the work a neat full stop, and the alternation of cadenzas and tuttis maps out an obvious symmetry (though one distorted by the length and density of the dawn chorus that develops up to figure 28).[2] Otherwise the work asks to be read, in structure as in detail, as a transcription from nature: Messiaen calls it 'a completely truthful work,'[3] and in his note to the musicians, also printed in the score, he insists that all the songs 'have been heard in the forest and are perfectly authentic', even advising the pianist, who has to offer an 'imitation of the attacks of a very large number of birds', to make 'a few forest walks, in springtime, especially early in the morning, to familiarize herself with her models'.

It is quite obvious, nevertheless, that Messiaen's own faithfulness to his models is bound to be limited by three factors: his accuracy in recording the songs, the concrete means of reproduction at his disposal (standard instruments tuned in semitones) and his tastes as a creative musician. As far as the first of these is concerned, there can be no doubt that he is far more conscientious an ornithologist than any earlier musician, and far more musical an observer than any other ornithologist. Early scientific studies of birdsong used only the most rudimentary onomatopoeic representation (a method employed occasionally in *Réveil des oiseaux* to give the performers added evidence of the sound required, but dropped in later birdsong works), and the arrival of sound recording virtually eliminated the need for ornithologists to attempt any transcription. Similarly, there are no parallels for Messiaen's exactness among other composers, as may be indicated by a comparison of his nightingale, from the start of *Réveil des oiseaux*, with notations of the same bird in Jannequin, Couperin, Beethoven and Stravinsky (see example 56).

Ex. 56   *Musical Nightingales*

   (a) Jannequin (c. 1530)

   (b) Couperin (1722)

   (c) Beethoven (1808)

(d) Stravinsky (1908–9)

(e) Messiaen (1953): Réveil des oiseaux

Even allowing for variation among individuals of the same species, it is clear that Messiaen's copy is on a quite different level of sophistication from the others, and that although there are agreements of detail, as when Beethoven concurs in the repeated major second fall, the Messiaen much more than the others has the appearance of careful imitation, as is natural when the musical aim is so different. The nightingale portraits of the earlier composers are essays in the picturesque: most especially in the 'Pastoral' Symphony, where Beethoven's stated intention was to communicate mood, not the exact song of a bird. The nightingale becomes a cipher for nocturnal quiet and contentment, as it does too in the Couperin piece, while in the Jannequin it is the excuse for vocal oddities that seem intended above all to charm and amuse, and in the Stravinsky it is hardly more than an invitation to exoticism. *Réveil des oiseaux,* though no doubt cognizant of all these predecessors (Messiaen even asks for a harpsichord sonority at some points in his piano nightingale imitation), is an essay of a different kind, and the composer, with no false modesty, has expressed an awareness of his originality in making scrupulous efforts to reproduce birdsong, to the extent of doubting that Couperin ever heard a real nightingale.[4] The absence of anything but birdsong is the absence of a human reaction: expressively the nightingale now means nothing but itself, and more generally in the work the superimpositions and juxtapositions of bird songs appear wholly unmotivated by anything other than the wish for them to be there in the right place at the right time.

Of course, the quest for exactness is not any guarantee that it has been achieved, and Messiaen has been sadly obliged to admit that his imitations are sometimes not recognized by professional ornithologists.[5] This is not really a fair test, however, since not only does it involve the problems of transcription already mentioned, it also depends on the listener's experience, whether ornithological or indeed musical. In places where Messiaen imitates a bird with a richer history in composed music even than the nightingale – the cuckoo – there may be difficulties of recognition which arise simply because his version is closer to nature than it is to the conventional stereotype: he agrees with the vast majority of his historical colleagues that cuckoos call in falling major thirds, but his Chinese blocks in semitones rather alienate the effect after so many woodwind cuckoos.

Ultimately, all that can be said about Messiaen's notation is that it is painstaking. He has detailed how he goes out into the country armed with binoculars, an identification manual, music paper and pencils, taking down the songs as if they were exercises in dictation or folk music to be collected; only in later years has he sought the assistance of a tape recorder.[6] The problem of accurate transcription thus enters his work at once, and he evidently has no illusions about the insufficiency of human musical means to record birdsong. 'Birds', he has said,

> sing in exceedingly fast tempos, which are absolutely impossible for our instruments, and so I have to transcribe the song in a slower tempo. Moreover, this speed is bound up with an extreme sharpness, birds being able to sing in exceedingly high registers that are inaccessible to our instruments, and so I notate them one, two, three or four octaves lower. And that is not all: for the same reason I have to suppress very small intervals that our instruments cannot execute. I replace these intervals of the order of a comma or two by semitones, but I keep the same scale of values between different intervals, which is to say that if a few commas correspond to a semitone, a true semitone will correspond to a whole tone or a third. Everything is enlarged, but the relationships stay the same, so that my version is still exact. It is the transposition of what I have heard on to a more human scale.[7]

This clearly suggests that Messiaen takes care of conformity with 'our instruments' at the stage of notation, which the available visual evidence would support,[8] and it also demonstrates his awareness of the frustrations to birdsong imitation, the charming impossibilities imposed by the second set of problems mentioned above, those of the means of performance. Again a comparative group of examples may help one to understand – in the absence of any more dependable transcriptions than Messiaen's own – how he tackles those problems. Among several birds who sing repeatedly in his output after 1940, the chaffinch has one of the longest histories as a Messiaen songster, since its call can be detected amid the relatively elementary imitations of the 'Regard des hauteurs' as well as in later works of various periods where it is named (see example 57).

Once more one has to allow for individual variation,[9] but what is most striking here is the consistency of treatment within an increasing

Ex. 57   Messiaen's Chaffinches

(a) Vingt regards sur l'Enfant-Jésus (1943–4)   8 'Regard des hauteurs'

(b) Réveil des oiseaux (1953)

(c) Catalogue d'oiseaux (1956–8)   9 'La bouscarle'

(d) Méditations sur le mystère de la Sainte Trinité (1969)   2

subtlety of transcription. The *Regards* motif gives the basic elements of
a trill ending in a quick flourish, to which *Réveil des oiseaux* adds the
initial jabbing repetitions. In *La bouscarle*, from the *Catalogue
d'oiseaux* for piano that followed later in the fifties, there is an attempt
to render shrill timbres by a liberal sprinkling of major sevenths and
minor ninths: Messiaen has said that in his birdsong imitations,
whether in the orchestra or on the piano, 'each note is provided with a
chord – not a classified chord but a complex of sounds whose purpose is
to give the note its timbre', and he has described the imitation of
birdsong coloration as 'the major difficulty'.[10] The quotation from the
Méditations sur le mystère de la Sainte Trinité might seem to indicate
that sound quality is not so critical a factor, but this is misleading, since
most of Messiaen's birds have a fixed instrumentation and a fixed
harmonic colouring, whether within a work or from one work to

another. Accordingly, when the chaffinch returns to the piano in *La fauvette des jardins*, it returns to very much the same chords and almost exactly the same rhythmic pattern as in 'La bouscarle'. The chords in the *Méditations* example might arguably be understood as attempting to make the same effect on a different instrument; it is also notable that the durations here follow very much the pattern of the violin solo from *Réveil des oiseaux*, whereas the piano versions give distinctly less time to the trill, though of course the tempo changes, here at a peak of nicety, will obscure any correspondence.

One may wonder whether these different interpretations of the chaffinch's song represent simply separate attempts to render different birds, or whether they mark stages in Messiaen's transcription of an ideal chaffinch of his imagination. Perhaps a study of his field notebooks would help towards an answer, but at least it is clear from the examples above that his transcriptions have become more finely detailed, like Bartók's transcriptions of folk songs, and that each new work profits, consciously or unconsciously, from works that have gone before: the resemblance between the notations in 'La bouscarle' and *La fauvette des jardins* is too close to be coincidental. One may imagine, therefore, that as time goes by so Messiaen's experience of the real chaffinch is coloured by how he has made his musical chaffinches sing. And it may be so also for his listeners, for if ornithologists fail to recognize familiar birds when they encounter them in Messiaen's music, admirers of the music may well find themselves recognizing fragments of Messiaen in the wild. Art, being of necessity selective, can imitate nature only in part. Nature has within itself all the possibilities of imitating art.

If Messiaen's birdsong imitations are thus doomed to being only partial, example 56 bears witness at least to the relative accuracy of his observation and example 57 to his readiness to do his utmost with the instrumental and notational means available. It remains to consider the participation of his musical taste, which these examples may already have suggested is not insignificant. Indeed, while insisting on the fidelity of his intentions, he has admitted as much: 'Of course, I am the one who is listening, and involuntarily I introduce something of my manner, of my way of hearing and reproducing the songs.'[11] A thorough analysis of that 'something' would again require a comparison with the models – and not just with any chaffinch or nightingale, but with the particular songs Messiaen heard, which, since he made no recordings, are forever lost except inasmuch as they survive in his notations. It is enough, however, to examine the imitations of a work such as *Réveil des oiseaux* to gain some idea of how far the songs have been redrawn in a new musical world, rather as plainsong quotations and Peruvian songs had been redrawn in earlier works. There are, for instance, a good number of songs circling prominently around the cell of a fourth or fifth plus a tritone, the cell noted as being important in earlier work (see example 58).

Ex. 58   Réveil des oiseaux

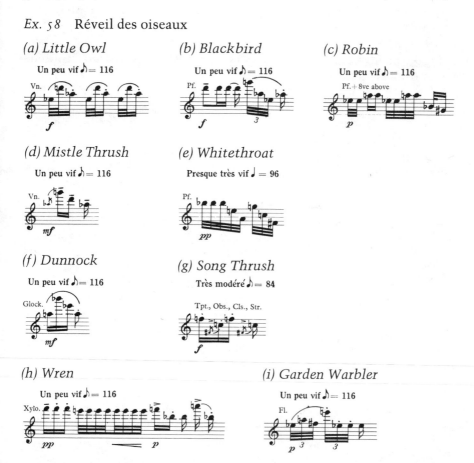

If one adds to these examples those of the nightingale from example 56 and of the chaffinch from example 57, the presence of the same motif has been illustrated in well over a quarter of the songs appearing in *Réveil des oiseaux*, and more could yet be added in support. One must therefore postulate either a high degree of harmonic concurrence among the birds of Petichet (which is perhaps not wholly absurd given the composer's presence in their midst) or else a substantial involvement of personal inclinations in the particular intervallic expansions Messiaen chooses to employ. Of course, those inclinations are no longer as closely allied to the modes of limited transpositions as they were in the works of the thirties, or even in those of the forties: the intervening twelve-note explorations had vastly widened Messiaen's understanding of modality, to the point where it could deal with material as tonally diffuse as birdsong. A mode is now not just a fixed repertory of notes, some having stipulated functions (those of tonic, or final, and dominant especially); rather it is an association of single notes and small motifs, which may include representatives of all twelve pitch classes, but which in preferring certain patterns and relationships gives them a feeling of rootedness. Bird songs could rarely have been brought into the old limited-transposition system without their being travestied, whereas, as has been shown, quite minor adjustments were all that were necessary for the songs of medieval monastics and Incas. But the new modality can deal with birdsong very adequately, which may be why the birds began to make their voices heard clearly only in the *Quatuor pour la fin du temps*, and why too one of the earliest and purest expressions of the new modality, *Neumes rythmiques*, sounds in large part like artificial birdsong.

Messiaen's wholesale attachment to birdsong in *Réveil des oiseaux* and its two successors, *Oiseaux exotiques* (1955–6) and the *Catalogue d'oiseaux*, may therefore be understood as an enthusiasm for material that suited the present state of his musical style – not just negatively in having intervals that demanded reinterpretation and fixing (pitch in most bird songs being a sliding phenomenon), but also positively in their quasi-neumatic repetitions of particular formulae (a connection Messiaen has admitted in speaking of the 'torculus' in the song of the Japanese bush warbler),[12] their adherence like Hindu theory and Greek verse to prescribed rhythmic patterns, and their toccata-style speed and insistence. At the same time, however, bird songs had the allure of coming directly from nature, and hence by implication from God. And if Messiaen could persuade himself that he was following nature as his model directly, as appears to have been possible for him in *Réveil des oiseaux* to judge from its preface, then he might imagine himself to be avoiding the expression of his own personality quite as much as Cage wished in his indeterminate compositions of the same period. 'It is', he has said,

> in a spirit of mistrust of myself, because I belong to this species – I mean the human species – that I have taken bird songs as a model . . . for despite my profound admiration for the folklore of all countries, I do not believe one can find in any human music, however inspired, melodies and rhythms which have the sovereign liberty of birdsong.[13]

The seriousness and zest with which Messiaen talks about birdsong[14] must make one suppose he was stimulated in *Réveil des oiseaux* and the next works by a wish to display that sovereign liberty, to draw his audience's attention to the music of their environment, doing so not like Cage by removing everything else but by offering an interpretation, for if the *Trois petites liturgies* bring a sacred office into the concert hall, *Réveil des oiseaux* no less surely brings a scene from nature.

But however much Messiaen thought himself to be copying nature, and however much his exactitude contrasts with that of earlier composers, *Réveil des oiseaux* belongs, as we have seen, within his own musical world. It is, in the context of his output, a 'reawakening of the birds' after their dormancy in the works of 1949–50, and one that uses the stylistic extensions of that avian night to invoke many more birds much more precisely than had been possible before. They are all, though, distinctively Messiaen's birds, singing in patterns characteristic of him, but distributing those patterns in complex aerated textures that he might never have invented without the model of the dawn chorus. That model provided too a formal shape, making this, like the *Mode de valeurs et d'intensités* which it resembles in point of self-repression, one of the very few Messiaen works not laid out in clear sections that correspond by repetition. Instead the accumulating forms of the *Turangalîla-symphonie* have been extended to accommodate a whole variety of different lines constantly playing on one another in motivic imitation, a tangle of threads pulling backwards and forwards through the eye of the present.

Messiaen's fellowship in the post-war avant-garde was signalled in the autumn of 1953 when *Réveil des oiseaux* had its first performance at the Donaueschingen Festival, which was already a principal forum for the music of Stockhausen and Boulez. It is puzzling that this delightful and extraordinary score should since then have remained one of his least-played works, far outstripped in popularity by its immediate successor, *Oiseaux exotiques*, which, however, was not started until very nearly two years after the première of *Réveil des oiseaux*. The gap was similar to the one that had intervened a dozen years before after the *Quatuor*, and possibly the reason for it was the same: that Messiaen had made a breakthrough in a work of a very particular kind, and that he took some while to discover what the implications of that work might be. In the event, answering a commission from the concert series that Boulez had recently started as a platform for new music and that would soon be known as the 'Domaine Musical', he returned to the medium of piano and orchestra, but created a work much more clean and compact in its scoring, length and form. The strings are displaced, the wind somewhat reduced and the percussion a little expanded, to create an energetic ensemble of the sort Varèse had favoured in his *Hyperprism* and *Intégrales*, though with the difference that Messiaen brings forward the woodwind rather than the brass and the tuned rather than the untuned percussion: his diagram for the orchestral placement, published in the score, asks that the xylophone and the pair of B flat clarinets, as well as the solo piano, be at the front of the stage.

On the level of form, *Oiseaux exotiques* exhibits a tighter opposition of tuttis and cadenzas, partly because Messiaen ends each section with a dynamic call that seems to demand something new. The pattern is as follows:

Tutti: Two shrieks of the Indian minah, each answered by other calls of the same animal, and then the 'vocifération implacable', as the score has it, of the Himalayan white-crested laughing thrush, landing weightily on repeated notes.

Piano cadenza (figure 3): More calls of the minah, giving way to an appeal from the American wood thrush and then to a steep determined descent from the veery, also from North America.

Tutti (figure 4): Counterpoint of four birds on woodwind, glockenspiel and xylophone.

Piano cadenza (figure 5): Repetitions of short motifs from the Virginian cardinal.

Tutti (figure 6): Continuation of the four-bird heterophony.

Piano cadenza (figure 7): Again a solo from the cardinal.

Tutti (figure 8): Rumbling and then fiercely strident calls from the American prairie chicken introduce and conclude a lively chorus of birds underpinned by untuned percussion stanzas in Greek and Indian rhythms.

Piano cadenza (figure 24): Dialogue of two American species, the catbird and the bobolink, ending with the latter at a high point of excited brilliance.

Tutti (figure 25): Vibrant calls of the Indian shama interleaved with heterophonies of shamas and other birds in an ABABA pattern.

Piano cadenza (figure 31): Brief returns of the wood thrush and cardinal.

Tutti (figure 32): Return of the minah's shriek and, immediately, the white-crested laughing thrush's heavy iterations.

Messiaen has admitted that in *Oiseaux exotiques* there is 'a certain element of composition within the "bird material" used',[15] but has limited his comments to pointing out that the work brings together 'exotic birds' from different continents, most of them being North American species but some coming from India, South America, China, Malaysia and the Canaries. Presumably some of the North American birds he notated on the spot during several visits to the United States during the late forties and early fifties; the others he would have transcribed from gramophone records.[16] In any event, one cannot imagine his purpose to have been a reproduction of nature as in *Réveil des oiseaux*, since the choruses of *Oiseaux exotiques* could exist only in an aviary. The invitation is thus all the stronger to consider the birds as symbols, or else as purely musical phenomena. The imitation of birds for magical purposes is common in shamanistic religions;[17] closer to Messiaen's spiritual world there is of course the common representation of the Holy Spirit as a dove, or such lines as those of Tertullian: 'Nay, the birds too, rising out of the nest, upraise themselves heavenward, and instead of hands, extend the cross of their wings, and sing somewhat to seem like prayer.'[18] Anthropomorphic interpretation of birdsong in this way is certainly not alien to Messiaen's thought,[19] and in the second preface to the score he writes of the wood thrush's 'sparkling fanfare' as being 'full of sunlight, almost sacramental'. It may not be inappropriate, therefore, to interpret the piece as a converse of mechanical birds, exaggerated from nature in the violent shapes and colours of music for wind and percussion, and calling to each other in divine praise.

Besides flying with the metaphors that Messiaen invites, however, one can also consider the musical substance, where again there is an element of composition that was kept to a minimum in *Réveil des oiseaux*. This will already have become apparent in the formal outline above, but it shows itself too in the construction of timbres, not only by means of different instrumental groupings but also by the choice of harmony, as already mentioned. Nearly all the songs in *Réveil des oiseaux* are monophonic, and the piano plays very often in octaves. In *Oiseaux exotiques*, by contrast, the piano harmonies are nearly always more complex, even if they still gain lustre from an awareness of resonance relationships, and the dense tangles of solo lines in the main and penultimate tuttis are contrasted with single calls elsewhere that bind large parts of the orchestra into strongly unified effects. Examples include the opening call of the minah, ripping upwards on brass and very high woodwind over a soft side-drum roll, or the exultant and eminently conclusive shouts of the shama, which join almost the whole ensemble in emphatic chords based on the line shown in example 59. Messiaen has remarked how the pursuit of birdsong timbres is 'one of the sources for the colouring of my orchestration', and no work better than this exemplifies the brilliance of that colouring, no doubt because he was attempting here to render not only the songs but also the plumage of his specimens, especially, as his first preface reminds one, the red of the cardinal.

At the same time, the line shown in example 59 is rather less than

Ex. 59   Oiseaux exotiques

arbitrary as a musical shape: but for the flattening of the C sharp and the addition of the A sharp, it is a theme in pentatonic E major, and other modal features characteristic of earlier Messiaen can be detected also in other parts of the score, presenting within its vivid and truly exotic colouring a groundwork of familiar modality, particularly of E-centred modality. (And E major in some modal variety was, one may remember, the key of the twin slow movements from the *Quatuor pour la fin du temps*, for instance, or of the finale from *Les offrandes oubliées*.) There is thus a harmonic identity to the score that may well be more significant than the scanning of the bird heterophonies against stanzas in Śārṅgadeva and Greek rhythmic patterns.[20] The 'sacramental' calls of the wood thrush resound again in E major harmony, typically formed from a 6–4 triad in the left hand with added notes (D sharp, G and A) sounding as upper partials in the right. Moreover, the brilliant ejaculations of the cardinal, which occupy two whole solo passages, positively abound in modal suggestions, even suggestions of the old modes of limited transpositions, as is indicated in example 60, a condensed transcript of the second of these cardinalatial cadenzas. (The notation has been slightly simplified rhythmically, and the numbers below each figure indicate how many times it is repeated.)

Ex. 60   Oiseaux exotiques

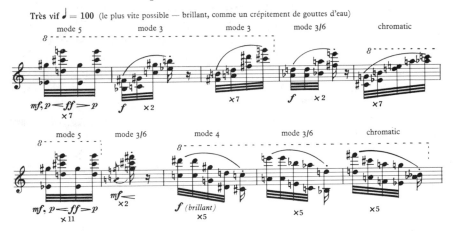

The repetition of motifs is more insistent than in *Réveil des oiseaux* (the repetitions go inevitably in prime numbers), and the choice so often of modal figures in fourths, tritones and fifths, always in the upper register, gives a bell-like clarity to the episode. Of course, these matters could be explained as resulting from the search for naturalism in the reproduction of the bird song, but that only leaves the question of why Messiaen should have chosen this particular song at this point. It seems wiser to assume, therefore, that the music's properties were dictated more by the needs of the work than by those of nature, especially when *Oiseaux exotiques* is so blatantly anti-naturalist in its selection of birds, in its use of certain songs for their rhetorical effects (the opening cry of the minah, the concluding, downward, tonally motivated call of the shama, the expectant dominant chord of the wood thrush) and in its form. Besides, in example 60 it can hardly be fortuitous that the two halves of the cadenza take similar courses through the modes, or that the mode of the penultimate bar of the second half is an inversion of that of the penultimate bar of the first half, at a transposition chosen to keep the maximum number of notes the same (five out of six). By contrast the same inverted mode earlier in the second half (bar 7) is at a transposition where it has least number of notes in common with its companions. On a grosser level, the predominantly upward shapes of the first half are replaced by downward shapes in the second, so that the entire solo is a symmetrical structure in its motifs as in its modalities.

Of course, by no means all of *Oiseaux exotiques* is so closely structured: passages like this are as rare as full-blown tonal expressions like the calls of the shama that invoke the ending, and both have their place as neumes of structural and harmonic clarity in music that has room too for complex choruses of figuration and for ideas that have no strong tonality at all. It is clear, nevertheless, that Messiaen's achievement of tighter structuring here, by comparison with *Réveil des oiseaux*, has required not only the rhythmic machinations of the central tutti but also, and more importantly, the return of his modes, in places at a strength unknown in his music since the *Turangalîla-symphonie*. Not that the effect is the same: the quick repetitions and abrupt changes of example 60 have little in common with the movement-long maintenance of mode in earlier works; what happens is that a particular harmonic colour is flashed at the ear and then replaced. Nevertheless, the modes are important in stabilizing parts of the music around certain chords and even certain central pitches, while at the same time they imply a return of the individual musical consciousness that *Réveil des oiseaux* had appeared to be doing without, since nothing could be more indicative of Messiaen's presence than the presence of his modes of limited transpositions.

His next project, however, has the superficial appearance of naturalism once more. It was an immense *Catalogue d'oiseaux* for piano, consisting of thirteen pieces each devoted to the portrayal of a bird from some region of France, and playing altogether for close on three hours. Here Messiaen tried, as he has said,

to give an exact rendering of the type bird of an area, surrounded by its neighbours from the same habitat, as well as the forms of the song at different hours of the day and night, accompanied in the harmonic and rhythmic material by the scents and colours of the country where the bird lives.[21]

This is an ambitious programme indeed, and it raises the question, even more insistently than do the preceding orchestral pieces, of the adequacy of understanding Messiaen's bird music in terms of its ostensible intentions. Of those there can be little doubt. Not only does he name all his singing birds as they contribute their vocalises to his score, following his regular practice since *Réveil des oiseaux*, but he also states the pictorial meaning of other elements in the pieces. Sometimes the illustrative effect is almost onomatopoeic in its directness, as when a soft, slow line works its way up the keyboard in thirds in imitation of the 'majestic flight of the Golden Eagle, carried on air currents' in the first of the pieces, 'Le chocard des alpes' (alpine chough). Then, on the next level of obviousness, there are cases where the musical character forms by its nature or its traditions a reliable evocation, provided the imagination has been primed in advance of the scene to be shown: hard, loud discords in irregular rhythms, for instance, make a fair image of a glacier in the same piece, or radiant dominant sevenths in C sharp major and chords of E major in its immediate successor, 'Le loriot' (golden oriole), are apt recollections of the warm summer sun of southern France.

More equivocal, perhaps, are the cases where Messiaen relies on his private mythology of colour values associated with sounds, as he does when heading a strain in 'Le merle bleu' (blue rock thrush) with the words 'the blue sea', or another in 'Le traquet rieur' (black wheatear) with 'joy of the blue sea', apparently relying for the colour effect on the use of mode 2 arrowed towards A major. ('Paysage' from the *Poèmes pour Mi* may be considered an earlier example of this usage if, as Messiaen supposes,[22] the E major here can be understood as dominant in its function.) In this case the luminosity of the harmony may well make its effect even if the particular colour goes unappreciated, but there are other passages that, in descriptive terms, would seem to be somewhat meaningless if their colouring is not understood: one clear example must be the passage portraying the plumage of the kingfisher in 'La bouscarle' (Cetti's warbler). Finally, in the scale of ease of comprehension, there are passages that one would scarcely presume to be pictorial at all were it not for the marginalia in the score. One instance is the three-part counterpoint in a mode of pitches, durations and intensities at the start of 'La chouette hulotte' (tawny owl), repeating a kind of music that had seemed wholly abstract in *Cantéyodjayâ* and the *Mode de valeurs et d'intensités*, but that now, admittedly held in the bass register throughout, is marked as representing 'the night'.

Since the *Catalogue d'oiseaux* is much occupied with times of day, representation of night has to come in other pieces too, and it can be quite different: a calm progression of chords folding into B flat major, for example, in the very next portrait, 'L'alouette lulu' (wood lark), or rumbling bass discords in 'Le merle de roche' (rock thrush). Of course, this diversity of depiction does not necessarily indicate a breakdown of pictorial effect, since there is no reason why a single phenomenon should not have a variety of musical expressions, or why the nights of the *Catalogue d'oiseaux* should not be as unalike as those of Scheherazade, the tawny owl inhabiting a night of woodland and roadsides, the rock thrush one of bare dolomite crags. Similarly, the converse confusion of two ideas in a single musical gesture does not of itself compromise the naturalist intention, since when, for instance, the blue rock thrush and the sea tend to spill over into each other's A major exultation in 'Le traquet rieur', the effect can be interpreted as a rendering of a real uncertainty about the nature of a flash of blue at the corner of the observed scene.

Less easy to explain as nature painting are the very many cases of obvious and deliberate compositional intervention, which range over the whole of the *Catalogue* from its large-scale forms to its harmonic and rhythmic details. On the largest scale, the thirteen pieces are organized into seven volumes according to a 'palindromic rhythm', 3–1–2–1–2–1–3, with the biggest piece, the half-hour 'La rousserolle effarvatte' (reed warbler), in the middle, and the two next longest, 'Le traquet stapazin' (black-eared wheatear) and 'Le merle de roche', in the other single-work volumes. As for the forms of the individual pieces, they are always made up characteristically of blocks in verse–refrain or palindromic patterns, even when the stated intention is to reproduce a diurnal cycle.

It could be argued that this is simply a question of musical style, and that Messiaen's use of forms so long typical of him is no more significant than Beethoven's choice of an F major symphony to contain his pastoral experience. But Messiaen had shown in *Réveil des oiseaux* that he was capable of following a natural course of time, speeding up the period from daybreak to midday as Debussy had done in *La mer*, and simultaneously slowing down the bird songs in order to make them playable and perceivable,[23] but not introducing wholesale recapitulations. In the *Catalogue*, however, his hand in the structure is much more decisive. All three of the longest pieces purport to follow the progress of a day, and yet in every case there are obvious patterns of verse and refrain, both in the arrangement of different bird songs and in the placing of larger sections.[24] Messiaen also interferes with the clock to the extent of concentrating on moments that are ornithologically interesting, so that in 'La rousserolle effarvatte', for example, a lengthily described sunrise is followed with remarkable swiftness by noon and then all at once by five o'clock in the afternoon, where the music again waits a while. If the work is measured against its subject, therefore, it must be found to have a dizzying power over time, occasionally racing through hours at several hundred times clock speed, but elsewhere, when it transcribes the morning and evening songs of its soloist, slowing time down in order to reproduce the details on a human scale. What the piece also conveys, in returning at the end to the music of its beginning, is a tranquil acceptance of each new day as identical with the last, an essential reproducibility of time that Messiaen's music had always maintained, and that is conveyed too by the verse–refrain construction at a lower level within the work.

The usefulness of birdsong to Messiaen thus resides not only in its musical material but also in its association with time in two quite separate ways: its speed, and its hour of performance. Yet in adapting those temporal associations, and also in adapting the material in quite personal ways such as have already been illustrated in the case of the cardinal from *Oiseaux exotiques*, Messiaen works not to reproduce nature but to alter it. After all, had he wished to create music directly out of birdsong, he could have worked with recordings, as Respighi had done to bring a nightingale into his *Pini di Roma* (1924) or as James Fassett had done at very much the same time as the *Catalogue* in his *Symphony of the Birds* (1955): it cannot even be objected that Messiaen had no experience of electronic music, though in *Timbres-durées* he had chosen the sounds of water and of percussion instruments as his sources.

Such an exercise in electronic birdsong would, however, have been beside the point. It may seem the grandest folly to attempt the transcription of thirteen bird songs – along with the songs of sixty-four other birds, the noises of other animals, the colours of feathers, the times of day, the sea, flowers and rocks – for two hands at a piano, and certainly it would be absurd to suppose that this is all Messiaen had it in mind to achieve, despite the detailed correspondences he draws between musical idea and natural phenomenon in the published scores and in his prefaces to them. Nor can one readily imagine his purpose was, like Beethoven's, 'more mood evocation than painting'. Because of its clear-cut structuring and bald oppositions, the *Catalogue* has the character more of an exhibition of musical objects than of an attempted inclusion of the listener in some emotional discourse: even in the single instance where Messiaen depicts a feeling and not an observation, in the 'fear' music of 'La chouette hulotte', the relevant episode is presented as one object among many. Altogether, indeed, the *Catalogue* is distinctly detached from its ostensible subject matter, often because the songs are so evidently composed into Messiaen's modal and rhythmic style, so that it seems more reasonable to speak of the collection not as a group of attempts at fidelity to nature but rather as a sequence of piano pieces whose realization nature helped facilitate.

What also helped was Messiaen's previous experience as a composer, which again must shadow his fidelity as a musical naturalist. The return of a mode in durations and intensities has already been mentioned; other twelve-note constructions include the passages working with thirty-two different durations marked out by chords in chromatic aggregates at moments in 'Le merle de roche' ('Soixante-quatre durées' here is the obvious parent) and the sketches of bird flight and of cold Breton sea water in non-parallel twelve-note successions in 'La buse variable' (buzzard) and 'Le courlis cendré' (curlew) respectively. There is also the frequent return of the modes of limited transpositions, not only in the realization of the bird songs as in *Oiseaux exotiques* but also in the additional material descriptive of time and situation. It happens too that the atmosphere of an earlier work may be recalled, as when 'Le merle bleu', with its A major and its splashing in parallel fourths (the injunction reads: 'imitate the large gongs and long drums of Bali'), moves towards the quasi-Oriental heterophony of the *Visions de l'Amen*. And resemblance can even become outright quotation: the apotheosis of 'Le loriot', for instance, takes place over a return of the music attached to the line 'tous les philtres sont bus ce soir' in the *Cinq rechants*.

The relative brevity and simplicity of 'Le loriot' make it a suitable piece to consider further, and though simple it is certainly not unvcharacteristic of the cycle: indeed, it might even be regarded as central, since the presence of the quotation from the *Cinq rechants* must indicate Messiaen's acknowledgement of the pun in the title, making this a portrait not only of the golden oriole but also, Couperin-fashion, of the intended performer. Its principal tonal centre of E major, established much more certainly than in *Oiseaux exotiques*, is one of union between heaven and earth (as in *Les offrandes oubliées* and *La Nativité du Seigneur*), of union, therefore, between the sphere of the birds and the sphere of men; it is also a key of praise (as in the *Quatuor pour la fin du temps*) and of a calmer expression of sexual love (as in the *Poèmes pour Mi*) than arises with a sharpening up the cycle of fifths to B major and, most especially, F sharp major. But though the comparative harmonic straightforwardness of 'Le loriot' is part of the work's unusual simplicity, it is not unknown elsewhere in the collection. The A major of the sea in 'Le merle du roche' and 'Le traquet rieur' has been mentioned; it is also the colour of the water in 'La bouscarle'. And the B flat major of the night in 'L'alouette lulu' points up by its diametrical opposition the connection of E major with the radiant summer sun of southern France in 'Le loriot' and also in 'Le traquet stapazin'. In no case, however, does

Messiaen bring back the key signatures that had disappeared from his music after the *Turangalîla-symphonie*.

In a sense, though, the nature of the modality of 'Le loriot' is stated at the start in a pair of chords, the second followed, as so often in Messiaen, by birdsong sporting in the upper partials; it is the golden oriole making its first call (see example 61). The oriole's call typically grows out of the chords in that the pedal maintains the second of them in resonance, but equally it could with justice precede them, since being based on an E major triad (with the addition of two precipitate falls through a minor ninth) it holds a place in the whole-tone scale before F sharp and G sharp. Much of the piece is concerned with this reciprocity between the chords and the bird song, until at the climax, when the oriole is visited with an apotheosis over the *Cinq rechants* reminiscence, the two are united and, as Messiaen's preface has it, 'The sun seems to be the gilded emanation of the oriole's song.'

Ex. 61   Catalogue d'oiseaux   2 'Le loriot'

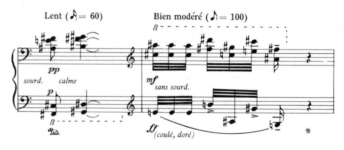

But it is not only the oriole that is drawn into and out of the chordal play. The first pair of chords, dominant sevenths on F sharp and G sharp, is sounded three times, each time calling up the oriole, but then the progression changes to F sharp seventh–E, which triggers new birdsong material (see example 62). The redstart's song picks up the B from the E major triad, and its melody belongs to the same transposition of the second mode as does the oriole's main line, though now it interprets B as dominant of F, not E, and accordingly substitutes a diminished-seventh chord for the major triad behind the oriole's call, while harmonically it echoes the minor sevenths that have featured in the chords. The wren squashes these to minor sixths, also emphasized in Messiaen's layout of his chords, and in insisting on a high F sharp it relates back to the opening chord of each little progression so far. Finally the robin, in its gentle cascade of black notes against white notes, compresses the harmony still further from a minor sixth to a major third, and then recalls the first chord pair backwards, in enharmonic spelling. The ball has been passed back to the chords, and at this point there is a longer string, of five chords, still moving in whole-tone steps, travelling from a ninth chord on F sharp to, once more, an E major triad. A different progression again summons a different bird, the blackbird, and a different set of relationships between chords and song: the blackbird lands forcefully on a high G sharp, for instance, and its second solo ends with the notes F sharp–G sharp–E, covering the whole harmonic space within which the chords and the oriole have their home.

Ex. 62   Catalogue d'oiseaux

Each group of chords thus acts like a search element in a computer programme to call up relevant bird songs, though there is not always a one-to-one relationship between chord group and songs: the two appearances of F sharp seventh–E, of which the second follows the blackbird's interruption, both draw on the redstart and its associated wren and robin (with the addition of a song thrush), but the three F sharp seventh–G sharp seventh couples elicit different responses each time, first the golden oriole, then the blackbird and finally the redstart. There

is, it would seem, a certain randomness written into the programme;
but its limits are set. In the first part of the piece the intial chord of each
sequence is always F sharp seventh and the final chord G sharp seventh
or E, except in the single instance of a progression longer than two
chords, where the starting point is F sharp ninth and the harmonic
journey takes in more of the whole-tone scale (ninth chords on E, D and
C) before arriving with complete propriety on an E major triad. These
constant elements are matched by constancy in the bird songs, all of
which take up some aspect of the chords, whether the tonality of E
major (golden oriole), the dominance of B (redstart) or the prominence of
F sharp (wren and robin), G sharp (blackbird) and E (song thrush).

   Then in the central part of the work, where the chordal progressions
become longer and more venturesome, leaving the whole-tone base as
they move from F sharp major to A minor and then from F sharp major to
F sharp minor, the answering bird songs are again new and now lacking
in a tonal centredness. They are the songs of a pair of garden warblers,
and they are stilled only once the chords have retraced their steps back
to more normal territory in going from A minor to G sharp major and
then from F sharp minor to E major. Now again there is a new song, that
of the chiffchaff, which splutters in a tight chromatic region from F to A
at the top of the keyboard, thus picking up the G sharp of the E major
chord and simultaneously preparing for the return of the golden oriole,
which has not been heard since the opening sequence, but which now
produces a torrent of calls leading into its apotheosis, where its song and
the chords merge their qualities while retaining enough character to be
identifiable. The melody in the first phrase (see example 63), for
instance, still has the oriole's E major arpeggio and its falling minor
ninth to conclude. It is the song thrush that awakens the music again,
with its accents on E and then on F sharp, bringing back the chords (F
sharp seventh and G sharp seventh) and songs (redstart, wren and oriole)
characteristic of the opening.

Ex. 63   Catalogue d'oiseaux   *2 'Le loriot'*

Like all the other members of the *Catalogue*, therefore, 'Le loriot' has more of art, specifically Messiaen's art, than of nature in its shaping: in the repeated dialogue of chordal refrains with birdsong verses, and in the return at the end to the music of the beginning. Even the smallest details reveal the hand of a composer, and quite particularly of this composer. As in the example from *Oiseaux exotiques*, there are traits derived from the modes of limited transposition, and the whole nature of the harmony – rich in added-note chords and symmetrical formations such as the diminished-seventh chord and the augmented triad, all used without much long-term regard for diatonic process – is thoroughly characteristic of Messiaen. This can be seen, for instance, in the choice of added resonances for the first call of the golden oriole in example 61: a strident diminished-seventh chord for the initial E, radiant triads for the other notes of the E major chord (major for the fifth, minor for the third) and obtuse discords for the pitches out of agreement with E major, so that each note is dosed with a harmonic quality in a way that had been Messiaen's since his very earliest music. The addition of timbre turns out to be an addition of a very personal sort of harmony, which marks the *Catalogue* and *Oiseaux exotiques* even more distinctively as Messiaen's than does the motivic and pitch correlation carried over from *Réveil des oiseaux*. (One may note, for example, the fifth–tritone set at the start of the oriole's call, the end of the redstart's and throughout the wren's in examples 61–2.)

If all this must cast doubt on the accuracy of the *Catalogue* as portraiture, the idea of birdsong is still important, on at least two counts. In the first place, the bird names give the composer a ready means of identifying what Johnson has aptly described as 'groups',[25] in the sense that Stockhausen used the term of his *Kontra-Punkte* (1952–3) and later works. One may suppose that, like Stockhausen and Boulez, Messiaen rapidly grew disenchanted with the music of individual points they had all essayed in works of 1949–51 (the *Mode de valeurs et d'intensités*, *Kreuzspiel*, *Structures Ia*), and that he was led to work with larger units, or groups, defined by a certain quality, which might be register, interval content or instrumental presentation, for example. But where Stockhausen in *Kontra-Punkte* and Boulez in *Structures Ib* worked with abstract groups, Messiaen preferred to associate his with bird songs, for reasons that draw attention to the second aspect of birdsong's importance as an idea in his music.

'For me', he has said, 'the only real music has always existed in the sounds of nature.' And he goes on: 'The harmony of wind in trees, the rhythm of waves on the sea, the timbre of raindrops, of breaking branches, of stones struck together, the different cries of animals are the true music as far as I am concerned.'[26] The 'always' in the first sentence suggests that, like Keats, he is attracted by what bird songs contain of the eternal, by the fact that in many respects they are the same today as they were thousands and indeed millions of years ago. They are therefore an image of the changelessness that had always been central to his musical and religious thinking. But it is clear also that the notion of copying nature is a justification for creative activity for him as it was for Debussy, or as it has been for musicians in other cultures, for birdsong imitations are not infrequent among the developed musical traditions of eastern Asia. His own choice of bird songs may have been affected, as has been suggested, by stylistic tastes and habits, but the appeal of nature goes deeper. In an article he wrote on the occasion of the first performance of the *Catalogue* he wrote:

> In my hours of gloom, when I am suddenly aware of my own futility, when every musical idiom – classical, Oriental, ancient, modern and ultra-modern – appears to me as no more than admirable, painstaking experimentation, without any ultimate justification, what is left for me but to seek out the true, lost face of music somewhere off in the forest, in the fields, in the mountains or on the seashore, among the birds.[27]

At a time when music could no longer be justified as an expression of the self, justification had to come from some outside authority: God, nature or mathematics, or, as in the *Catalogue d'oiseaux*, all three at once.

The suggestion that the *Catalogue* is a religious work has to be made somewhat circumspectly, since Messiaen's poetic prefaces are keys rather to interpreting the works as illustrations of nature, of a natural habitat presented quite dispassionately ('La bouscarle', heard beside the Charente, is perhaps the most vividly detailed musical ecology), or of nature coloured by human reaction ('La chouette hulotte'), or in the extreme case of 'Le merle de roche', of landscape transformed by the mind into fantasy. But elsewhere he has described the birds as 'little servants of the immaterial joy',[28] and it may not be too presumptuous to regard him as concurring in the Franciscan vision, to which he gives voice in *Saint François d'Assise*, of birds as presages of the agility of the resurrected. To imitate them, therefore, is to imitate the divine, the 'unique bird of eternity' as the *Trois petites liturgies* have it.

However, his transcription of bird songs for the piano inevitably involves not only a human instrument and human scales of pitch and time but also an individual language of rhythm and harmony. The *Catalogue* could never be a mirror to nature; instead, and much more interestingly, it is a fusion of imitation and imagination, as much as the birds of Ernst or the eagle-headed gods of the ancient Near East or the angels of Jewish-Christian mythology. In this perspective, the accuracy of the copy seems rather beside the point. What matters is that the *Catalogue* is a vast store of piano music, exceeding the *Vingt regards* in range and formal richness as much as in duration, a treasury of different musical environments in which the composer can sing songs that are his own.

The very length of the *Catalogue* rather militates against its being performed entire in the concert room, and it is much more a collection than a cycle such as the *Vingt regards* had been: certainly the constituent pieces now have enough weight to count as separate works rather than as movements. In that respect as well the *Catalogue* invites comparison with the contemporary efforts of Messiaen's pupils Stockhausen and Boulez, since like the former's *Klavierstuck XI* (1956) or the latter's Third Piano Sonata (1956–7), though in a simpler way, if offers the performer a choice of material. There are works here of sonata proportions (the three largest); alternatively one may imagine bird song sonatas put together from among the rest, for example from 'Le traquet rieur', 'Le loriot' and 'Le merle bleu' to make a quite conventional and tidy A major sonata with a slow movement in the dominant. It was, however, in its entirety that the collection was first presented to the public, by Yvonne Loriod at a Domaine Musical evening on 15 April 1959, bringing an end to the period of eight years during which all of Messiaen's composing had been associated with birdsong. The death that same month of his first wife closed another chapter.

CHAPTER 11

The Colour of Time

Up to now Messiaen's life had not changed much since the war. There was the regular activity of teaching his class at the Conservatoire, to which he gave all his instructive energy: there were no more visits to Darmstadt after the fateful encounter of 1951. Then on Sundays there was the equally regular activity of playing at La Trinité, though the organ was now far from the centre of his enthusiasms as a creative musician: having given concrete form to his improvisatory discoveries in the *Messe de la Pentecôte* and the *Livre d'orgue*, he stopped improvising,[1] and he also again stopped composing for the organ, as he had in the period between *Les corps glorieux* and the Pentecost mass. The summers meanwhile were spent as usual at Petichet, though some time must have been given to other areas for the collection of bird songs. (A note prefixed to the *Catalogue d'oiseaux* indicates that the period of collection extended some years back before the period of composition, which was from 1956 to 1958.) New works, composed at Petichet or in Paris, were then introduced at Boulez's Concerts du Petit Marigny (later Domaine Musical), whose evenings Messiaen supported assiduously. *Cantéyodjayâ* had its strangely belated première at the second of these concerts, on 23 February 1954, when Messiaen himself also appeared on the platform to play his *Quatre études de rythme*. In 1956 there was the first performance of *Oiseaux exotiques*, commissioned by the Domaine Musical; in 1957 there was a Domaine excursion to La Trinité to hear Messiaen play his *Livre d'orgue*; and in 1959 the première of the *Catalogue d'oiseaux* took place under the Domaine's aegis. Two of these 'Domaine works', *Cantéyodjayâ* and *Oiseaux exotiques*, were brought out by Boulez's publisher, Universal.

There was also continued interest from what was at this time the most prestigious festival of new music, Donaueschingen, following the first performance there in 1953 of *Réveil des oiseaux*: the orchestral *Chronochromie* was commissioned for the 1960 festival and *Couleurs de la cité céleste*, for piano and small orchestra, for that of 1964. The latter's première was again in the hands of Boulez's Domaine Musical ensemble, who also gave the first performances of the *Sept haïkaï* in 1963 and of *Et exspecto resurrectionem mortuorum* in 1965. At the same time interest in Messiaen's music was quickening beyond the circle of the avant-garde. Most of his works became available on gramophone records during the 1950s and early 1960s, including the entire corpus of organ music, which he himself recorded at La Trinité in 1956. Introductory books on the composer were published by Claude Rostand (1957), Antoine Goléa (1961) and Pierrette Mari (1965), and performances of the major works, including most especially the *Turangalîla-symphonie*, brought a sea change in his international reputation. Where even positive responses in the 1940s and early 1950s had tended to be guarded about what was detected as vulgar in his art, appreciation now began to focus on what is resplendently new: the forms, textures and harmonic movements that present a fresh way of hearing time.

It is tempting to suppose that this widening, deepening recognition affected the new mood of confidence apparent in *Chronochromie* (1959–60), which celebrates Messiaen's emergence from a decade during which he had turned inwards to private genres, those of twelve-note and rhythmic speculations and birdsong notation. For *Chronochromie* is a public work of a kind he had not essayed since the *Turangalîla-symphonie*, having the same immensity of gesture and almost the same scoring, except that the conditions of the commission dictated that there be no ondes martenot and, for once, no solo piano[2] (though the aura of the former is recalled when the strings lead two passages of slow modal melody, and the absence of the piano is countered by an increase in the 'gamelan' ensemble to include glockenspiel, xylophone, marimba, bells, gongs and cymbals).

As its title suggests, *Chronochromie* is a colouring of time, effected not only by a highly variegated use of its large instrumental ensemble but also by the placing of quite different kinds of music in succession. On the largest scale, the succession is in seven parts, which cannot properly be considered as separate movements since they are divided only by short measured silences. Together they make up a structure that Messiaen had already identified in his preface to 'Le chocard des alpes': a Greek triad, characteristic of the choral odes of the ancient drama, and consisting of a strophe, a balancing antistrophe and a contrasting, concluding epode. In *Chronochromie*, though, there are two pairs of strophe and antistrophe, as well as a framing introduction and coda, which is enough to obscure the model more than somewhat, especially when there do not seem to be any of the references to Greek metres one might expect in such a form. The single importance of the Greek triad, indeed, lies in its suggestion of a structure based on contrasts in equipoise, rather than on the development that the title of the

Turangalîla-symphonie had implied; and in *Chronochromie* as in that earlier work Messiaen totally alters his archetype by repetition.

One of the fascinations of *Chronochromie*, however, is how differently it can interpret repetition. For though three whole sections ('Strophe II', 'Antistrophe II' and 'Coda') are essentially replays of earlier sections ('Strophe I', 'Antistrophe II' and 'Introduction' respectively), exact repeats are curiously rare: the images are sufficiently complex and sufficiently characterized for details to be changed while the larger profile is still immediately recognizable. A simple example is the music headed 'the rocks' in the introduction and the coda, where the preservation of harmonic type (twelve-note chords), instrumental opposition and dynamic is bound to be more striking than the alteration of pitches; the use of the whole sound space, either in simultaneity (the widespread chords) or in succession (the instrumental blocks) is highly characteristic of the work (see example 64).

Ex. 64   Chronochromie

1 'Introduction'   *7 'Coda'*

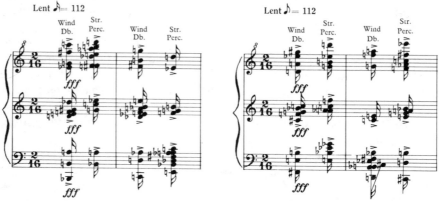

If this suggests that pitch is less important in *Chronochromie* than other musical qualities, the suggestion is fair. Messiaen has insisted on the prime importance here of interversions worked on a sequence of thirty-two 'chromatic' durations,[3] as in 'Le merle de roche'. The number of possible permutations of thirty-two different values is colossal, of the order of two thousand (European) quintillion, and to play all of them at the tempo of the strophes would take something like a trillion times the entire history of the universe so far. Instead of that *Chronochromie* uses a mere thirty-six interversions,[4] and then by no means all of those: a set of three unfolding simultaneously underlies each of the strophes, and the arrival of fragments of other interversions is marked in all the other sections except the 'Epode', though the fact that this has a notational length almost exactly three times that of the strophes (101 bars of 4/8 against 33 with the same signature) must hint that there are hidden interversions going on here too.

But then all the interversions are hidden. In the strophes they are marked out by solo percussion lines coloured by string chords, which Messiaen identifies as 'turning chords', 'chords on the dominant' and 'chords of contracted resonance' without stating the criteria that characterize the first and third of these varieties:[5] they are both complex harmonies, of eight and seven notes respectively, quite lacking any diatonic sense. This kind of string-tinged percussion pattering had appeared before in 'Turangalîla III' as one stream in a heterophonic texture, but in *Chronochromie* it risks becoming reduced to the merest background presence by the vivid calls of French birds from woodwind and tuned percussion soloists, each imitating a particular species, as generally in the choruses of *Réveil des oiseaux* and *Oiseaux exotiques*, and the whole assembly numbering up to ten birds singing at once. Thus although the strophes have the firmest rooting in the work's rhythmic mechanism, they impress themselves largely as woodland re-creations of the sort Messiaen had created before, and was quickly to create again in the thrice longer 'Epode', which consists entirely of French bird songs played by eighteen solo strings in an almost seamless tangle. (There is one point of thinning and restart just before the halfway stage.) Although it plays for less than four minutes, this section marks an extreme of stasis in Messiaen's music. Time stops because the forward movement of the music thoroughly baffles any attempt to comprehend it: there is no direction here, only a tissue of motivic connections operating horizontally and vertically, forwards and backwards.

The 'Epode' and the strophes are segments of time given a single colour, since perpetual change gives the impression of constancy; the other sections colour their smaller units to create instead patterns of abrupt change, appealing again to birdsong models, but usually to single calls rather than dawn choruses. There was the same distinction in *Oiseaux exotiques*, and the sensation there of great mechanical birds in full throat is even stronger in *Chronochromie*, where in the introduction and coda, for example, the full weight of a large symphony orchestra is brought to bear on the calls of two Swedish species, the osprey and the white-tailed eagle (these have the same roles of initiation and conclusion taken by the minah and the laughing thrush in *Oiseaux exotiques*): there can be no question of a natural effect when the eagle's cry is enunciated by an orchestra of over a hundred playing giant chords fortissimo.

In that it relates to birdsong at all, *Chronochromie* obviously, and in ways that have been indicated, relates to the works of 1953–8, but it also looks back further. The operation of system here is a connection with a certain aspect of the *Turangalîla-symphonie*: one instance of this has been pointed out, but there is also the similarity of the 'rock' chords of example 64 to the brusque chordal exchanges at the start of 'Chant d'amour I', or of the twelve-note successions of sound, points in the antistrophes to similar successions in 'Turangalîla II'. And allowing for the maturing of a quarter-century, the calls of the song thrush in neumes from the woodwind ensemble are an expression of the same image that lay behind the alleluias of the second movement of *L'Ascension*. There is even a similarity of form here, for as in that movement the woodwind chant is interleaved with contrasting music in an ABABA pattern, the B material consisting in the *Chronochromie* antistrophes of another bird song, that of the skylark, but with a complete change to tuned percussion declaiming over a soft texture of string harmonics.

Following an indication of Messiaen's own,[6] one may describe the skylark as singing in B with E flat as its dominant, and some tonal centredness, unusual in the other sections of the work, is continued in the second portions of the antistrophes, after the antiphonies of song thrush and skylark. First in each case comes a melody held by second violins, violas and cellos in unison, a melody whose typical wide-intervalled modal character cannot be disguised by the twelve-note chords in the rest of the strings (see example 65, in which, for clarity, the time signature have been omitted). The first part of the melody is whole tone, the latter part in the third mode, allowing the tonal centre to move from C sharp to what the final plunge clinches as a sort of C minor. After this comes a different variety of slow music, a chorale that moves again in twelve-note chords over a wide register, this time surmounting a bass line in D flat that similarly sets out from a whole-tone figure but that ends by returning to its initial D flat. These moments of relative agreement in speed and tonality are followed by a spirited chase of more Mexican birds, athletic violin motifs and the already mentioned twelve-note sound points around slowly progressing fractions of interversions. Five-part symmetry in the first part of the section thus gives way to triune dissimilarity in the second, echoing the triune character of the entire work.

Ex. 65   Chronochromie   *3 'Antistrophe I'*

'Antistrophe II' takes the same course, but with a variation and uneven amplification of the elements. Sometimes the extension looks to be calculated – the first skylark solo plays for exactly three times as long as in 'Antistrophe I', and the final segment is almost precisely twice as long (117 semiquavers against 58) – but in other cases the factor is not so simple, and whether the relationship between the two sections was derived according to some numerical rule or not, the effect is of unpredictable stretching, or more of denying time by showing that quite different lengths of it, and quite different proportions, can be used to produce the same form. Details too can be altered without loss of structural force or integrity. The string melody ends on the same low C, but after starting out from F sharp, and the chorale starts out from the same D flat but now ends on B flat: the present bends towards concurrence with the past in the area where the melody ends and the chorale begins, then bends away again. But the final passage, though much longer, still ends with the reiterated C of its equivalent before.

In the case of the other mirroring sections, the introduction and the coda, the later member is not expanded but abbreviated, and not by a shortening of the elements but by a reduction in their number, though not to the extent that the coda misses the mosaic variety of the introduction: both have their Swedish and Japanese birds, contrasting with the French species of the strophes and 'Epode', and the Mexican fauna of the antistrophes; both also have brief sections founded on interversion forms, a spray of five-part woodwind counterpoint matching the first 'Pièce en trio' of the *Livre d'orgue* in inscrutability, and images designed to imitate sounds and sights of the mountains: the massive, stone-hard chords of 'the rocks' and a 'combination of rotating figures suggesting the complex sonority of water in the falls and streams of the Alps (a double homage to Berlioz and Pierre Schaeffer)'.[7]

The homage to Berlioz is to a musician whom Messiaen had admired since childhood[8] and respected as an earlier master of the music of nature,[9] whose natal region he shared and with whom, among French composers of the past, he is most obviously to be associated, not least with respect to *Chronochromie* and its combination of fierce imaginative reflex (in the outer sections especially) with immense ceremonial (in the chorales, which have few parallels outside Berlioz's *Grande symphonie funèbre et triomphale* and *Grand messe des morts*). Schaeffer is a less obvious target for Messiaen's tribute, except that the unsatisfactory experience of *Timbres-durées* by no means prejudiced him against electronic music, and he maintained his regard for the pioneer of *musique concrète* as a 'great discoverer of new sonorities'.[10] The torrent music of *Chronochromie* is no less new and strange, depending as Messiaen has said on

several circling movements (which pivot on themselves with various changes and different rhythms), given to solo violas and cellos: this is the moving mass that rolls and flows on. The little subsidiary noises of the foam and of sheaves of droplets are provided by bass-clarinet figures, dives from the bassoon and pizzicatos from the double-basses. A trilled chord, stationary in the violins and changing on the double basses, expresses the colour of the resonance against the rock walls. Sometimes that resonance generates a powerful deep humming: this is the bassoon and the tuba in their bottom-most notes.[11]

The observation is scrupulously detailed, and if Messiaen's efforts at transcribing water are, like his bird songs, difficult to accept just as accurate mimesis, the passage does prove his readiness to range widely over his acoustic experience in search of materials to produce the strongest possible images and the strongest possible contrasts. No longer is the outcome justified as musical topography, as in the *Catalogue d'oiseaux*, or as pure birdsong composition, as in *Réveil des oiseaux* and *Oiseaux exotiques*. *Chronochromie* is not a portrait of any region outside its composer's head, and though bird songs certainly dominate much of the surface, there are a great many other things going on in the music: so many that it is hard to discern any unifying factor other than that of Messiaen's creative personality, which is at its most characteristic here in surrounding essentially simple, single ideas with layer upon layer of disinterested heterophony, in working and reworking the same musical objects, and in giving an equality of treatment to slices of time that range from the few milliseconds of a quick staccato to the lazy minutes of the 'Epode', all being arranged as distinctive episodes (Stockhausen would by this date be calling them moments)[12] in a balance of symmetries. Time is thus coloured, and in that colouring lies the music's claim to be operating in a time where time is still, the frozen present of the time when the music was composed. It may be the lack of performances that has moved composers in the twentieth century to interest themselves in this time, in notation more than execution (witness the *Mode de valeurs*), in the static score rather than the dynamic sounding entity. *Chronochromie*, however, in its alterations achieved at the time of composition and momentously displayed at the time of performance, transfers a static conception of music back into the large concert hall.

One result of Messiaen's enhanced public status, apart from perhaps the supreme confidence of *Chronochromie*, was that it gave him the opportunity to travel more widely. The Japanese birds of *Chronochromie* had entered that work by way of recordings, but in 1962, soon after his marriage to Yvonne Loriod, he was able to visit Japan on the occasion of the first performance there of his *Turangalîla-symphonie*, conducted by Seiji Ozawa, who was two decades later to be in charge of the world première of *Saint François d'Assise*. The impressions he received on this journey – impressions of new birds, new places, new musical traditions – were evidently strong, for before the year was out he had worked them into the *Sept haïkaï*, subtitled 'Japanese sketches' and scored for piano with a brilliant small orchestra similar to that of *Oiseaux exotiques*, but with the addition of eight violins to the ensemble of wind instruments and percussion.

One main reason for their inclusion seems likely to have been the readiness with which they can be made to imitate, in complicated chords played *sul ponticello*, the acid discords of the shō, or mouth organ, in the central haiku, 'Gagaku': Varèse had done rather the same thing in his *Nocturnal* (1961), though there is no reason why the two composers should not have come independently to the same imitative effect. Outside 'Gagaku', however, the presence of strings may point up the fact that the *Sept haïkaï* have less in common with *Oiseaux exotiques* than they have with *Chronochromie*, in terms of variety of experience and of the form into which that variety is frozen. Once again there are seven sections – independent movements now – starting with an introduction and ending with a closely related coda. Within this frame there are again two answering pairs, each consisting here of an impression of place (movements 2 and 5) followed by a bird chorus with piano cadenzas in the manner of *Oiseaux exotiques* (movements 3 and 6), and also a lone movement standing out from the rest: in *Chronochromie* it is the 'Epode', in the *Sept haïkaï* 'Gagaku', both finding the composer in the role of listener to an alien music.

Messiaen's sample of gagaku sports imitations not only of the shō but also of the shawm of the court ensemble, the hichiriki, whose piercing tone is approached by a solo trumpet playing in unison with two oboes and a cor anglais. Its melody – Messiaen marks it 'noble, religious, nostalgic', evincing here, as in his remarks on birdsong, a personal interpretation that may have nothing to do with any original intention – is in five phrases in an ABCAB pattern, which may possibly have been borrowed from the gagaku piece *Etenraku*, recorded on the only commercial gramophone record of gagaku music likely to have been available to Messiaen at this date (Everest 3322). Apart from the structural similarity, there are resemblances of motif, as may be seen in the first phrases played by Messiaen's reed-imbued trumpet and the Japanese instrument. (See example 66; *Etenraku* has been transposed up a third to be in the same G sharp tonality).[13] Whatever the source, though, Messiaen presents his gagaku memories with respect. He makes no

Ex. 66 (a) Sept haïkaï 4 'Gagaku'

(b) Etenraku

attempt to copy the wavering pitch of gagaku, but he comes much nearer Japanese modality than had the crudely pentatonic essays in the genre by earlier Western musicians, and he provides for his hichiriki and shō an environment of woodwind and percussion that is not in gagaku style at all, fusing the borrowed music with his own but acknowledging its separate identity. The movement thus looks forward to the Japanese works of Stockhausen, beginning with his *Telemusik* (1966).

In reverse, the other four internal movements of the set may show something of Stockhausen's influence in their abundance of irrational rhythms producing simultaneous accelerations and decelerations at different speeds, or bewildering conflicts of pulse. The effect is most acute in the second bird movement, 'Les oiseaux de Karuizawa', where it loosens the regular jittering of earlier avian gatherings, and in the first piece of scene painting, 'Le parc de Nara et les lanternes de pierre'. This extraordinary movement, with its flat presentation of timelessness in slow string chords (already sounding like the shō) and chinking marimba reiterations together with time-driven, almost Schoenbergian expressions in the clarinets, may give a clue to the appeal of Japan for Messiaen, for though no doubt the *Sept haïkaï* are marked by a common Western excitement at the formal perfection of Japanese art, they suggest too a community of spirit with the Japanese ability to exist on different time-scales at once, to participate in unchanging ceremonial and yet at the same time to operate at the forefront of advancing technological and commercial expertise.

This sort of double focus had, however, been a feature of Messiaen's music since long before his visit to Japan (its first appearance had been two decades before, in the 'Liturgie de cristal'), and though the intention of this movement is to evoke a Japanese scene, the means are his own. The violins and crotales follow an interversion of thirty-two, 'chromatic' durations from the set partly explored in *Chronochromie*, while bells follow another, and like the strophes of the preceding work, the movement ends when the rhythmic repertory has been exhausted. Meanwhile the rhythm of the bass clarinet, though apparently moving freely, is declared in the score to be an irrational interpretation of Greek metres, as in the first movement of the *Messe de la Pentecôte*, and since the angular melodies of E flat and standard B flat clarinets are stylistically similar, the attribution to Cretic tetrameters and other feet seems to serve as a cover for all this extremest jumble of unstable rhythms, in which the individuality of each moment is stressed against the eternal music of the strings, crotales and bells (see example 67).

Ex. 67   Sept haïkaï   2 *'Le parc de Nara et les lanternes de pierre'*

[Modéré ♪= 100]

This same contrast of an onward-moving music with a static exists too in the outer movements, of which the second is the double of the first. Here it is the melody of the violins in unison that belongs on the time-scale of human emotion, but Messiaen's footnote advises that the rhythmic processes unfolding in the wind and percussion are more important, and that the two movements are 'highly wrought and grimacing, like the two guardian gods framing the entrances of Buddhist temples'. The first has the violins repeating a short melodic formula with constant change of detail; the second gives them a 'second strophe' which starts differently but returns to the same figure. The processes on the other levels correspond more mechanically. In the introduction the rhythm of the piano is played backwards by the woodwind, and in the coda the roles are simply reversed. The bell music, coloured by brass and other percussion, operates a similar system. In the introduction it works with, as the score states, the 'rhythms of the three shakti', these being female avatars of the gods: the first, associated with the shakti of Brahma, is a quickening in values of eight down to two demi-semiquavers played in pairs (bars 1–5); the second, for the shakti of Vishnu, is the deçi-tâla *lakskmîça* (bars 10–11); and the third, for the shakti of Siva, is another deçi-tâla, *simhavikrama* (bars 14–18). In the coda these formulae are turned backwards and differently treated. Finally, in this jostling of independent patterns, the xylophone and marimba state another deçi-tâla twice, Messiaen's favoured *miçra varna*, and then start out from *simhavikrama* again to reach *miçra varna* by a process of gradual change, which Messiaen names after the Greek process of metabolē. The stages are set out in example 68, and they shed some light on Messiaen's technique of distorting rhythmic cells by regular or irregular augmentation or diminution. In the coda the whole sequence is turned back on itself, so that the retrograde of *miçra varna* is metabolized into the retrograde of *simhavikrama*.

Ex. 68 Sept haïkaï 1 'Introduction'

♩ ♩ ♩ ♪♩. ♩ ♩. (simhavikrama)

♪. ♪. ♪ ♪♪. ♪. ♩.

♪ ♪ ♪ ♪. ♩♪ ♪. ♩ ♪

♪ ♪ ♪ ♪ ♩♪ ♪♪ ♩♪

♪ ♪ ♪ ♪♪ ♪ ♪ ♪♪ ♩.. ♩ ♪♩

♪ ♪ ♪ ♪ ♪ ♪ ♪♪♩. ♪ ♪♪ ♩ ♪♩

♪ ♪ ♪ ♪ ♪ ♪ ♪ ♪ ♪ ♪ ♪ ♪ ♩. ♩ ♪♪♩ ♪♩ (miçra varna)

In his preface to the score Messiaen translates *simhavikrama* as 'lion's might' and *miçra varna* as 'colour mixture', which might suggest he was beginning to use the Śarṅgadeva formulae not just as intriguing patterns but also as bearers of symbolic meaning, for if leonine strength is contained in these guardian movements at each end of the work, colour is very much a quality of its fifth movement, 'Miyajima et le torii dans la mer', notionally descriptive of what the preface recalls as:

> An island, a mountain covered in dark green Japanese pines and maples (red in autumn). A shinto temple, white and red. In the blue sea, opening on to the invisible (which is the real temple), a great red gateway, or torii.

Here, for the first time, Messiaen marks in the score the colour he associates with a particular chord or stretch of harmonized refrain, preparing for the eruption of colour in his next work, *Couleurs de la cité céleste* (1963), which, as a vision of the New Jerusalem revealed to the writer of the Apocalypse, makes a return to the sacred concert after a gap of almost twenty years since the *Vingt regards*.

Indeed, *Couleurs* was Messiaen's first religious work at all since the *Livre d'orgue*, excepting only an organ piece he had written in December 1960 as a test exercise for the Conservatoire, *Verset pour la fête de la Dédicace*, where verses on adapted plainsong are answered by refrains from the song thrush. Possibly the experience of writing this work played some part in reopening the composer to a direct invocation of the sacred, since *Couleurs* too is deeply imbued with plainsong, and even with the same alleluia from the mass of the Dedication that had been used in the *Verset*. However, the theological nature of the new work was apparently influenced too, in more mundane fashion, by the circumstances of the commission from Donaueschingen. Henrich Strobel had asked Messiaen, somewhat bizarrely, for a work for trios of trombones and xylophones, and though he had accepted the plan, he had understandable misgivings about it.[14] But eventually he decided that the trombones had an 'apocalyptic sonority' while the xylophones wanted to speak of birds, and so, expanding the former to an orchestral brass ensemble and adding to the latter three clarinets, metal percussion and once more a solo piano, he arrived at the ensemble for a work that would return to the subject matter of the *Quatuor pour la fin du temps*, but with all the musical means he had acquired in the intervening twenty years or more.

The piano-wind-percussion constitution of *Couleurs de la cité céleste* suggests a companion work to *Oiseaux exotiques* and the *Sept haïkaï*, but in fact the piano is now much less a soloist; the orchestra is tilted considerably more towards the brass than towards the woodwind, and the short, separate sections of the earlier works are replaced by a single-movement form of kaleidoscopic variety. The nearest precedent for such a form in Messiaen's music is *Cantéyodjayâ*, and as in that piece there are elements of verse–refrain structure starting to lose themselves in larger cyclic patterns, to the extent that, as his first prefatory note to the score has it, 'The work does not end, having never really begun: it turns on itself, interlacing its temporal blocks, like the rose window of a cathedral with its vivid invisible colours.'

Among the 'temporal blocks' that revolve in the work are the imitated calls of exotic birds (from New Zealand and the Americas), choruses of wind or percussion instruments in harmonized plainsong, inscrutable rhythmic patterns derived as usual from Hindu formulae, Greek metres and *Chronochromie* interversions, and images stimulated by what Messiaen has called the 'extraordinary, extravagant, surrealist and terrifying' superscriptions from the Apocalypse placed in the score. Of these last, the seven angels with seven trumpets (Rev. 8:6), who have their dance in the *Quatuor*, are more immediately pictured in short bursts of seven-part brass writing, and another vision – 'And the fifth angel sounded, and I saw a star fall from heaven unto the earth: and to him was given the key of the bottomless pit' (Rev. 9:1) – gives rise to two ideas: a quick piano flurry for the star, and a minor-third fall from D flat to B flat in the cavernous region below the bass staff (there is the same fall an octave up between the 'Antistrophe' chorales of *Chronochromie*), this played by horn and trombones while the clarinets, cencerros (Cuban cowbells) and tubular bells add resonances three and four octaves above.

A footnote in the score indicates that the impression must be one of height as well as depth, the one being dependent on the other as partials are dependent on their fundamental, or as the colours of the celestial city blaze only by contrast with the blackness of the abyss. Aloyse Michaely[15] has pointed out that the image is close to one from Berlioz's Requiem, in two passages of intimate prayer (the Hostias and the Agnus Dei), where the gap yawns between sepulchral trombones and a chord for three flutes. One is reminded of Messiaen's stated admiration for this work, along with *Roméo et Juliette* and the *Symphonie fantastique*, which he describes together as containing 'passages which have nothing to do with nineteenth-century music; passages which are already *musique concrète*'.[16] (The linkage with Schaeffer begins to seem more reasonable.) They are so in Messiaen's terms, of course, not because they use the sounds of everyday experience but because they evoke those sounds; and if the musical image is powerful enough, it may even persuade us that it corresponds to a reality that can exist only in the imagination, though in the case of the Messiaen work the low D flat is not only a striking pictorial image but also a moment of clearing in the fabric of the music, revealing a fundamental for the giant flickering of resonances within which it has its being.

Messiaen has said that it was the attempt at approximating birdsong timbres that led him to an extraordinary colourfulness of orchestration,[17] but it seems fair to assume too that the resonance model played its part: the interconnection of birds and bells in his music has already been noted, and the first large section of *Couleurs de la cité céleste* even has a refrain from the New Zealand bell bird, singing in carillons on clarinets, piano and xylophones. More generally, resonance phenomena are suggested by chords which, in this work as in many of its predecessors, cover a wide register, use octaves and fifths to enhance particular notes and have wide intervals in the bass and narrow ones in the treble. Even harmonies containing all twelve pitch classes thus gain a clarity of sound, a clarity that for Messiaen shines with a definable visual colour. Hence the title of the work, and the appeal in the three remaining inscriptions from the Apocalypse to the 'rainbow round about the throne' (Rev. 4:3), to the holy city's light 'like unto a stone most precious, even like a jasper stone, clear as crystal' (Rev. 21:11) and to its foundation stones of jasper, sapphire, chalcedony, emerald, sardonyx, sardius, chrysolyte, beryl, topaz, chrysoprasus, jacinth and amethyst (Rev. 21:19–20).

This was by no means the first time Messiaen had concerned himself with the musical mirroring of colour – there had been the 'jumble of rainbows' in the *Quatuor* – but it was certainly the first composition to have a preface beginning, 'The form of this work depends entirely on colours', and the first in which, following on from the fifth of the *Sept haïkaï*, musical ideas are marked with their colour values all through. This is a problem. The language of musical discussion is deeply penetrated by visual analogies; the word 'chromaticism' itself implies some kinship in experience between harmony and colour, and relations between the two had been sensed since Aristotle. However, detailed interest in these connections on the part of composers is a phenomenon of the twentieth century, beginning with the work of Mikolajus Čiurlionis and with Skryabin's notation of a part for light organ in his *Prometheus* (1908–10), continuing with the stage compositions of Kandinsky (*Die gelbe Klang*, 1912) and Schoenberg (*Die glückliche Hand*, 1910–13), proceeding by such byways as that of Bliss's *Colour Symphony* (1921–2) and eventually reaching the precision of *Couleurs de la cité céleste* where single chords are marked as matching the colours of the celestial city's precious foundation stones.

There is a clinical condition of synaesthesia in which the patient suffers, if that is the word, a confusion of auditory and visual perceptions, so that sounds excite a sensation of colour. Messiaen has remarked on this as affecting his friend the painter Charles Blanc-Gatti,[18] but he has said too that this is not the origin of his own feeling that colour and music are linked: instead, as he has tried to explain, 'When I hear music, and also when I read a score, I see internally, with the mind's eye, colours that move with the music.'[19] In the case of the movement from *Sept haïkaï*, the colours are marked against particular chords for the violins and for the piano (see example 69). In harmony as in sonority the two chord streams are complementary, twelve-note aggregates being formed by the addition of the 'vert pâle et argent' chord to the 'orangé', the unmarked to the 'gris et or' and the 'bleu' to the 'rouge'. The complementation of colour, obviously, is not so exact,

Ex. 69 Sept haïkaï 5 'Miyajima et le torii dans la mer'

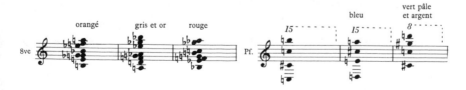

since the opposite of red ought to be green, but as symbols of cold and heat, in Messiaen's own interpretation,[20] blue and red are diametrically opposed, and twelve-note complementation is obviously important in parts of *Couleurs* where high chords in the piano and cencerros touch in the pitch classes that have been omitted from chords of brass and clarinets. The representation of two of the precious foundation stones – topaz and chrysoprase, together with crystal – offers evident instances, recalling Messiaen's statement that his favourite painter is Robert Delaunay,

> . . . not only because he is the forerunner of abstract painting, and so very close to what I see when I hear music, but above all because he created a very subtle and at the same time very violent way of treating relationships between complementary colours, especially by the principle of 'simultaneous contrast' and 'Orphism'.[21]

The intended correspondences of colour and sound in example 70 are not easy to determine: perhaps the only clue is to be found in Messiaen's remark apropos Beethoven, 'The colour of violet and G major make an absolutely frightful dissonance!'[22] – which could suggest either clear green or topaz yellow as the hue of the last bar. In any event, it is probably mistaken in most instances to look for a direct correlation of colour and harmony, for despite the above comment Messiaen has said, 'One cannot speak of an exact correspondence between a tonality and a colour.' Instead the creation of a colour effect seems to depend on the play of complementation, which may be why Messiaen has been happier to ascribe colours to his modes of limited transpositions, where complementary tonalities so readily surface. The second mode, he has said, 'turns through certain violets, certain blues and violet-tinged purple', while the third mode 'corresponds to an orange with pigmentations of red and green, touches of gold and also a milky white with

Ex. 70   Couleurs de la cité céleste

iridescent reflections like those of opals',[23] and these associations are duly borne out in *Couleurs* (figure 75) where there are chords in mode 2 marked 'blue violet', in mode 3 marked 'orange, gold, milky white' and in mode 4 marked 'violet'.

However, there is one very clear correspondence between colour and key in the blueness of A major, as is established in example 69, in 'Le merle bleu' and 'Le traquet rieur', and again in *Couleurs* where the mode 2 passage mentioned above is a cadence on to an A major triad with added D sharp, which one may imagine adds the hint of red to change the colour from the pure blue of example 69 (where the low D acts to enhance the A by resonance). There is even support for that supposition in the less certain association between E flat (enharmonic equivalent of D sharp) and red, as seen in example 69 or in places in *Couleurs* where Messiaen marks the effect as one of red sardonyx (e.g. figure 24): in both cases there is a 6–4 chord of E flat major in the bass. Moreover, at figure 74 in *Couleurs* the 'red' chord from the *Sept haïkaï* reappears exactly in a passage marked 'red touched with blue', the blue coming from a piano–percussion chord identical with the 'blue' chord from the same source, except that the A is brought down two octaves. The complementary colours of blue and red would thus seem to be connected in Messiaen's mind with the complementary tonalities of A major and E flat major, which produce, when their added-sixth chords are combined, the violet-tinged second mode with its tendencies towards blue on the A major side and red on the E flat.

Of course, there is no reason to suppose that the internal experience of colour will communicate itself to Messiaen's listeners. For Skryabin, it appears, A major was green and E flat steel; F sharp was his vivid blue[24] (though perhaps it is significant that both composers are agreed that blueness goes with ecstatic joy). Nevertheless, consideration of the intended colour effects goes some way towards explaining Messiaen's harmony and discerning its symbolic meaning. For instance, the frequent appearances of blue and red chords in *Couleurs de la cité céleste* – the same blue and red used for the score's striking cover – can be seen as looking not only to the jewels of the New Jerusalem but also to the prefigurings of those splendours in the windows of the Ste Chapelle and of Notre Dame de Chartres, the two churches in which, to Messiaen's great satisfaction, his next work, *Et exspecto resurrectionem mortuorum*, had its first performances. He has also confessed his personal attachment to violet, apparently natural in a son of Sagittarius,[25] and his awareness of the medieval colour lore by which reddish violet, or purple, represents the Love of Truth and bluish violet, or hyacinth, the Truth of Love. That symbolism is not at all in conflict with the nature of such A major–mode 2, therefore hyacinth-coloured, works as the *Trois petites liturgies* or the *Visions de l'Amen*.

At the same time, the doctrine of colour complementation provides another means of interpreting Messiaen's predilection for the modes of limited transpositions and his technique, not only in *Couleurs* and *Sept haïkaï* but also in *Chronochromie*, of spacing and orchestrating twelve-note chords so that smaller units, often with some feeling of tonality, are distinguished: examples 69 and 70 are constructed entirely on this basis. Messiaen thus acquires for himself a modal passage through a totally chromatic universe, keeping all twelve notes in play but preferring to focus on particular modes, tonics and triads. And just as the usefulness of birdsong may lie partly in its labelling of different 'groups' for the composer (and for writers on his music), so the colour associations may lighten his task in fortifying his sense of a work's harmonic qualities. This, though, is still a more personal realm of analogy, which may well be meaningless for anyone but the composer; and though some colours are so firmly connected with tonal and modal features that their use guarantees a certain harmonic feel, in other cases, as in example 70, the harmony seems arbitrary except in its aspects of complementation. Others will hear these stones differently, and the presentation of this material as isolated chords heightens its alterability, bringing out the extent to which the work's lattice of strong, definite harmonic processes is filled with panes that one can imagine being different, so that although Messiaen was not moved to follow the aleatory routes of his younger colleagues at this time, *Couleurs de la cité céleste* incorporates the aleatory in its movement between what must be as it is and what could conceivably be otherwise.

The fixed features of the work are a result of the restitution here of tonal centres and of the modes of limited transpositions, which are themselves connected with the reintroduction of plainsong. Earlier, in *Les corps glorieux* and the *Messe de la Pentecôte* for example, it had been Messiaen's habit to alter plainsong quotations so that they fitted one of his own modes, and he had done the same more recently in the *Verset pour la fête de la Dédicace*, where the alleluia is reinterpreted in the third mode. But in *Couleurs* the same melody is unchanged, making a place for itself in the work by virtue of its instrumentation and its harmonization with parallel major chords having an added tritone. Since the Dedication alleluia appears also, and unadorned, in the *Méditations sur le mystère de la Sainte Trinité*, the different processes of melodic and harmonic alteration can be illustrated all within Messiaen's output (see example 71; time signatures have been removed in the *Couleurs* extract).

There are other plainsong quotations in the work that are melodically changed, notably the alleluia for the Eighth Sunday after Pentecost, which runs through the work as a refrain; or that for the Fourth Sunday after Easter, which is twice presented (figures 41 and 61) in an extraordi-

Ex. 71   *Alleluia for the Dedication*

(a)   Méditations sur le mystère de la Sainte Trinité   2

(b)   Verset pour la fête de la Dédicace

(c)   Couleurs de la cité céleste

nary antiphony of timbres, its notes distributed among bells, solo horn, clarinet trio and piano in treble chords. Much more usual are choruses of the kind illustrated in example 71, whether scored for wind instruments or an ensemble of tuned percussion, or for colossal tuttis of wind and bells in the harmonization of the Pentecost VIII alleluia that represents mode 4 in the colour sequence mentioned above, as well as in the concluding chorale that more complexly harmonizes the Corpus Christi alleluia. The instruments are thus brought into Gregorian choirs, and made to sing alleluias that have a bearing on the work's poetic subject matter, looking forward to the splendours of the celestial city (Pentecost VIII and Dedication) or else celebrating the redemptive sacrifice of Christ (Easter IV and Corpus Christi).

The same fundamental idea of the resurrection into glory, already treated in *Les corps glorieux* and *L'Ascension* as well as less centrally in other works, is at the base of the work that followed *Couleurs: Et exspecto resurrectionem mortuorum* (1964). This is again music for wind and percussion, but so differently balanced as to bring about a wholly particular musical style. The agile wind choirs of *Oiseaux exotiques*, the *Sept haïkaï* and *Couleurs de la cité céleste* have been replaced by an army of thirty-four players, and the omission of keyed instruments from the percussion leaves an ensemble of bells and gongs, 'these metal percussion instruments for which I have a particular affection'.[26] This is an orchestra on the monumental scale of Berlioz's *Grande symphonie*, and it lends itself to music of a monumental character: Messiaen in his preface to the score recounts how while writing it he surrounded himself with 'strong and simple images: the stepped pyramids of Mexico, temples and statues of ancient Egypt, Romanesque and Gothic churches', recalling Berlioz's description of his *Te Deum* as 'colossal, Babylonian, Ninevite'. But close though Messiaen is once more to his admired fellow countryman in this work, *Et exspecto* lacks the self-aggrandizement of Berlioz's comparable pieces: despite the first person singular in the title, this is not a personal meditation on death but a ceremonial, and it is so, once more, because its form is liturgical rather than dramatic.

Indeed, no work since *L'Ascension* has so rude and strong a structure, built in great blocks that are placed beside one another in schemes of symmetry and repetition. Perhaps this is because the two works are both concerned with the expectation of eternity from the viewpoint of the here and now, not with that existence in eternity which had been the subject of *Les corps glorieux*, or the *Quatuor*, or *Couleurs de la cité céleste*. Like *L'Ascension*, *Et exspecto* begins with a prayer from the temporal world (the movement is headed with the opening words from the psalm *De profundis*) and ends with a long, slow ascension which climbs on rungs of repetition.

The second movement, inscribed with St Paul's words on Christ's dominion over death, finds an image for that dominion in an unmistakably palindromic form, ABCBCAB (the last B curtailed). The A sections consist of a six-note streak of lightning in the woodwind followed by the same six notes transposed down by two octaves and compressed into a chord, from which they are removed one by one in the order of the original idea: Messiaen calls this a 'melody by losses', and it can be understood to express the interchangeability of the successive and the simultaneous. In the B sections, a woodwind quintet plays litanies of imitation and answer (see example 72). This quotation falls entirely within the ambit of mode 4, but more thoroughly characteristic of the

Ex. 72   Et exspecto resurrectionem mortuorum   2 'Le Christ, ressuscité des morts, ne meurt plus. . .'

work is the frequency of intervals of a major second, fourth, tritone and minor sixth. These are common too, for instance, in the melody of the first movement and in the trumpet line that provides the second movement with its c material, the theme being harmonized with complex chords (Messiaen's preface speaks of Grünewald's resurrected Christ, 'who seems to be flying in a rainbow generated by his own light') and overlaid by manipulations in the cencerros on the Śarṅgadeva rhythm *simhavikrama*, whose presence here, as in the *Sept haïkaï*, adds the symbolic meaning of 'lion's might'. Moreover, as the preface also points out, the second half of *simhavikrama* is identical with another Śarṅgadeva pattern, *vijaya*, which means 'victory', and the whole formula contains fifteen durational units, so that it multiplies Siva, whose number is five, by the Christian Trinity, and celebrates Christ in his Hindu transposition: an emblematic instance of Messiaen's willingness to find Christian images in the products of other cultures.

The third movement brings the voice of Christ calling his people to resurrection, that voice being heard in three awesome forms: an Amazonian bird call on the whole woodwind ensemble, a slow pattern of change ringing on four bells in tritones, and an immense chord in triple crescendo that seems to pick out notes from the last bell resonance and bring them to a huge amplification. This trinity of ideas is then repeated in slightly altered form, complete with its coda in which the bell pattern is sounded by the lowest wind instruments and finished off by rolls on the lowest of the gongs, and tam-tams.

Rather similar in its stark divisions, the fourth movement looks forward and backward to a time outside time when 'the morning stars sang together, and all the sons of God shouted for joy' (Job 38:7). As in *Couleurs de la cité céleste* the music of heaven is imagined in terms of its two earthly adumbrations, plainsong and bird calls, separated by long reverberations from the three tam-tams in descending order of pitch: spectacular announcements of sonorous mysteries that Stockhausen at the same date was subjecting to scientific examination in his *Mikrophonie I* for tam-tam and electronics. The antiphony of Easter chant and Calandra lark is played through and repeated; there is then a heterophony of chants with the melody of the first movement returning, and finally a sequence of eight massive chords, preparing for the enormous chorale with which the work ends. This is a long consideration of the fragment of monody from the second movement quoted above, with the principal note in each chord well defined by octave doublings, and with at the end a great rise to the G sharp that the melody had touched in its previous incarnation before falling to F sharp. If this G sharp is expressively an arrival at the gates of the celestial city, it is musically a completion in melodic terms of the symmetrical harmony G sharp–D–C–A–G–D flat, and a grand release thereby from the asymmetries that give tonal harmony its bass-bound gravitation, a release even from the emphatic but contested D flat major of the last chord (see example 73).

Ex. 73   Et exspecto resurrectionem mortuorum   5 'Et j'entendis la voix d'une foule immense'

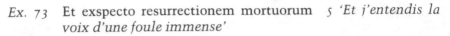

CHAPTER 12

Tota Trinitas Apparuit

The first performance of *Et exspecto resurrectionem mortuorum*, in the Ste Chapelle, is evocatively recalled in Messiaen's preface, where he writes, 'The blues, the reds, the golds, the violets resounded in each window with the music.' 'It was', he goes on,

> an ideal environment for the work, because of the marriage of the sound complexes with the dazzlement of the colours and also because of the crossed resonances due to the windows on every side. It was eleven in the morning, and the sun also played its part, bringing here and there new touches of colour with the rebounding of the sounds.

But the suitability of ecclesiastical performance is a matter of acoustics as well as colour: the stupefying chords, which sound, as has been suggested, like abstractions from the resonance of some great bell or gong, are intended themselves to resound, which is why much of the work is slow, why it waits through notated silences in the second and third movements, and why Messiaen advises a gap of a minute be left between movements, so that the five monoliths are clearly marked off from one another. The scale of the piece, however, fits it also, as the preface confirms, for performance out of doors, even 'among high mountains' – a proposition that must have affected many of the score's imagined performances if not yet any of its actual ones.

Within two months of the première of *Et exspecto* Messiaen had begun the ascent of his own mountain of the imagination in the composition of *La Transfiguration de Notre-Seigneur Jésus-Christ*, where the orchestra of the preceding work finds itself joined by strings to match, by a choir of a hundred voices and by a septet of solo instrumentalists. The subject of Christ's Transfiguration, though not rich in iconography or previous musical treatment, appears in retrospect to have been almost inevitable for Messiaen. In the first place it is, as a literary event, unequalled in the Gospels for its grandeur and strangeness. Moreover, it is set among mountains, and it represents – like those other moments in the Christian story that Messiaen had already contemplated in his music, the Incarnation and the Ascension – an instant of contact between God and man, between the celestial and the mundane, the eternal and the temporal. Finally it embodies a complete manifestation of the divinity, for, as St Thomas Aquinas writes in words Messiaen sets in his penultimate movement, 'In the Transfiguration, which is the mystery of the second generation, the whole Trinity appears: the Father in the voice, the Son in the man, the Holy Ghost in the bright cloud.'

Besides Aquinas, the textual sources for *La Transfiguration* are the Bible and the missal, including the passage in St Matthew dealing with the miracle (17: 1–9) and other texts associated with the liturgy for the feast of the Transfiguration. All these are assembled to make not a telling of the story but a showing of it, a liturgy and not a drama. The Gospel narrative is dispersed as the seed of the work, in four short movements chanted by the chorus with momentous introductions and more discreet support from the percussion. The other ten movements are all meditations, not necessarily relating either musically or theologically to the adjacent Gospel texts, but expanding on the central mysteries: the brilliant light of the Transfigured Christ, which is the announcement and the promise of the clarity of the resurrected condition; the intervention of the divine in the human; and above all, presupposed by these others, the affiliation of men to God.

Because *La Transfiguration* is the first of Messiaen's works (excepting the unpublished mass) to take sacred words into its substance, it might seem to require, and has indeed received,[1] discussion in terms of its subject matter. But it is a contribution to art before it is a contribution to theology, and perhaps it is suspicion about the point of art – the same suspicion from which Messiaen removes himself creatively through his appeal to outside arbiters from God to Śārṅgadeva – that encourages a valuation of the work for its conceptual rather than its musical ideas. Of course, the two cannot be separated. The doctrine of affiliation is expressed not only in the choice of texts but also in the choice of key for the work, E major, the same as in 'Dieu parmi nous' from *La Nativité*, or flickeringly in the compactest gathering of Messiaen's earthly angels in his *Oiseaux exotiques*, or gradually achieved in the heavenward urges of the first movement of *L'Ascension* or the twin slow movements of the *Quatuor pour la fin du temps*. And, quite apart from these personal associations of tonality and meaning, *La Transfiguration* finds musical means to present a miracle in which things of the earth are revealed as eternal and beautiful, or rather it rediscovers means that Messiaen had used in his musical beatifications of the 1930s and 1940s: means by which, through modality, triads are unloosed into new relationships, by which rhythmic progress is released from regularity of metre, by which forms are disjointed out of the continuity that mimics clock time. The difference is that these means are now employed on a vaster scale, and that the result, incorporating so much choral chanting, is a ritual in effect as well as in design, adumbrated in Messiaen's output only by the *Trois petites liturgies*.

The fourteen movements are divided into unequal 'septenaries', the second almost twice as long as the first, but both alike in executing the perfect number that had been counted out too in *Les corps glorieux*, the *Visions de l'Amen*, the *Livre d'orgue*, *Chronochromie* and the *Sept haïkaï*. Briefly the form is as follows:

1 'Récit évangélique': There is a descending, loudening introduction for gongs, tam-tams and other percussion, out of which a tritone F–B sounds on bells to provide the intonation for the tenors who begin the choral recitation at the unison or in octaves of the narrative, starting in mode 2 and then moving into other modes.

2 'Configuratum corpori claritatis suae': Framed by the exultant sounds of the African great indicator and other birds, the chorus extol eternal light and attribute to it already its majestic chords of E major, which are the focus for the first of the several chorales in the work.

3 'Christus Jesus, splendor Patris': The texts speak of the terror of illumination as well as the joy, and the birds are now hardier species of the mountains, enjoining the chorus to fierce accentuations of the word 'illuxerunt', though the central part of the movement is again in the chorale style.

4 'Récit évangélique': As 1.

5 'Quam dilecta tabernacula tua': A slow movement incorporating sections of chorale and also taking up again the sweetness of the 'Jardin du sommeil d'amour' in rapt phrases for the solo cello and in passages where the choir hum triads with aureoles from muted strings and bird songs from the other six soloists: piano, flute, clarinet, xylophone, marimba and vibraphone.

6 'Candor est lucis aeternae': The women sing again of eternal light within a heterophony of woodwind–percussion birdsong and string drapery; brass and untuned percussion are omitted.

7 'Choral de la sainte montagne': Massive movement for all except the percussion in block chords, progressing up the mountain in stages that always come to rest on an E major chord, though one differently laid out each time and not receiving its E in the bass until the end.

8 'Récit évangélique': The second septenary starts as the first had done, but with skeins of string glissandos and trilled harmonics to represent the bright cloud.

9 'Perfecte conscius illius perfectae generationis': Where the meditations of the first septenary had concentrated on the phenomenon of light, those of the second are more concerned with the Transfiguration as an image of man's affiliation to God. This first of them is in two parts, corresponding to the earthly and the celestial life in the quotation from Aquinas that it sets. In both a patchwork of choral chant, solo recitative, birdsong and other material is capped by a chorale in octaves marching towards a final C.

10 'Adoptionem filiorum perfectam': A Transfiguration hymn is set in choral strophes punctuated by ripe solos from the cello. Five of the soloists then have a birdsong cadenza over rhythmic operations in untuned percussion, and the movement is completed by a warmly harmonized alleluia.

11 'Récit évangélique': As before.

12 'Terribilis est locus iste': As the work comes towards its end, the meditations become both longer and more closely focused on the actual event. Here the mountain summit is evoked as a place of majesty and dread, with the weighty summons of Bonelli's eagle and the honk of the peregrine falcon among other mountain birds, with a solo baritone declaiming awesome words from Aquinas on how the clarity of the risen Christ will surpass that of the saints as the splendour of the sun surpasses that of snow, and with two luminous Glorias, the first in E major pentatony coming to rest on a chord of A flat major, the second in A flat major pentatony coming to rest on a chord of C major: a third, perhaps to be imagined as taking place in heaven, would complete the traverse of an augmented triad and return to E major. As it is, the movement ends with a mighty choral shout of the word 'Terribilis' that finishes on C in octaves, greeted by tam-tam and gong crashes coloured by wind and strings, and then almost covered by a bass-drum roll in colossal crescendo.

13 'Tota Trinitas apparuit': This hugest movement of the work is a liturgy within the liturgy, having three large sections in which the orchestra acts largely to frame and acclaim the chant of the chorus, who sing in the first two sections texts from the Transfiguration mass. Choral alleluias intensify the ritual atmosphere, as do great strokes on bells, gongs and tam-tams, which Messiaen colours, as he had in *Et exspecto*, with chords in the sustaining instruments of the orchestra. The third section comes to Aquinas's words on the appearance of the entire Trinity on the mountain of the Transfiguration, and the three persons are named in monumental chords that move slowly in the directionless universe of the third mode before arriving at a pure, clamorous E major, which they do only after the procession has been three times interrupted. (One hesitates to draw

any conclusions from the comparison with the only mention of birdsong in the New Testament.)

14 'Choral de la lumière de gloire': The second chorale treads a slow path similar to that of the first, but its dimensions are still vaster and it ends not on a pianissimo achievement of E major but on a triad of this central key multiplied across six octaves and reiterated fortissimo.

It may be clear from this brief synopsis that *La Transfiguration* embodies a wholesale return to the diatonic concords of Messiaen's earlier style, and to the same manner of bringing those concords into new relationships by means of the symmetrical features – the tritone, the augmented triad and the diminished-seventh chord – contained in the modes of limited transpositions, which had been pushed back into an incidental status in the works that had intervened since the *Turangalîla-symphonie*. On the other hand, the twelve-note constructions and rhythmic manipulations of such works as the *Livre d'orgue* and *Chronochromie* play a vey much smaller part, though they leave their residue in an immense enlargement of Messiaen's harmonic vocabulary by comparison with the symphony: *La Transfiguration* is rich in complex chords, often containing all twelve notes, but disposed, as in *Couleurs de la cité céleste*, so that very frequently a particular note is accentuated, either by octave doubling or by the clear isolation of a triad in treble or bass. The other outstanding difference from the music of the 1930s and 1940s is the prominence of birdsong. Halbreich counts a total of eighty-seven species imitated and named in the score, which is ten more than in the whole of the *Catalogue d'oiseaux* and for the first time includes representatives from the fauna of every continent.

Even if few listeners will be able to identify all these avian voices, the presence of birdsong in close proximity with hallowed chorales or severe enunciations from Aquinas gives *La Transfiguration* an unmistakably personal quality. Arguing from Messiaen's point of view,[2] one might suggest that the birds are more adequate to sing the divine praises than is fallen man, but there is clear evidence in the work – perhaps most obviously in those sections where a song is altered to induce some variation in a repeat – that birdsong here is a model that the composer has felt at liberty to adapt. He had already admitted to submitting birdsong 'to all sorts of manipulations, in the manner of composers of *musique concrète* and electronic music'[3] in *Chronochromie* and *Couleurs de la cité céleste*. *La Transfiguration* would seem to offer more instances of this, as, for example, when the song of the Mexican greyish saltator in the ninth movement becomes a cello melody in the third mode (see example 74).

This same movement provides other instances of Messiaen's hand-

Ex. 74   La Transfiguration de Notre-Seigneur Jésus-Christ   9 'Perfecte
conscius illius perfectae generationis'

ling of birdsong and other materials so that they function in a strong
musical scheme. The piece begins with loud repetitions of an eleven-
note treble chord made exotically tinny by the addition of xylophones,
cymbals, bell and gong, and picking out the first part of the rhythm of
simhavikrama. Messiaen speaks of the cymbals as 'powerful and
chaotic, like the music of Sikkim',[4] and it is to another territory of the
high mountains that he turns for his next image: a B flat in the deepest
bass of the brass, joined by a C from the choral basses and low strings a
ninth above, the whole 'black and fortissimo, like the trumpets and bass
voices of Tibet'. Together these make an 'attempt to speak the height
and depth of the mystery', but the images are more than picturesque.
There are connections with other works, in the *simhavikrama* rhythm
or in the low B flat that forcefully echoes the abyss of *Couleurs de la cité
céleste*. There are also matters of musical structure, for B flat is the
single pitch class not represented in the 'Sikkimese' chord, and so the
two Himalayan evocations are linked in chromatic complementarity.

What happens next is that Messiaen completes the whole-tone scale
begun with B flat and C, and does so by means of bird songs that
accentuate the remaining four notes. Then the opening is repeated, the
high chords now shifting about but still omitting B flat, the bass voices
again singing 'A' and so inscribing the first name of God into the work.
But the bird song is different: the golden oriole, previously joined by
other species, now sings alone in its E major. A deepening march of
gongs and tam-tams, expanded from the fourth movement of *Et
exspecto*, reintroduces the choral basses and their low brass and strings
on the same low C, from which the voices descend in whole-tone steps
to B flat and then G flat, singing a fragment of the Aquinine text.

So far the same whole-tone scale has governed everything in the
music, but now there is a turn to the diminished-seventh chord on C,
which adds two new notes, A and E flat. A new birdsong episode leads to
a low A with resonance in the percussion and upper strings. Then a solo
baritone chants more of the text on F sharp. (Like the other solo
episodes, all brief, this brings no suggestion that a character is being
assumed: the work avoids anything at all so dramatic, and picks its
soloists from the choir when it wants passages to stand out in black
lettering against the illuminated capitals of the rest.) The recitative

sparks off an ensemble of birds from Mexico, Africa, Greece and France, before a solo tenor in E flat, last note of the diminished-seventh chord, ushers in a choral psalmody in octaves. This is accompanied with lustrous harmonies which Messiaen sees in a delirium of colour – 'blue striped with green to black spotted with red and gold, by way of diamond, emerald, purplish blue, with a dominant pool of orange studded with milky white', as the prefatory notes have it – all of which may suggest a rainbow of modes and tonalities (see example 75).

Ex. 75   La Transfiguration de Notre-Seigneur Jésus-Christ   9 *'Perfecte conscius illius perfectae generationis'*

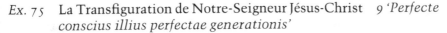

So it is. But the detail is not so unmeasured as its colour scheme. The melody begins back in the central whole-tone scale of this movement, now anchored to D by Messiaen's characteristic omission of the step next above. (See example 19, p. 81, for a comparable instance in the *Poèmes pour Mi* of thirty years before.) However, the addition of C sharp and later of G converts the scale from whole tone to mode 6, still with D as pivot, until at the end there is a turn into mode 3 so that the line can end on a low B, accentuating a note that has not until this point played any important part in the movement: perhaps this final rooting in the third mode is responsible for Messiaen's 'pool of orange studded with milky white'. But it is not only the fall to B that calls into question the status of D in the melody: the first accompaniment chord makes it the dominant of G major, while the last in example 75 suggests it might be the mediant of B minor. In both cases, and throughout this passage, the chant note is emphasized by octave doubling, but it may either crown the harmony as dominant and so give some sense of movement, or else be enfolded as mediant at points of rest. The effect in either event is of harmony touched off as resonance by the melodic note, and of course this effect is enhanced by the scoring for vibrato strings with bells and vibraphone – scoring that recovers the sound world of the *Trois petites liturgies* (compare example 33, p. 114), even including the ondes martenot, of which the vibrato cello gives a reasonable imitation. The main difference from such earlier compositions lies in the greater complexity of the harmony, and the correspondingly lesser degree of injected function: example 75 may be compared in this respect with the harmonization of similar whole-tone images in example 19 and also in example 41, p. 128 from the *Turangalîla-symphonie*, both having a definite goal, whereas the D centre of the extract from *La Transfiguration* is uncertain and the episode knows no rest until it drops to the low B.

This whole passage of chant is repeated, and there is then another intercontinental birdsong conversation, including the greyish saltator on the cello, before the whole ensemble of voices, wind and strings takes up the chant begun fragmentarily near the beginning by the basses. The same whole-tone scale is now expanded to make a version of the third or sixth mode (C–D flat–E–G flat–A flat–B flat), and the harmony settles into pure octaves as this culminating music moves slowly to rest on C. Then the 'Sikkimese' clamour returns to initiate a large-scale repeat including almost everything that has happened so far, though with some omissions (notably of the tenor soloist, whose E flat becomes a chanting note for the baritone) and many alterations of detail, especially in the birdsong passages: it is enough here, as in the *Catalogue d'oiseaux*, that the harmonic and gestural quality of birdsong be retained for the repetition to be felt.

This is not insignificant, for it points up how much Messiaen's music allows infinite capacity for variation within a fixed framework. Over the widest area in this movement such a framework is provided by the whole-tone scale C–D–E–F sharp–A flat–B flat, to which can be related the other modes that appear (mode 6 and mode 3 in the main sections of choral chant) and the tritones that pervade so much of the melodic and harmonic texture, and not only of this movement. However, this scale hardly does more than authorize the ground plan. It certainly does not engender anything that could be described as a harmonic process: the dynamic of the work comes rather from contrast than from continuity, and from contrast made as complete as possible by means of twelve-note and modal complementarities, as well as by widely divergent materials being used in juxtaposition. This is 'moment' form again, and, as in examples by Stockhausen and Boulez, there is no binding reason why one particular event should follow another, except the rule of contrast: indeed, sometimes Messiaen alters an original plan in its repetition, either by leaving passages out (as here) or by interpolating new ones.

Even so, *La Transfiguration* is much more a closed form than are *Cantéyodjayâ* and *Couleurs de la cité céleste*, and it is so for two main reasons. In the first place, much more of the music is organized in blocks that match one another in symmetry or repetition, like the two similar blocks from which the ninth movement is constructed. Secondly, a sense of finality is achieved in many instances by an appeal to the chorale model, which has that sense by virtue of its history (in Bach's cantatas and Passions) and also, one may conjecture, by virtue of its musical nature: the even rhythm and the secure harmony that dissolve the memory of whatever diversities have passed the mind before, as Stravinsky had found in his *Symphonies of Wind Instruments*. Most conspicuous in *La Transfiguration* are the chorale movements at the end of each septenary, but several of the other movements end in chorale style too: Nos. 2, 3, 9 and 13. Of these, the very ending of the thirteenth movement, 'Tota Trinitas apparuit', (see example 76) provides an exemplary instance of Messiaen's habitual movement in such music from obscure, tritone-heavy density into diatonic clarity.

Ex. 76   La Transfiguration de Notre-Seigneur Jésus-Christ   13 'Tota Trinitas apparuit'

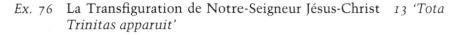

(+ cymbal and gong *crescendo*)

The first two chords here pile up notes from the third mode, though with a fifth or minor triad at the top to highlight the melody note. Melodically the whole phrase circles within the confines of an augmented triad, whose symmetry is that of the third mode, ending on a chord of E major with added sixth. The second phrase, of two chords, uses a different transposition of the third mode, complementary to the augmented triad of the first, and now without the diatonic enhancement of particular notes: instead the emphasis is on tritones, fittingly for the image of the cloud. But then the chorale starts out again from the added-sixth chord of E major, and though the bass steps down chromatically as the treble moves up on the rungs of a C sharp minor triad, the aim of both is the triumphant affirmation of E major, now without its sixth and with its tonic in the bass. By the change of one note, the melodic augmented triad of the first phrase has been changed into a minor one, and rhythmically too there is a correspondence between the final phrase and the first, but with a sixfold extension at the end that brings the total duration of the passage to twenty-seven quavers, or three to the power of three. Such things are unlikely to be accidents of a musical imagination so prone to trinitarian symbolism, but perhaps the outstanding image of the Trinity here is the E major triad, a triune phenomenon whose luminescence *La Transfiguration* is concerned to reveal with ever increasing certainty as it proceeds.

Messiaen's next work was a further examination of the same theological and musical idea, extended over a not dissimilar span of time, but with the great choirs of *La Transfiguration* replaced by a solo organist: it was the *Méditations sur le mystère de la Sainte Trinité* (1969). Writing for the organ, Messiaen is writing for himself, and writing too for his own instrument: it may be the merest happy accident that he found himself working in a church dedicated to the central mystery of the Christian faith (one cannot imagine anybody getting very excited about Ste Clotilde), but the published edition of the *Méditations* includes specifications of his organ at La Trinité, and it was on that instrument that he chose to record the work, even though he had given the first performance in Washington, DC, at the Basilica of the Immaculate Conception, and even though the suggestion that he should compose another large-scale organ work had come from the German player Almut Rössler.

The personal character of the *Méditations* is a matter of style, for just as the piano works after 1943 are coloured by the knowledge that they are to be played by Yvonne Loriod, so there are common qualities in the organ music that seem to be dictated by Messiaen's preferences as a practising musician. (The secondo part of the *Visions de l'Amen* calls out to be taken into account here as well.) In order to have more certainty in this thesis one would need recordings of the composer playing music other than his own, and unfortunately there are none. It is clear, however, that the *Méditations* contain sound images that had been particularly associated with his organ music: very slow processions of triadic harmonies guided by the modes of limited transpositions, toccatas in dense chords, measurings of the Trinity in three-part counterpoint, unusual choices of stops to produce slightly strident combinations of harmonics. (As Messiaen has suggested,[5] his practice of adding resonance in piano and orchestral works may have grown out of this technique.) Even the new things in the work turn out to belong to the world of the old. For instance, the long monodies of the garden warbler in the second and last meditations jump on to repeated notes in very much the manner of the játi music in *Les corps glorieux*.

If such correspondences come about because the work belongs to Messiaen the organist as much as to Messiaen the composer, then his own recording[6] ought to be a valuable addition to the published score. In fact it raises more questions than it answers. The tempo markings in this work are all given only in words, and so organists will have to decide for themselves whether Messiaen's own quaver = 80 is a fair interpretation of 'Un peu vif' for the All Saints alleluia at the start of the eighth meditation, for instance – especially when it offers hardly any contrast of speed with the 'Très modéré' that follows. Less open to argument is his distortion of rhythmic shapes, including for example the much favoured *miçra varna* in this same movement. There are similar problems in his recordings of the earlier organ works, but they seem particularly crucial in the case of the *Méditations*, since here the recording was made within a year of the first performance, and should therefore, so one might suppose, capture the music in a state close to that it had achieved when it was notated.

But if there are difficulties in deciding how far the published edition is the vessel of Messiaen's musical intentions, there are special difficulties here too in determining to what extent, and in what manner, it represents his theological scheme. This gap between music and programme has already been mentioned, but it widens in the *Méditations*, partly because the music has become so much a language of symbols, which are simply presented one after another in repeating patterns, and partly because Messiaen introduces what he calls a 'communicable language', which extends the ciphering of Bach and Schumann to make a whole musical alphabet, and then uses that alphabet to 'transliterate' sentences from Aquinas in the first, third and seventh movements. Example 77 gives the word 'humaine' from the seventh movement.

Ex. 77   Méditations sur le mystère de la Sainte Trinité   7

Even allowing for the fact that the letters are distinguished not only by pitch but also by duration, it is not reasonable to suppose that a code of this sort is going to be understood, least of all when there are other things happening in the music: the top line is a birdsong imitation, the bottom a fragment from a long ostinato based on a fragment of the tala that had served for the shakti of Brahma in the *Sept haïkaï*. One must therefore conclude either that the *Méditations* are not intended for human listeners, or else that the intention of the 'communicable language' is other than Messiaen states it to be. In fact he does interfere with its vocabulary to no little degree by using themes for the three persons of the Trinity, as also for grammatical moods and for the verbs 'be', 'have' and 'love', all of which together account for a sizeable proportion of the sacred texts, but perhaps the real value of the conceit is that it gave him a justification for returning to the partly randomized triple counterpoint of the *Mode de valeurs et d'intensités* or – a nearer parallel – the abruptly vaulting melodic line of 'Reprises par interversion'.

Although the sections in 'communicable language' may be unintelligible as such, they form some of the most substantial passages in the work, since elsewhere Messiaen's composition in symbols results in a very fractured form, reaching an extreme at the first page of the penultimate meditation. Here the ideas and their stated meanings are as follows: All Saints alleluia ('God is simple'); a three-chord figure played three times ('the three are one'); three monodic themes (Father, Son, Holy Spirit); melody in the bass, sequence of chromatic chords closing in contrary motion and another chord sequence marking out *miçra varna* (these three together: 'O the depth of the riches both of the wisdom and knowledge of God!' (Rom. 11: 33)). Possibly it was his awareness of the meanings associated with the Śarṅgadeva formulae – an awareness first evidenced in his remarks on the *Sept haïkaï* – that prompted the abundance of symbols in the *Méditations*, though as his preface points out, there was also the example of Wagner. Indeed, there was also his own practice, in works from at least the *Visions de l'Amen* onwards. The difference now is that symbols often constitute the entire musical substance, and if the work is not understood merely as a message in code (if it were only that, one might as well just read the composer's explanations, printed before each movement) then it may be approached as a grouping of images like those of *Neumes rythmiques*, with some longer ones that function as refrains.

In most of the movements, nevertheless, the form is even more firmly left open than it is in *Cantéyodjayâ* or *Couleurs de la cité céleste*. Most remarkably, four of the movements, including the last two, end with major triads against which the song of the yellowhammer picks out discordant notes, leaving the possibility that more is yet to be said. It may be in response to this openness that Messiaen declines to give his movements titles, as he had almost invariably before. (The *Cinq rechants* represent the only other exception.) A reading of his verbal commentaries quickly shows that the nine pieces do have separate theological concerns, and that these are reflected in a musical symmetry: for instance, the second and eighth meditations are both occupied with qualities of God, holiness and simplicity, in the presentation of which they use plainsong and bird calls, both ending with the yellowhammer, while the next pair in, the third movement and the seventh, treat of the relationship among the three persons in 'communicable language'. However, it remains perfectly possible for ideas and sonorities to be taken from one movement into another, and the piecemeal presentation of the material encourages a view of the movements not as independent entities but as simply different selections from a common store of elements.

This formal dispassionateness in the music even suffuses those movements that have some degree of musical or pictorial integrity in the manner of the older cycles, for the two which are most musically unified, the third and the seventh, are unified in their concentration on the most objective material, the 'communicable language', and the single piece based on a narrative image, the fourth, is a statement of the unknowableness of God. As Messiaen's note points out, 'Almost the whole of this piece creates an atmosphere, preparing for the final vision.' It is an atmosphere of expectation broken by some weird bird inventions: fortissimo clusters after the black woodpecker, the soft hoot of Tengmalm's owl, a long solo in the style of the song thrush. Then loud chords rush past in the iambic rhythm of God's words to Moses on Mount Sinai (in the French Bible), 'Je suis!', after which there is a long pause broken by the return of the owl, wholly ignorant of what has happened.

If this may be taken as a metaphor of nature's ignorance of God, other parts of the work would suggest that the whole of nature, represented as usual by bird calls, is joined in a celebration of him: the ignorance is the ignorance of innocence, the ignorance in nature of the fact that it manifests the divine. And that divine manifestation is perhaps contained within the music, when the birds sing at whirring speed themes that the work has attributed to the Trinity (see example 78). Correspondences of this kind – between quite different places in the music,

Ex. 78 Méditations sur le mystère de la Sainte Trinité

(a) 'Fils'   (b) 'Fauvette des jardins'

quite different pulses (one might cite also the G major of the 'God is love' passage in the central meditation and the G-centred whole-tone character of the 'love' theme in the 'communicable language') – contribute to the openness of the *Méditations*, but another factor here is the difference in the degrees to which ideas are composed into the fabric of the cycle. The song of the blackcap, for instance, is always heard over an added-sixth chord of A major, whose notes it duly emphasizes, and the final irritations of the yellowhammer have so plain a musical function that they cease to sound like bird impressions at all. On the other hand, the direct quotation of plainsong, either in unadorned monody or in octaves (see example 71, p. 207), is a newly immediate opening to a source beyond the work in which it is contained. As the loops of time of the *Méditations* revolve, therefore, they bring with them, like genes in a chromosome, temporal particles that belong in the medieval era of plainsong, in the eternity of the birds and in the 1969 of the 'communicable language'. And as usual in Messiaen, there is no attempt to forge from these separate objects a continuity: indeed, they are more than ever before left to be distinct, and therefore to belie by their independence any suspicion that the composer is, as the title might suggest, conducting a train of contemplative thought. In that respect the cycle is not at all personal, but rather offers images that will ask for interconnection in the memory of the hearer. The real meditation takes place after the *Méditations* are over.

CHAPTER 13

From the Canyons to the Stars

In 1970, the year after the *Méditations sur le mystère de la Sainte Trinité*, Messiaen wrote a new birdsong piece for his wife, a pendant to the *Catalogue d'oiseaux* just as, in inverse measure, the *Méditations* were a pendant to the similarly titled last movement of *Les corps glorieux*. The piece was *La fauvette des jardins* (garden warbler), bringing forward as star soloist a creature that had already sung in all those works where Messiaen turns to the French fauna, including the *Méditations*, which in this respect, as in their nature as organ music, constitute a homecoming. (The common bulbul is the only non-French bird given a place in the cycle.) *La fauvette des jardins* is a homecoming too, since it transforms impressions received among the fields of Petichet: like the larger members of the *Catalogue d'oiseaux*, which it surpasses in length, it follows the course of a day, with the long solos of the principal bird, now warbling in harmony, interleaved with the songs of other birds and with symbols of mountains and lake. Of these, the lake is represented six times in different colourings by a chordal theme in different modes, the bright blues of mid-afternoon resounding once more in A major (and here a yellowhammer steals in, exactly as at the end of the *Méditations*).

It was to a very different landscape that Messiaen looked in his next work. According to his own account,[1] he was at first reluctant to accept the commission from the American patron Alice Tully for a work to celebrate the bicentenary of the Declaration of Independence, but he was won over by her personality, and thereupon consulted an encyclopedia in search of a suitable subject. He came up with the canyons of Utah as being the most marvellous natural phenomenon in the United States, and his American agent arranged a trip there: since he mentions that he was currently working on the recording of *La Transfiguration* with Antal Dorati in Washington, this must have been in the spring of 1972. He duly visited the canyons, and made there notations not only of bird songs but also of colours: 'Red-violet, a red-orange, rose,

dark red carmine, scarlet red, all possible varieties of red, an extraordinary beauty.' These then formed the basic materials for the commissioned work, *Des canyons aux étoiles . . .*, a 100-minute suite of twelve
movements for solo piano with an orchestra of full woodwind, brass and
percussion sections but just thirteen strings – an ensemble, therefore,
mediating between the sumptuous array of the *Turangalîla-symphonie*
and the sharply focused groupings of *Oiseaux exotiques*, the *Sept haïkaï*
and *Couleurs de la cité céleste.*

Nor is it just in its scoring that *Des canyons aux étoiles . . .* seems a
balance of Messiaen's orchestral endeavours, for if the songs and
choruses imitated from American and other birds establish close links
with *Oiseaux exotiques* in particular, the harmony, like that of *La
Transfiguration*, is much more inclined to favour the triadic sonorities
of an earlier period. And this affects the birdsong. For instance, where
the shama in *Oiseaux exotiques* landed on an E firmly but grimly
harmonized with its fifth, its tritone and its fifth's tritone, the same bird
in *Des canyons aux étoiles . . .* arrives at a brilliant chord of E major (see
example 79). This impresses itself rather less as birdsong than as

Ex. 79   Des canyons aux étoiles . . .   *11 'Omao, leiothrix, elepaio,
shama'*

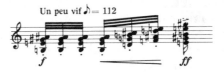

harmonic progresssion: a comparison with example 76, p. 219, from *La
Transfiguration* is not irrelevant. And so *Des canyons* continues the
process of musicalizing birdsong begun, as a serious undertaking, in
Réveil des oiseaux with its volatile motivic connections. But where the
earlier works, especially *Oiseaux exotiques* and the *Catalogue
d'oiseaux* find the composer stimulated by birdsong to new ideals of
colour, harmony and rhythm, in *Des canyons* it is rather that bird songs
are embraced in a human harmonic language, that of the diatonic
system. The lustrous E major of *La Transfiguration* and the innocent A
major of the *Trois petites liturgies* and the *Visions de l'Amen* are very
clearly the principal tonalities, the one ending the second part of the
work and the other the third. They are also the principal colours. A
major as always is blue, here the blue of heaven, and E major is the
orange-red of the rocks of Bryce Canyon, bearing out Messiaen's contemporary contention that a complementary colour is associated not
with complementary harmony but with the relationship of a fifth.[2]

The division into three parts provides a non-retrogradable rhythm of five, two and five movements, and also makes it possible for a scene at one of the Utah sites to conclude each part. However, performances of the work, which like *La Transfiguration* occupies a whole programme, have naturally taken an interval after the second part, so dividing the work into two approximately equal halves, each ending in exultant major concord. The contents are, briefly, as follows:

1   'Le désert': A quotation from Ernest Hello signals that Messiaen would have his desert interpreted as a spiritual one, an emptiness that is the precondition for any attempt to apprehend the divine. The imagery, however, is that of the physical desert (without any obvious influence from Varèse). A slow incantation on the solo horn – recalling the theme of God from the *Méditations*, but ending with an upward rather than a downward tritone – introduces and concludes the piece, which also includes long, quiet solos for the wind machine, sounding as if across the wilderness. In the middle of the piece there are calls from a bird of the Sahara desert, punctuated by the phrases of an extraordinary whistling melody that passes from bowed crotales to piccolo to violin harmonics.

2   'Les orioles': A movement consisting almost entirely of birdsong imitations for piano and orchestra, announcing the importance of E major but giving at least equal weight to the added-sixth chord of G major, with which the piece ends: this is most particularly the harmony of the orchard oriole, whose voice the piano takes as its own in several miniature cadenzas: the tenth movement is thus prepared.

3   'Ce qui est écrit sur les étoiles . . .': What is written in the stars turns out to be the fatal sentence written on the wall of Belshazzar's palace: 'Mene tequel parsin', as it is in the version Messiaen uses. He inscribes the text in his music again by means of the 'communicable language', with the same pitches and durations as in the *Méditations*, but now also with a fixed instrumentation and stridently discordant harmony for each letter: the orchestra is cut about in savage blocks in the manner of the 'rock' music from *Chronochromie*, though with the addition of unevenness in the rhythm, so that the message of astrology is one that has also been written into the fabric of the earth. And it is the music of the earth that comes next, in a crescendo–diminuendo for Messiaen's invented 'geophone', a large flat drum filled with lead beads and rotated to make a sound like that of the sand. (*Le Transfiguration* had made a similar introduction in the 'luminophone', consisting of a steel vessel filled with ball bearings and used 'to add "body" to effects of light'.) After this there is a brass chorale framed by the piano imitating Townsend's solitaire, and then a long bird chorus which

is brought to an end by the solo horn on the song of the cañon wren. This brings back Townsend's solitaire on the piano and a symmetrical closure of the movement as it had begun.

4   'Le cossyphe d'Heuglin': The bird of the title is the white-browed robin, which provides all the material for the first of two movements entirely confided to the piano. Messiaen's preface mentions three distinct sorts of call this bird makes – shapely phrases repeated from two to four times, accelerating figures becoming either louder or quieter, and bass rumbles – and these he uses to create a roughly palindromic form.

5   'Cedar Breaks et le don de la crainte': Hello again provides the superscription: 'To replace fear by awe opens a window for adoration.' Messiaen's preface speaks of Cedar Breaks as 'a vast amphitheatre, sliding down toward a deep abyss', and so providing a reminder of damnation. But as the preface also states, 'In the scale of feelings, the fear of punishment ranks rather low', which is perhaps why those parts of the movement that appear to deal with fear are wilfully absurd or banal: there are strange effects on the strings, the still stranger sound of a trumpeter making squeaks through his mouthpiece alone, and a simple descent given the corrupt sound of a trumpet with wa-wa mute doubled by glockenspiel and bells. Adoration, on the other hand, would seem to be voiced by the American robin in what Messiaen regards as neumes, spilling into E major harmony, and the gift of awe is certainly evoked by another passage in the 'communicable language', this time spelling out Greek praises of God. The transliteration, the robin's song and the wa-wa episode are the main elements in three parallel sections that Messiaen prefers to describe as a strophe and two antistrophes, to be followed by an epode suggesting the wind, on wind machine and string trills, bringing the songs of more birds. Finally, as in *Chronochromie*, there is a coda that abbreviates the introduction.

6   'Appel interstellaire': The second part starts with a horn solo that may well have been the first part of the work to be composed. The young French composer Jean-Pierre Guézec, a pupil of Messiaen and more recently a colleague on the Conservatoire staff, had died in March 1971, and Messiaen was among those who contributed to a 'Tombeau pour Jean-Pierre Guézec' at the Royan Festival three months later, his contribution being, according to one report, 'a five-minute piece for solo horn: fanfares and signals, shot through with long pauses, surround a slow, sad melody that is as full of pathos and expressive purpose as the war memorial of a French city'.[3] With the possible exception of that last metaphor, this is a fair description of the 'Appel interstellaire', in which case the prominent role of the horn in *Des canyons*, giving a new focus to

Messiaen's instrumentation not only here but also in the first, third and tenth movements, may have been prompted by its use for a memorial. As an 'interstellar call' the piece includes a variety of messages: slow melodic phrases, arpeggios, flutter-tongue and trilled notes, hunting calls returning to the antique fingering of the horn in D (but characteristically using G sharp as an alternative dominant along with A), and the bizarre waverings in pitch created by half raising or lowering the keys.

7   'Bryce Canyon et les rochers rouge-orange': A big finale moving through various modal circles around E major, forming in Messiaen's view another expression of the Greek triad, with a strophe, two antistrophes, an epode and a coda.

8   'Les ressuscités et le chant de l'étoile Aldebaran': This is almost a recomposition, within the more crystallized orchestral style of a quarter-century on, of the 'Jardin du sommeil d'amour'. This time the song folds repeatedly into chords of A major with added sixth rather than similar chords of F sharp major, suggesting that its message is one of serene joy rather than ecstasy, and the form is that of a rhyming quatrain ABAB. But it is again the strings that carry the main burden, coloured not by an ondes martenot but by woodwind and by bells and solo violin harmonics doubled by crotales, a mixture of string and tuned percussion sound that recalls the ondes as it had in the ninth movement of *La Transfiguration*. The birdsong figuration, provided in the *Turangalîla* movement by piano, flute and clarinet is now taken by an extreme treble trio of piccolo, glockenspiel and again piano, but playing in its top register. The birds, of course, are the resurrected bodies; the song is that of the star Messiaen has adopted as his own: he notes Stockhausen's attachment to Sirius[4] (curiously, the latter's *Sirius* was another commission for the American bicentenary) and confers his own choice on the principal star of Taurus, even though it was Arcturus that was mentioned in the *Trois petites liturgies*, and even though, for all the blueness of its song, Aldebaran is a brilliant red. More special effects – high harmonics executed *col legno* on the double-bass and glissandos in harmonics on open strings on the violins – greet the end of each phrase of the song with, as Messiaen's preface puts it in characteristically evocative terms, 'their sprinkling of water, their rustling of silks'.

9   'Le moqueur polyglotte': A second long piano solo. The species, the mockingbird, is one that had appeared in the first movement, but now it extends itself over four long verses and displays a formidable repertory: brilliant repeated ejaculations, thuds in the deep bass, long trills and – a new effect in Messiaen's piano music – resonances sounding from silently undamped strings. While all

these things are in rotation, there are more spasmodic appearances of other birds: Australian complements to the American soloist.

10 'La grive des bois': The bright simple call of the American wood thrush – a C major arpeggio on piccolo, high tuned-percussion and violin harmonics – is an image of the 'new name' promised for each soul in the Apocalypse (Rev. 2:17). It is preceded in the piece by a duller, earthly representation from stopped horn and alto flute, and the two forms are heard in alternation with other bird songs until at the end the horn-led version is reduced to a basic pattern, G–E–C, repeated against climbing white-note chords in the strings: resurrection has been achieved, as it has at the end of the eighth movement of the *Méditations*.

11 'Omao, leiothrix, elepaio, shama': As the title implies, this is another birdsong movement, bringing together Hawaiian and other species: the former include the first and third in the title, while the leiothrix is a Chinese bird and the shama is the exultant animal already encountered in *Oiseaux exotiques* and in example 79. Their various convocations, with nineteen other birds, are punctuated by varied repetitions of a refrain carried mainly by the bassoons and horns in unison. One statement of it is counterpointed by a return of the *râgavardhana–candrakalâ–lakskmîça* tala encountered in so many works of the late 1930s and 1940s, providing the only acknowledged intervention of the deçî-tâlas in the cycle.

12 'Zion Park et la cité céleste': According to Messiaen's preface: 'Those who discovered the pink, white, mauve, red, black walls, the green trees and the limpid river of Zion Park looked on it as a symbol of paradise.' He does the same. The piece is built around a wind chorale that slips from one to another of the two transpositions of the third mode including all the notes of the A major triad, in which it seeks its resolution. Repeatedly that resolution is interrupted by choruses of birdsong figures, but at the end the pure triad is held firmly by the strings, greeted by whooping horn glissandos and chimes in the tuned percussion, and finally taken up by the whole ensemble fortissimo.

Taken together, the twelve movements thus complete a tour not only of the sights and sounds of Utah, but a tour indeed from the canyons to the stars. It begins in the chromatic desert and it ends in the gloriously diatonic celestial city, but it is not otherwise a sequential journey, not a pilgrim's progress: such would have been unthinkable given Messiaen's predilection for a sense of time that slows, stops, rotates and turns back on itself. The celestial city, for example, has already been inhabited in all its A major splendour by the eighth movement, and the depth of the canyons is not properly felt until the seventh. Moreover, many of the movements contain within themselves the ascension from darkness into light, bass into treble, chromatic into diatonic that is the musical embodiment of the programme.

None shows this more clearly than the seventh, the finale to the second part and effectively to the first half of the piece. The superscriptions here include a phrase from St Paul to the Ephesians, where he prays that they 'may be able to comprehend with all saints what is the breadth, and length, and depth, and height' (Eph. 3:18), and also a fragment from St John's catalogue of the New Jerusalem's foundation stones, picking out sardius, topaz and amethyst, and naming their colours as red, yellow orange and violet: these will provide, according to the now very detailed listing of colour schemes in the preface, the predominant tints of the movement. However, above the two Apostles Messiaen places a quotation from the mystic Romano Guardini that could serve as epigraph not only for this movement but for everything he has written: 'Worldly concerns will not be erased, but will be translated into eternity.'

The translation takes place, as so often before, within a form that encapsulates eternity in repetition, and that may be represented as follows:

STROPHE
  i   Short dialogue for four Utah birds.
  ii Rock music in 'red-orange' culminating in a cadence into E major and continuing with chorales for wind and strings in alternation.
  iii Vigorous dance in octaves in the manner of the 'Danse de la fureur' and 'Amen des étoiles'.
  iv The preface refers only to 'Bells' sounds', passing over the fact that this is a shrill distortion of section ii.
  v   Chase of chords finishing on B flat harmonized with 'contracted resonance'.
  vi Tutti in asynchronous ostinatos on a grid of even semiquavers.
  vii Image of the abyss with trombones on bottom B flat as in *Couleurs* and *La Transfiguration* but now falling to G flat.

ANTISTROPHE I
  i   Extended.
  ii Slightly altered and ending on a C minorish dissonance instead of an E major chord.
  iii Very slightly altered.
  iv Slightly altered.
  v   Reaching a similar chord under E.
  vi In different modes.
  vii Very slightly altered.

ANTISTROPHE II
  i   Further extended.
 ii   The opening is confused by the fact that its eight bars are played
      simultaneously by the strings in the order 4–3–2–1–8–7–6–5 with
      different but parallel chords; the chorales are interrupted and
      overlaid by birdsong.
viii Descending chimes in high woodwind and tuned percussion, over
      E major chords in the brass, are repeatedly cut off by birdsong.

EPODE
 ix   Piano cadenza on Utah birds.
  x   An alleluia, as the preface has it, in string chords.
 ii   Massive return of the chorale leading to cadence figure into E
      major and tutti affirmation.

   The characteristic 'block' formation of the music is obvious from this
synopsis, but it is also clear that Messiaen's analysis of the form is not
entirely helpful. In leaving unstated the relationship between iv and ii it
obscures an important source of the movement's dynamism, for once
the distortions of iv have been heard there is a crucial need for the return
of ii. The need is exacerbated by the repetition of the process in the first
antistrophe, after which section ii has itself been infected by distortion
as it appears in the second antistrophe, which stops before it would
come to iv and offers instead a foretaste of E major harmony, interrupted
though it is by birdsong. The piano cadenza breaks the pattern; the
alleluia, in the Lydian mode on E, foresees the triumph; and at last the
cadence is able to happen as it should.
   This dynamic is strong and sure, but it is not really a process of
development. After all, the cadence has been heard in its elemental form
at the start in the second section of the strophe (see example 80). What
follows is a disturbance and then a reachievement of the E major
sublimity, taking place within a context where the key is never truly
lost but where it may be differently embodied as a result of different
modalities at play. The cadence in example 80 is in E major coloured by
the third mode (only the F is foreign); the ostinato sections vi combine
different modes, at first the third and the sixth in transpositions that
exclude E and its major third, and then the third and the second in
transpositions that exclude only A and concur in the dominant-seventh
chord on E with added minor third and tritone. To take a final example,
the string alleluia chooses a mode that has only one note not found in
the original transposition of mode 3. Messiaen thus works with different modal colours around the third mode E major of his principal
image (example 80), reserving the black of exclusion for the section that
precedes the first sounding of the trombone's voice from the abyss – on B

flat, the tritone opposite of E – and that follows a chordal arrival also at B flat. (It would seem that the 'chord of contracted resonance' is defined by containing all the notes of the added-sixth chord with the addition of the minor third and both seconds, but its function would seem to be, like that of many of Messiaen's complex chords, to allow the illumination of diatonic features – here a B flat major triad in the treble – within dense harmony.)

Ex. 80   Des canyons aux étoiles . . .   7 'Bryce Canyon et les rochers rouge-orange'

The harmony of *Des canyons aux étoiles* . . . clearly links it with Messiaen's earlier works, up to and including the *Turangalîla-sym-phonie*, bypassing much that had happened in between except the influx of birds. On the plane of form, too, it joins with *La Transfiguration* in exposing sectional repetitive types of the kind outlined in the consideration of the seventh movement above: the freer patterning of *Cantéyod-jayâ* or *Couleurs* has been left behind, as has the rhythmic virtuosity of the *Sept haïkaï* or the weighing of time-lengths to be found in the *Livre d'orgue* or *Chronochromie*. But there is also much that is new in the score, especially in the use of special instrumental effects, to which Messiaen had not been much given in earlier compositions, and the generally lean and strident sound-world, eschewing the rich blends of the *Turangalîla-symphonie* in favour of combinations where, even in homophony, individual strands of colour stand out. The work is therefore not so much a synthesis, as has sometimes been suggested, but more a step into the future that also joins the circle with the composer's past.

It does so even with his distant past, since the melodic assertion of a tritone dominant given harmonic diatonic support in example 80 is a repetition under different circumstances of example 9(a), p. 55, from *L'Ascension* as well as of innumerable similar progressions in intervening works, not least the whole of *La Transfiguration*, whose first pitched sound is a B–F tritone and whose last an E major chord in which that B has been given 'proper' dominant status. In this case too, the resolution comes not at the end of a process of development but all at once, to be then more or less obscured by shifts of mode: as in the tenth movement of *Des canyons*, the 'new name' is given from the first, and it is the business of the music to clear away whatever impediments there may be to its recognition, just as for Messiaen the truths of Christianity are given, unquestionable and unalterable, requiring only to be expounded. Indeed, the musical idea may, like the theological principle, antedate the work in which it is espoused, as with the '*Boris* motif' of earlier years, or as here when, in finding the cadence of example 80, Messiaen went back to a time before his own musical awakening and remembered the horns from the orchestral masterpiece of his teacher Dukas, *La péri*.

CHAPTER 14

The Saint, the Sinner and the Angel

In 1975, the year following the completion and first performance of *Des canyons aux étoiles . . .*, Messiaen was asked by the administrator of the Paris Opéra, Rolf Liebermann, to write a work for that house. Believing, as he has said,[1] that he had no gift for opera, the composer demurred, but he was eventually persuaded, and in the summer of the same year he began writing the libretto for what would, eight and a half years later, reach the Opéra as *Saint François d'Assise*.[2]

During this period Messiaen worked intensively at his task, despite spells of ill health. The composition of the opera was, by his own account, also begun in 1975 and finished in 1979, whereupon he went on to the orchestration and completed the score in 1983. (It is of course interesting to have this evidence that he regards composition and orchestration as distinct tasks, though one can hardly believe works like *Couleurs de la cité céleste* were plotted in every detail before a thought had been given to their instrumentation.) The result was a full score of 2,000 pages for an opera containing more than four hours of music, laid out for forces far beyond any normally accommodated in a theatre pit: the orchestra is of 120 players, including very large wind and percussion sections as well as three ondes martenot, these returning after a gap of three decades since the *Turangalîla-symphonie*; there is also a choir of 150. (At the first performance the huge instrumental ensemble spilled out of the pit into the boxes nearest the stage, for the brass and two of the ondes martenot, and on to platforms at either side of it, woodwind on the left and percussion on the right, presenting the work not inappropriately as an action within the orchestra.) Very evidently *Saint François* is a monument whose architectural details, decorations and inscriptions will begin to reveal themselves only when an edition of the score is available.[3] Meanwhile it is impossible to do much more than glimpse the broad outlines.

Messiaen has said that he chose the subject because Francis is 'the saint who most resembles Christ'[4] and therefore offers an image for the

Passion he would not presume to undertake,[5] and also for the more personal reason that St Francis spoke to the birds. One may note too the prominence of the Francis theme in French music of the twentieth century: in, for example, Pierné's orchestral *Paysages franciscains* (1920), or in Tournemire's trilogy *Les combats de l'idéal* (1916–29), where Francis is introduced as spiritual hero to stand supreme over Faust and Don Quixote, or in the latter's opera *Il poverello di Assisi* (1936–8). Messiaen's claim, though, is that his opera 'resembles nothing else, and owes nothing to anyone, unless to the birds'.[6]

Otherwise its only debts are to the source documents: to the lives of Thomas of Celano and St Bonaventure, and to the texts attributed to Francis himself, including the *Cantico delle creature*, whose verses are distributed through the libretto. Inevitably, too, it owes much to Messiaen's earlier music, establishing, like *Des canyons aux étoiles . . .*, the *Méditations sur le mystère de la Sainte Trinité* and most especially *La Transfiguration*, a firm connection with his style of the 1930s and 1940s. In the case of the vocal writing this is quite natural, since aside from brief moments in *La Transfiguration* he had written nothing for solo voice since *Harawi*, and indeed the singers have access most frequently to a style of evenly paced modal chant that goes back through *La Transfiguration* to the song-cycles, each character having a theme of his own. The orchestra can be harmonically more adventurous, ranging from a warming enfoldment of the voices in the manner of example 75, p. 217, from *La Transfiguration* (though now with the ondes martenot available to sweeten the strings as it had in the *Trois petites liturgies*) to brilliant toccatas and (for the Leper) an abandoned dance recalling Messiaen's very earliest works for orchestra, or to birdsong choruses of the kind he had placed in almost all his orchestral scores since *Réveil des oiseaux*, with the difference that now the birds are uncaged from the bar lines in the Sermon scene and allowed to fly independent of the conductor's beat.

There are in all eight 'Franciscan scenes', as the opera's subtitle has it, three in each of the first two acts and two in the last. The first scene, 'La Croix', discovers St Francis (baritone) walking along a road with the closest of his followers, Brother Leo (also a baritone). Three times the brother sings of his fear, and three times the saint points out that 'perfect joy' (Messiaen had wanted to call the scene 'La joie parfaite' but feared this would not be understood)[7] is not to be found in worldly things, not even in the divine gifts of healing, prophecy and understanding. The repetitions in each case are to very much the same music, Brother Leo singing his theme for each statement of his anxiety, and it becomes clear at once through this that *Saint François* has very much more in common with the body of Messiaen's other works than it has with the body of other operas, despite the composer's attention to the operatic repertory in creating a very long main part combining the 'vigour' of Golaud with the 'declamatory solemnity' of Boris.[8]

After Francis has thrice said what perfect joy is not, Leo asks him in what then it does consist. He answers with a parable. If they were to be exhausted, rain-drenched, filthy and hungry, if they were to knock at the door of a monastery and be refused admittance by the porter, if they were then to be beaten by the porter, and if they were to suffer these hardships in thinking of Christ, that would be perfect joy. The parable is pronounced to a dynamic toccata in the strings, spattered with decoration from wind and metallic ondes martenot. Brother Leo is amazed into silence and the two men go on their way, while the lighting increases on a large black cross at the top of a high stairway in the middle of the rear of the stage. The chorus, unseen (though visible on steeply raked platforms for all their contributions in the original production), sing Christ's words that those who wish to follow him must take up the cross.

The second scene, 'Les laudes', has the young Franciscan community singing the morning office in alternation with St Francis taking verses from *Cantico delle creature*. Three of the brothers, Silvestro, Rufino and Bernardo, all basses, are accompanied in their chant by low ondes martenot and double-bassoon, while the saint receives, as so often in the opera, his halo of violins. The three brothers and the chorus depart, to a bell theme heard at the start of the scene, and Francis is left to pray for help in overcoming his horror of lepers. The curtain falls on his 'theme of decision', an emphatic double-octave descent.

In the third scene, 'Le baiser au lépreux', Francis's prayer is answered. The Leper is found alone, singing of his spiritual desolation and physical suffering: he is, according to the composer's exact stipulation of costuming, dressed in tattered rags, his limbs covered with black spots and blood, as lepers appear in the scene of the Temptation of St Anthony in Grünewald's Isenheim altarpiece. (Similarly, Francis is intended to have the features of his portrait by Cimabue and the gestures of Giotto's representations of him in the Assisi frescos.) Francis enters and, surmounting his disgust, speaks with the Leper of offering his suffering in patience to God; but the Leper is concerned only with his bodily condition.

A new bird call – that of the gerygone, one of several from a territory not previously heard in Messiaen's music, New Caledonia, which he visited himself to make notations – announces the arrival of the Angel (soprano), who should resemble Gabriel in an Annunciation by Fra Angelico to be seen in the Museo San Marco in Florence: he has long blond hair, a golden halo, a long pink-mauve robe with gold embellishments, and wings in five colours: red, black, yellow, blue and green. He sings, in A major coloured by the third mode, words adapted from 1 John 3:20: 'Leper, your heart condemns you, but God is greater than your heart. He is love. He knows all.' The Leper becomes contrite, and Francis recognizes that the fault is his in not loving the man enough. He embraces him, to a slow soft phrase from the ondes martenot and muted solo strings, and the Leper is miraculously transformed: now whole, he wears the red and orange costume of a medieval nobleman, and executes a wild dance of triumph. Both men then become aware of their unworthiness, but the chorus concludes the scene, and with it the first act, in singing that those who greatly love will be pardoned.

The fourth scene, 'L'ange voyageur', brings the Angel back to catechize the brothers, who are introduced by their themes in the orchestra: Leo by his song of fearfulness, Bernardo by a melody on horns, strings and ondes martenot and by woodwind calls of the New Caledonian monk bird, Elias by more abrupt, intemperate bird calls and by glissandos in strings and trombones. Leo asks Masseo to be porter for the day while he takes care of some building work, and he goes, singing his song. The Angel appears, with orchestral sonorities that establish him as belonging to another world: chords in the seven flutes, cold shrieks from E flat clarinet and high oboe in the style of the Noh theatre, and calls from the gerygone. He strikes at the door in a dochmiac rhythm $(\smile - - \smile -)$ sounded by the whole orchestra in loud, low chords: it is, in Messiaen's terms, the formidable appeal of grace.

The brothers, however, do not recognize their visitor as anything but a traveller. Masseo lets him in, and he asks, singing smoothly in E flat major coloured by the second mode, to talk to Elias. Eruptive sounds in the orchestra prepare the entrance of the latter (tenor), who is irritated to be brought from his work, and still more irritated to be asked questions of faith. He pushes the Angel back out through the door. But the Angel makes his dochmiac knock again, and is again admitted, asking this time for Bernardo, the doyen of the community. Bernardo accepts the interrogation more philosophically, and to the Angel's questions about readying his soul for resurrection he replies that he will answer to God that he is an image of God. In turn he asks a question of the Angel, the question of Elsa to Lohengrin: 'What is your name?' The Angel cannot reply ('Do not ask my name: it is miraculous!') but says that he has come from far to speak with Francis. He goes, and the brothers realize what it is they have been entertaining.

The fifth scene, 'L'ange musicien', is the interview between St Francis and the Angel foreseen at the end of the last. Francis is at prayer, singing more of his *Cantico*, in his cell on the hill of La Verna: when he speaks of the resurrection, Messiaen inserts songs of a blackbird and a song-thrush notated there. The saint asks for a presage of immortality, and his guardian kestrel calls out on trumpet in D, double-bass tuba and bassoon. An added-sixth chord of A major, glazed with a glockenspiel gerygone, warns of the imminent arrival of the Angel, who seems from this to be coming from the Aldebaran of *Des canyons*. Unlike his followers, Francis recognizes the Angel at once, and the Angel sings again in E flat major coloured by the second mode a central idea taken from Aquinas: 'God dazzles us by an excess of Truth. Music transports us to God by its want of Truth.' He then plays on his treble viol, the music in fact provided by the trio of ondes martenot in calm modal melody floating throughout the theatre. The birds of the forest join their songs to his, and night falls, leaving only his right arm and his instrument visible. The saint faints. He is found by Leo, who calls Masseo and Bernardo to come, whereupon Francis wakes and tells them he was overcome by the celestial music, which, if it had continued longer, might have caused his soul to leave his body. The curtain falls slowly as the brothers look up and seem to catch sight of something in the sky.

If the fifth scene would be a gift to any composer (and it must be said Messiaen comes near achieving the stupendous expectations he sets up for the angelic music), its successor thrives on talents more peculiar to Messiaen: it is 'Le prêche aux oiseaux'. The orchestral introduction brings forward several species; Francis himself identifies more for his brothers: the turtle dove, the wren, the robin and the blackcap. He then has a vision of the colours and birds (orchestrally figured) of New Caledonia, which of course was unknown to Europeans of the thirteenth century: the vision is therefore testimony to Francis's spiritual elevation. Afterwards a birdsong chorus brings back European species and prompts the saint's decision that he must preach to the birds. He does so, telling them of God's blessings on them in giving them flight as an earthly image of resurrected agility, in providing them with food and habitation, marvellous plumage and song, so that they may sing without words, like the angels. He makes the sign of the cross over them, and after a moment of silence there begins Messiaen's grandest bird concert, featuring two skylarks (xylophone trio and woodwind ensemble), a garden warbler, two blackbirds and a blackcap (violins), and, freed from the main tempo, another garden warbler (ondes), another blackcap (ondes), a lyre bird (ondes), yet another blackcap (trumpet in D) and a golden oriole (horn trio and tuned percussion). At the end the birds fly off to the four points of the compass, creating a cross in the sky. Francis speaks to his disciples of what they can learn from the birds in abandoning themselves to divine providence, and they depart.

The final act begins with the seventh scene, 'Les stigmates'. St Francis is again on La Verna, but now in a cavern, and an atmosphere of dread is evoked by an amplification of 'La chouette hulotte', bringing back the owl's cries and the mode of durations, timbres and intensities. Francis prays to be blessed before his death with the knowledge of the sufferings of Christ and the love of Christ; the orchestra presents a further sequence of bizarre sounds, recapitulating the chasmal trombone of

Couleurs, La Transfiguration and *Des canyons*, the geophone and wind machine of this last work, and new effects in the ondes and strings. The chorus, singing for Christ, tell Francis that he must accept the five wounds of the cross and become himself a second Eucharistic sacrifice. He exclaims that he is undeserving, but the great black cross reappears and the chorus sings in accelerating Balinese rhythm: 'C'est moi!'

Five rays of light come from the cross and implant in Francis's body the stigmata, with a return of the violent dochmiac rhythm of the fourth scene to signal the violent entry of the eternal into the temporal. Christ's words in the chorus, in a rare passage of the libretto that is wholly Messiaen's invention, propound the mystery: 'I am that afterwards that was before. I am that before which shall be afterwards. . . . It is I who thought time and space.' The stage is bathed in red-orange light and the cross turns to scintillating gold, producing a colour scheme fit for a finale in E major tinged with various modes. Christ in the choir calls to Francis, and tells him in a long chorale that he must carry his cross for the sake of eternal life. So the scene ends with a beatific audition achieved in music similar to that which had ended each part of *La Transfiguration*, for Francis too is transfigured by grace.

The ultimate scene, 'La mort et la nouvelle vie', may be considered to project a sevenfold entity into the eternity of an eighth member, as in the *Quatuor pour la fin du temps*.[9] The basses of the chorus recall the quasi-Tibetan gravity of *La Transfiguration*, and Francis makes his farewells to the Umbrian landscape, the birds, his town and his community. Bernardo, Masseo and Leo are cast down, but Francis points out that though it is night, still as always, the nightingale is singing, and he urges them to join in its praise; he sings the last verses of his *Cantico*, those concerned with sister Death. The chorus of brothers calls out in distress, and the Angel appears once more, visible only to Francis. The Angel recalls his A major theme from the third scene, which brings back the Leper in the rich dress of his earthly resurrection. He also recalls his E flat melody of the fourth and fifth scenes, and promises that Francis will soon be hearing forever 'the music of the invisible'. Francis calls on Christ with a repetition of the Aquinine thought: 'Music and Poetry have led me towards you: by image, by symbol and by want of Truth. . . . Deliver me, intoxicate me, dazzle me forever by your excess of Truth.' He dies. Brother Leo sings, like Arkel, of the silence of death, and then all leave, taking the saint's body with them. There remains only an intense light on the place where it lay, becoming more dazzling as the chorus sings a vast resurrection chorale ending in C major with full orchestral support.

There the opera ends, and with it, so Messiaen has intimated, his life's work (though he has begun another composition): his seventy-fifth birthday took place a dozen days after the première, and while acknowledging that he would have liked to compose a second *Catalogue d'oiseaux*, he has said that the project would have needed ten years' work, and 'death will stop me midway'.[10] The temptation is therefore almost irresistible to consider *Saint François d'Assise* as a summa, especially when it lasts for as long as the *Turangalîla-symphonie*, *La Transfiguration* and *Des canyons aux étoiles*... put together, and especially when, much more than any of the other late works, it incorporates materials from the whole of Messiaen's music: harmonies that had first sounded in *Le banquet céleste* and weird brass mouthpiece playing that had arrived in *Des canyons*, bleak inventions on the twelve notes and resplendent major chords, rhythmic processes and bird songs, psalmodies and chorales.

There are, however, problems in according it the status of crowning glory, and they arise from the nature of the genre, from Messiaen's unique attempt to transpose what he has called 'the most immaterial of the arts' into the very material world of the theatre. And though the history of opera shows that this is a transposition likely to produce friction, in Messiaen's case there is the special difficulty that not only his art but also his subject matter is of its essence immaterial.

On the most banal level this difficulty expresses itself in the figure of the Angel. Messiaen's wish for a creature out of Fra Angelico, with 'marvellous wings' and a 'magnificent costume', a being 'appearing to dance without touching the ground', is an appeal more to the imaginative faculty than to theatrical possibility. It may be that the element of the supernatural in *Saint François* could be satisfactorily presented on stage, as it has been on occasion in Wagner, but that would probably require some amendment to the composer's very literal directions for costumes, sets and staging – directions that had clearly lain heavy over the Paris production, with its painted scenes adapted from the Franciscan frescos of Assisi. The clue might be taken from the Angel's music, which, with its Noh woodwind and high treble birdsong, is the product of an imagination less bound by conventions of Christian art.

That is the crucial point. Messiaen as scenographer and dramatist operates with the ideas and symbols bequeathed him by a very particular tradition of Catholic piety; whereas Messiaen as composer gives himself the freedom to take up ideas and symbols from other cultures and to invent his own. Of course, his interpretation of those ideas and symbols is very often in terms of the same Catholic devotion, but if the immateriality of music gives it leave to speak of religious truths, it also allows audiences to understand it independently of those truths. One may thus consider Messiaen an artist to be working on two levels of intention, like all artists with aims beyond that of making art. His creations are in the first place a mythology of the glory of resurrected existence in the celestial city, and in the second place a body of musical compositions. The problem with *Saint François d'Assise* is that, being theatrical – and still more importantly, being narrative – it binds the two in a way that perhaps only *La mort du nombre* had done before.

Only the convinced atheist would assert that the theological can ever be wholly separated from the musical in Messiaen's art, and only the devout Christian would be able to maintain that they are necessarily united. For the vast number in between there is no reason to deny the widespread acceptance of Messiaen as a great master of religious music – indeed, as one of the very rare religious artists of his time: possibly only the *Sagrada Familia* of Gaudi offers a comparable experience among all the works of art imagined in this century. However, it would be an impoverishment to understand his music only as a language of symbols, as his remarks and prefaces on the later works, in particular, would indicate is his intention on the level of theology. Art is not a 'communicable language', precisely because its elements are not neutral objects like the letters of an alphabet but rather things with meanings beyond the literal: otherwise there would be no reason to distinguish the Winchester Bible from any pocket edition. And though one may argue that the artists of the Winchester Bible would not have produced the same images if they had been illustrating Catullus, though one may argue in Messiaen's case too that the artistic intention carries with it a flavour of the religious, still the making of a single penstroke intelligible as word or music is evidence enough of intentions to do other than praise God.

As we have seen, Messiaen's own statements of his artistic intentions, as contained in his *Technique de mon langage musical* and the prefaces to his scores, are often incomplete and sometimes misleading. No doubt this must always be the case, since any individual's response to a work of art includes, in retrograde canon as it were, the creation of an image of the artist, at least in Western culture; and no two individuals will posit quite the same creator. (An examination of the Messiaen literature is enough to assure oneself on this point.) And so if Messiaen's version of his artistic intention is at best partial and his version of his religious dimension beyond analysing (simply because the phenomena to which it relates have no objective status), one is left with the music, which is not without its own clues as to what he is about.

One prime feature stands out in every work and on every level: a conception of music in terms of individual events, distinct from any context. This is reflected in much that has been discussed already: a use of chords as single things at instants, to impart a particular function or colour, but without establishing the sort of integrated relationship among chords essential to dynamic tonality; a creation of rhythmic patterns out of individual durations, whether in imitation of Hindu and Greek types, in completion of number sequences or otherwise; a consideration of melody, rhythm, harmony and instrumentation as independent; a whole musical outlook that is rooted in the concept of mode, implying selection of items from a fixed repertory, rather than that of key, which implies fixed relationships among different repertories (the fixed relationship between the E major triad and the A major triad for example).

This entails, by comparison with symphonic diatonic music, a separation of the individual idea from its context, and indeed such a separation is graphically displayed when Messiaen takes an idea that would have a context-dependent function in more normal music – a cadence, for instance – and uses it as an object that can appear at any point in a movement. The result, inevitably, is an absence of development, which is context-dependent through and through. Hence Messiaen's customary presentation of his music in repetitive forms, where the absence of development is unashamedly celebrated, as well it might be, since it is the absence of development – the dislocation from a forward-moving time sense – that gives Messiaen the means to offer new experiences of time: experiences of great slowness or great speed, experiences of time reversing itself or circulating in repetition, experiences of time disposed in the irregular impulses of changing time signatures and mixed values.

New ways of experiencing time in music are equivalent to new ways of experiencing space in painting, sculpture and architecture, or to new ways of experiencing thought in writing. It is through these equivalences that Messiaen finds it in himself to respond to the surrealist challenge to reinvent the world according to the pattern of the mind, not to represent reality as brought to us by history and by the senses, but to create new realities from within. What may have helped him to become a greater artist than Breton or Dali, however, was his realization that those new realities could come also from a source that had been overlooked in the twentieth century – Christianity, the greatest surrealist conception of them all: a view of the world at odds with perceived reality, exactly as Magritte's flaming tuba could never exist, or as Messiaen's second mode has no place in the everyday reality of the diatonic system. All are expressions of the mind rampant in its independence from the ordinary things of the world; all provide for the mind experiences beyond the normal. The difference is that Christianity is a body of thought and imagery that has grown in the minds of some of the outstanding geniuses of two millenniums, and not a trick dreamt up in a moment, so that it cannot but have stabilized and tested Messiaen's creative endeavours besides stimulating them. He himself would argue that there is the even greater difference that Christianity is the vehicle of the Truth. But to point to that Truth, 'by want of Truth', it may be enough that purely with the means of his art he has made the irrational real.

Notes

1 CHILDHOOD AND BEFORE

1 In *Tandis que la terre tourne* (Paris, 1912).
2 Antoine Goléa: *Rencontres avec Olivier Messiaen* (Paris, René Julliard, 1960), p. 19.
3 Ibid., p. 23.
4 Sleeve note for *L'âme en bourgeon: poèmes de Cécile Sauvage*, Erato STU 71104.
5 O my son, I'll take your head in my hand,
And I'll say: this small human world I planned;
This brow as it traces the line of first dawn
Conceals a whole universe I placed, new born,
To mirror, to water the sky when he cries.
And I'll say: I gave that flame to his eyes,
I drew from the moon's ambiguous smile,
From sea glints and from a plum's velvet pile
Two stars that stay at endlessness addressed.
And I'll say: I formed that cheek and that nest
Of a mouth where his voice stirs like a bird;
This man-faced world arose to my word.

O my son, I'll take your head in my hand,
And thinking the day grow, brighten, expand,
I'll see beneath this rose silk of your flesh,
Whose petal cover might the bees enmesh,
I'll see orbits plunging into the void,
Teeth grin in ranks on a jaw destroyed,
Ossature of nose with shadows gaping . . .

Your death's head: that too is my shaping.
6 Claude Samuel: *Entretiens avec Olivier Messiaen* (Paris, Pierre Belfond, 1967), pp. 121–2.
7 Goléa, p. 25.
8 Samuel, p. 39.
9 Ibid., p. 122.
10 Ibid., p. 122.
11 Ibid., p. 10
12 Harry Halbreich: *Olivier Messiaen* (Paris, Fayard/SACEM, 1980), p. 204.
13 Samuel, p. 18.

14 Ibid., p. 19.
15 Ibid.
16 Goléa, p. 19.
17 Samuel, p. 124.

2 THE CONSERVATOIRE

1 See Halbreich, p. 28.
2 Samuel, p. 128.
3 See Samuel, p. 206.
4 See Yvan Wyschnegradsky: 'Musique et pansonorité', *Revue musicale*, ix (1927–8), pp. 143–52; and Marcel Orban: 'Un musicien mystique: Nicolas Obouhow', *Revue musicale*, no. 158–9 (1935), pp. 100–8.
5 *An Autobiography* (London, Calder and Boyars, 2nd ed., 1975), p. 54.
6 See Samuel, p. 68.
7 Goléa, p. 28.
8 See Samuel, pp. 14–15.
9 Samuel, p. 143.
10 See Goléa, p. 28.
11 'Maurice Emmanuel: ses "trente chansons bourguignonnes"', *Revue musicale*, no. 206 (1947), p. 108.
12 Goléa, p. 28.
13 See, for example, Messiaen's *Technique de mon langage musical* (Paris, Leduc, 1944; English translation, Leduc 1957), pp. 71–4 (all page references are to the English translation).
14 See Halbreich, pp. 266 and 348. (The formulations are slightly contradictory.)
15 Samuel, p. 138.
16 See Paul Fraisse: *Les structures rythmiques* (Louvain, Publications Universitaires, 1956), p. 14.
17 *Technique*, p. 59.
18 Ibid.
19 See Donald Street: 'The Modes of Limited Transposition', *Musical Times* cxvii (1976), pp. 819–23.
20 See, for example, Samuel, p. 74.
21 See especially Pieter C. van den Toorn: *The Music of Igor Stravinsky* (New Haven and London, Yale University Press, 1983).
22 *Technique*, p. 58.
23 Pierrette Mari: *Olivier Messiaen* (Paris, Seghers, 1965), p. 39.
24 *Technique*, p. 65.
25 Samuel, p. 125.
26 Ibid., p. 71.
27 Ibid., p. 125.
28 Ibid.
29 Goléa, p. 29.
30 *Technique*, p. 62.
31 Ibid., p. 51.
32 Ibid., p. 13.
33 Ibid., p. 55.
34 Goléa, p. 30.
35 Arms extended, sad unto death,
   on the tree of the Cross you shed your blood.
   You love us, sweet Jesus: that we have forgotten.

Impelled by folly or the serpent's tongue,
on a panting, frantic, unceasing course,
we went down into sin as into the tomb.

Here is the spotless table, the spring of charity,
the banquet of the poor, here the Pity to be adored,
    offering the bread of Life and of Love.
You love us, sweet Jesus: that we have forgotten.

36 Sleeve note for Erato STU 70673.
37 See Robert Sherlaw Johnson, *Messiaen* (London, Dent, 1975), p. 55; and Halbreich, p. 321.
38 Sleeve note for Erato STU 70673.
39 *Technique*, p. 14.

3 LA TRINITE

1   *Revue musicale*, no. 138 (1932), pp. 128–9.
2   Olivier Messiaen: *Conférence de Notre-Dame* (Paris, Leduc, 1978), p. 3.
3   Samuel, p. 11.
4   Goléa, p. 38.
5   *Conférence*, p. 2.
6   Samuel, p. 16.
7   Note for EMI 2C 153 16291/6.
8   Samuel, p. 173.
9   See A. H. Fox Strangways: *The Music of Hindustan* (Oxford, Clarendon Press, 1914), p. 201.
10 *Technique*, p. 46.
11 Ibid., p. 40.
12 Ibid., p. 31.
13 Ibid., p. 33.
14 Ibid., p. 42.
15 Johnson, p. 48.
16 *Technique*, pp. 41–2.
17 Ibid., p. 42.
18 Ibid., p. 41.
19 Ibid., p. 41.
20 Note for EMI 2C 153 16291/6.
21 *Technique*, p. 33.
22 See Goléa, p. 47.

4 LA JEUNE FRANCE

1   Programme for the group's opening concert.
2   Sleeve note for Erato STU 70673.
3   Samuel, p. 205.
4   Halbreich, p. 209.
5   'Le rythme chez Igor Strawinsky', *Revue musicale*, no. 191 (1939), pp. 91–2.

5 THE HOLY FAMILY

1   *Technique*, p. 50.
2   Ibid., p. 45.

3 Ibid., p. 33.
4 Note for Argo ZRG 703.

6 TECHNIQUE FOR THE END OF TIME

1 Goléa, p. 61.
2 Ibid., p. 63.
3 See Goléa, p. 66.
4 *Technique*, p. 50.
5 Ibid., p. 34.
6 Ibid., p. 27.
7 Ibid., p. 16.
8 Ibid., p. 17.
9 Ibid., p. 36.
10 See Samuel, p. 126.
11 See *Technique*, pp. 38–9.
12 Goléa, p. 70.
13 Sleeve note for Adès 21 007.
14 See *Technique*, p. 7.

7 ARROWS AND AMENS

1 'Hommage à Messiaen', *Melos*, xxv (1958), p. 387.
2 Samuel, p. 129.
3 See preface to score.
4 *Technique*, p. 39.
5 Samuel, pp. 13–14.
6 See sleeve note for Erato STU 70200.
7 Goléa, p. 43.
8 Johnson, p. 74.
9 Published with EMI SLS 793/2.
10 See Goléa, pp. 106–7; and Samuel, pp. 130–1.
11 Samuel, p. 130.
12 See Samuel, pp. 133–4.
13 See notes with EMI SLS 793/2.

8 THE TRISTAN TRILOGY

1 See the preface to the published score.
2 See Goléa, p. 154; and Samuel, p. 21.
3 See Goléa, p. 157.
4 See Goléa, p. 156.
5 Goléa, p. 147.
6 Ibid., p. 156.
7 Ibid., p. 149.
8 R. and M. d'Harcourt: *La musique des Incas et ses survivances* (Paris, Paul Geuthner, 1925), pp. 332–3.
9 Goléa, p. 82.
10 Ibid.
11 Ibid., p. 84.
12 See Goléa, pp. 90–1.
13 See 'Le rythme chez Igor Strawinsky'.

14 Note for RCA SB 6761–2.
15 Ibid.,
16 See note for RCA SB 6761–2.
17 Ibid.
18 Johnson, p. 99.
19 See sleeve note for Erato STU 70457.
20 See Goléa, p. 176.
21 See Johnson, p. 99.
22 See Goléa, p. 176.
23 See sleeve note for Erato STU 70457.
24 See Goléa, p. 176.

9 NEW MODES OF THOUGHT

 1 See Goléa, p. 247.
 2 See Johnson, p. 103.
 3 See Halbreich, p. 39.
 4 See Johnson, p. 108.
 5 See Goléa, p. 247.
 6 See note on *Kreuzspiel* in Karlheinz Stockhausen: *Texte*, ii (Cologne, Du Mont, 1964), p. 11.
 7 See Samuel, pp. 186–91.
 8 Ibid., p. 190.
 9 'Stravinsky demeure', *Musique russe*, i (Paris, Presses Universitaires de France, 1953), reprinted in Pierre Boulez: *Relevés d'apprenti* (Paris, Seuil, 1966), pp. 75–145.
10 'Kadenzrhythmik in Werk Mozarts', in *Texte*, ii, pp. 170–205.
11 See Richard Toop: 'Messiaen/Goeyvaerts, Fano/Stockhausen, Boulez', *Perspectives of New Music*, xiii, no. 1 (1974), pp. 141–69.
12 See Mari, p. 63.
13 Ibid., p. 213.
14 See Samuel, p. 17.
15 Boulez, p. 68.
16 See, for example, *Conférence*.
17 Goléa, p. 212.
18 See Johnson, p. 114.
19 See Samuel, p. 108.
20 For Messiaen's own view, see Halbreich, p. 291.
21 Goléa, p. 211.
22 See Samuel, p. 194.
23 In Erhard Karkoschka: *Notation in New Music* (London, Universal, 1969), p. 164.
24 See Richard Toop: 'Stockhausen's *Konkrete Etüde*', *Music Review*, xxxviii (1976), pp. 295–300.
25 Samuel, p. 211.

10 BIRDSONG

 1 *Technique*, p. 34.
 2 See Johnson, p. 122.
 3 Samuel, p. 152.
 4 Ibid., p. 117.
 5 Ibid., pp. 111–12.

6 See Samuel, pp. 110–11.

7 Ibid., pp. 113–14.

8 See *Olivier Messiaen et les oiseaux*, a film by Denise Tual and Michel Fano (1973).

9 See Samuel, p. 100.

10 Ibid., p. 113.

11 Ibid., p. 112.

12 Ibid., p. 106.

13 Goléa, p. 234.

14 See, for example, Goléa, pp. 223 ff.; and Samuel, pp. 95–118.

15 Samuel, pp. 151–2.

16 See Samuel, p. 99.

17 See Edward A. Armstrong: 'Aspects of the Evolution of Man's Appreciation of Bird Song', *Bird Vocalizations*, R. A. Hinde (ed.) (Cambridge, Cambridge University Press, 1969), pp. 343–65.

18 *De spectaculis*.

19 See Samuel, p. 102.

20 See Johnson, p. 123.

21 Samuel, p. 111.

22 *Technique*, p. 65.

23 See Goléa, p. 226.

24 See Johnson, pp. 141–57, for comprehensive diagrams of the contents of the *Catalogue d'oiseaux*.

25 See Johnson, p. 138.

26 Goléa, p. 223.

27 *Le guide du concert* (3 April 1959), quoted in Johnson, p. 117.

28 Halbreich, p. 87.

11 THE COLOUR OF TIME

1 See Samuel, p. 17.

2 See Goléa, p. 280.

3 See Samuel, p. 157.

4 See table in Johnson, p. 177.

5 See Samuel, p. 160.

6 See note for Argo ZRG 756.

7 Ibid.

8 See Samuel, p. 127.

9 See Samuel, p. 29.

10 See Samuel, p. 211.

11 *Traité du rythme*, quoted in Halbreich, p. 403.

12 See Stockhausen's *Kontakte* and *Momente*, and writings on these works in *Texte* i–ii.

13 After transcription in the entry on mode in the *New Grove*, xii, p. 444.

14 See Samuel, pp. 164–5.

15 L'abîme: das Bild des Abgrunds bei Olivier Messiaen', *Musik-Konzepte*, no. 28 (1982), p. 44.

16 Goléa, p. 274.

17 See Samuel, p. 113.

18 Samuel p. 30.

19 Ibid., pp. 37–8.

20 Ibid., p. 43.

21 Ibid., pp. 44–5.
22 Ibid., p. 41.
23 Ibid., p. 42.
24 See *The Blaue Reiter Almanac* in the 'documentary edition' by Klaus Lankheit (London, Thames & Hudson, 1974), p. 131.
25 See Samuel, p. 42.
26 Samuel, p. 169.

12 TOTA TRINITAS APPARUIT

1 From Alain Michel, in a contribution to the programme of the Messiaen Festival held in Paris in November–December 1978 (Paris, La recherche artistique, 1978); see also Halbreich, pp. 432–49.
2 See Goléa, p. 234.
3 Samuel, p. 114.
4 Halbreich, p. 441.
5 See Samuel, p. 57.
6 Erato STU 70750–1.

13 FROM THE CANYONS TO THE STARS

1 See Harriet Watts: 'Canyons, Colours and Birds: an Interview with Olivier Messiaen', *Tempo*, no. 128 (1979), pp. 2–8.
2 Ibid., p. 5.
3 Rudolf Hollweg's review of the Royan Festival in *Melos*, xxxviii (1971), p. 250.
4 See Watts, p. 6.

14 THE SAINT, THE SINNER AND THE ANGEL

1 See Philippe Godefroid: 'Entretien avec Olivier Messiaen', *Opéra de Paris*, no 12 (1983), pp. 8–13.
2 See the programme book of this production for Messiaen's synopsis and commentary, on which much of the present chapter is based.
3 Publication is not expected before 1988.
4 Programme book, p. 22.
5 See Marcel Weiss: 'Messiaen et ses apôtres', *Le monde de la musique*, no. 62 (1983), pp. 30–1.
6 Ibid., p. 31.
7 See Godefroid, p. 10.
8 Godefroid, p. 10.
9 Preface to the published score of *Quatuor pour la fin du temps*.
10 Weiss, p. 31.

Chronology

YEAR	LIFE	WORKS
1908	Olivier Eugène Prosper Charles Messiaen born (10 December) at Avignon, first son of Pierre Messiaen and Cécile Sauvage	
1914	Pierre Messiaen joins the army; Cécile Messiaen takes Olivier and his younger brother Alain to live with her mother in Grenoble	
1917	First piano lessons	*La dame de Shalott*
1918	Pierre Messiaen returns to his family and takes them to Nantes	
1919	The family moves to Paris, where Olivier enters the Conservatoire	
1921		*Deux ballades de Villon*
1924	Second prize in harmony with Jean Gallon	
1925		*La tristesse d'un grand ciel blanc*
1926	First prize in counterpoint and fugue with Caussade	
1927	First prize in piano accompaniment with Estyle	*Esquisse modale*
1928		*Le banquet céleste; Préludes* begun
1929	First prize in organ playing with Dupré. First, unsuccessful attempt at Prix de Rome	*Préludes* completed
1930	First prize in composition with Dukas. Second, unsuccessful attempt at Prix de Rome	*Diptyque, La mort du nombre, Les offrandes oubliées, Trois mélodies*
1931	Appointed organist of La Trinité in Paris. Public début (19 February) with *Les offrandes oubliées* conducted by Straram. Hears Balinese gamelan at the Exposition Coloniale	*Le tombeau resplendissant*
1932	Marries Claire Delbos. Monteux conducts *Le tombeau resplendissant*	*Apparition de l'église éternelle, Hymne au Saint Sacrement, Fantaisie burlesque, Thème et variations*

YEAR	LIFE	WORKS
1933	Straram conducts *Hymne au Saint Sacrement* (19 March)	*L'Ascension* (orchestra)
1934		*L'Ascension* (organ)
1935	Siohan conducts *L'Ascension* (February)	*La Nativité du Seigneur*
1936	Foundation with Jolivet, Daniel-Lesur and Baudrier of 'La Jeune France'. Begins teaching at the Ecole Normale de Musique and the Schola Cantorum	*Poèmes pour Mi*
1937	Birth (14 July) of son Pascal. *Poèmes pour Mi* given their first performance (28 April) and orchestrated	*Fêtes des belles eaux, O sacrum convivium!*
1938	Plays two pieces from *La Nativité du Seigneur* at the ISCM Festival (June) in London	*Chants de terre et de ciel*
1939	Called up for military service	*Les corps glorieux*
1940	Captured (May) and imprisoned at Görlitz in Silesia	*Quatuor pour la fin du temps* begun
1941	First performance (15 January) of *Quatuor pour la fin du temps* before release from prison camp. Appointed to harmony class at the Conservatoire	
1942	Begins *Technique de mon langage musical*	
1943	Begins private classes in composition attended by Yvonne Loriod, Pierre Boulez and others	*Visions de l'Amen, Rondeau*
1944	Publication of *Technique de mon langage musical*	*Trois petites liturgies de la Présence Divine* completed; *Vingt regards sur l'Enfant-Jésus*
1945	First performance of *Vingt regards sur l'Enfant-Jésus* (26 March), *Les corps glorieux* (15 April) and *Trois petites liturgies de la Présence Divine* (21 April)	*Harawi*
1946		*Turangalîla-symphonie* begun
1947	Appointed to analysis class at Conservatoire. First visit to the USA, where Stokowski conducts *Hymne au Saint Sacrement* and Koussevitzky *L'Ascension*	
1948		*Turangalîla-symphonie* completed
1949	Teaches at Tanglewood and at the Darmstadt summer school. First performance (2 December) of *Turangalîla-symphonie* in Boston	*Cantéyodjayâ, Cinq rechants, Mode de valeurs et d'intensités, Neumes rythmiques*
1950	Teaches at Darmstadt. European première (25 July) of *Turangalîla-symphonie* at Aix	*Ile de feu 1, Ile de feu 2, Messe de la Pentecôte*
1951	Teaches at Darmstadt, where Stockhausen is impressed by *Mode de valeurs et d'intensités*. Records of *Quatre études de rythme* issued	*Livre d'orgue, Le merle noir*

YEAR	LIFE	WORKS
1952		*Timbres-durées*
1953	Premières at Stuttgart of *Livre d'orgue* (23 April) and at Donaueschingen of *Réveil des oiseaux* (11 October)	*Réveil des oiseaux*
1955	Plays *Livre d'orgue* for Domaine Musical (21 March)	*Oiseaux exotiques* begun
1956	First performance (10 March) of *Oiseaux exotiques* by Domaine Musical in Paris	*Catalogue d'oiseaux* begun
1958		*Catalogue d'oiseaux* completed
1959	First performance (15 April) of *Catalogue d'oiseaux* in Paris. Death of first wife	*Chronochromie* begun
1960	First performance (16 October) of *Chronochromie* in Donaueschingen	*Verset pour la fête de la Dédicace*
1962	Marriage to Yvonne Loriod. First visit to Japan	*Sept haïkaï*
1963	First performance (30 October) of *Sept haïkaï* by Domaine Musical under Boulez in Paris	*Couleurs de la cité céleste*
1964	First performance (17 October) of *Couleurs de la cité céleste* by Domaine Musical under Boulez in Donaueschingen	*Et exspecto resurrectionem mortuorum*
1965	First performance (7 May) of *Et exspecto resurrectionem mortuorum* in Ste Chapelle	*La Transfiguration de Notre-Seigneur Jésus-Christ* begun
1966	Appointed to class in composition at Conservatoire	
1967	Elected to Institut de France	
1969	First performance (7 June) of *La Transfiguration de Notre-Seigneur Jésus-Christ* in Lisbon	*Méditations sur le mystère de la Sainte Trinité*
1970		*La fauvette des jardins*
1971	Awarded Erasmus Prize	*Des canyons aux étoiles . . .* begun
1972	First performance of *Méditations sur le mystère de la Sainte Trinité* (20 March) in Washington, and of *La fauvette des jardins* (7 November) in Paris	
1974	First performance (20 November) of *Des canyons aux étoiles . . .* in New York	
1975		*Saint François d'Assise* begun
1978	Retires from Conservatoire. Messiaen Festival (November–December) in Paris. White Cliffs in Utah renamed Mount Messiaen (5 August)	
1983	First performance (28 November) of *Saint François d'Assise* at Paris Opéra	

Catalogue of Works

This catalogue includes the following information (where applicable), set out in the following order: title (and subtitle); forces; individual movements or section titles; date and place of composition, orchestration, etc.; dedication; first performance details; duration; publisher; commercial recording(s); any additional data. Unless otherwise stated, texts set are by Messiaen himself. The catalogue makes no pretensions to providing a complete discography. Messiaen's piano and organ works in particular have been much recorded, and the intention here has been to select versions that are of particular historical or aesthetic value.

The works are arranged in seven categories:

I   Opera
II Orchestral
III Vocal
IV Chamber and Instrumental
V   Organ
VI Piano
VII Electronic

I OPERA

Saint François d'Assise

scènes franciscaines
Solo roles Saint François (bar), Frère Léon (bar), Le Lépreux (t), L'Ange (s), Frère Massée (t), Frère Elie (t), Frère Bernard (b), Frère Sylvestre (b), Frère Rufin (b)
Choir s.s.m-s.a.a.t.t.bar.b.b. (15 voices to each part)
Orchestra 7.4.8.4 – 6.4.3.3 – 5 idiophones, 5 percussion, 3 ondes martenot – 16.16.14.12.10
  Act I   scene 1: La Croix   scene 2: Les laudes   scene 3: Le baiser au lépreux
  Act II scene 4: L'ange voyageur   scene 5: L'ange musicien   scene 6: Le prêche aux oiseaux
  Act III scene 7: Les stigmates   scene 8: La mort et la nouvelle vie
Composed 1975–9
Orchestrated 1979–83
First performance 28 November 1983, Paris Opéra; José van Dam (Saint François), Michel Philippe (Frère Léon), Kenneth Riegel (Le Lépreux), Christiane Eda-Pierre (L'Ange); Chorus and Orchestra of the Paris Opéra, conducted by Seiji Ozawa; production by Sandro Sequi, designed by Giuseppe Crisolini-Malateste

Duration Act I – 80 minutes; Act II – 120 minutes; Act III – 60 minutes
Publisher Leduc: libretto

II ORCHESTRAL

Fugue in D minor

Composed 1928, Paris

Le banquet eucharistique

Composed 1928, Fuligny
First performance Paris Conservatoire; student orchestra, conducted by Henri Rabaud
Note Related to *Le banquet céleste* for organ

Simple chant d'un âme

Composed 1930, Paris

Les offrandes oubliées

méditation symphonique
Orchestra 3.3.3.3 – 4.3.3.1 – timpani, percussion – strings
Composed 1930, Fuligny
First performance 19 February 1931, Théâtre des Champs-Elysées, Paris; Orchestre Straram, conducted by Walter Straram
Duration 11½ minutes
Publisher Durand: study score, piano reduction
Recording Erato STU 70673 (Marius Constant)

Le tombeau resplendissant

Orchestra 3.3.3.3 – 4.3.3.1 – timpani, percussion – strings
Composed 1931, Fuligny
First performance 1932, Paris; Pierre Monteux

Hymne au Saint Sacrement

Orchestra 3.3.3.3 – 4.3.3.0 – timpani, percussion – strings
Composed 1932, Paris
First performance 13 March 1933, Paris; Orchestre Straram, conducted by Walter Straram
Duration 13 minutes
Publisher Broude Bros (reconstructed from memory of an original score lost during the war)
Recording Erato STU 70673 (Marius Constant)

L'Ascension

méditations symphoniques
Orchestra 3.3.3.3 – 4.3.3.1 – timpani, percussion – 16.16.14.12.10   1 Majesté du Christ demandant sa gloire à son Père   2 Alléluias sereins d'une âme qui désire le ciel   3 Alléluia sur la trompette, alléluia sur la cymbale   4 Prière du Christ montant vers son Père
Composed May 1932, Paris – July 1932, Neussargues
Orchestrated May–July 1933, Monaco
First performance February 1935, Paris; Robert Siohan
Duration 30 minutes

Publisher   Leduc: study score
Recordings   Columbia ML 4214 (Leopold Stokowski); Erato STU 70673 (Marius Constant)
Note   Arranged for organ, 1934

Turangalîla-symphonie

Orchestra   3.3.3.3 – 4.5.3.1 – piano solo, ondes martenot solo, glockenspiel, celesta, vibraphone, 5 percussion – 16.16.14.12.10
1 Introduction   2 Chant d'amour I   3 Turangalîla I   4 Chant d'amour II   5 Joie du sang des étoiles   6 Jardin du sommeil d'amour   7 Turangalîla II   8 Développement de l'amour   9 Turangalîla III   10 Final
Composed   17 July 1946 – 29 November 1948
First performance   2 December 1949, Symphony Hall, Boston; Yvonne Loriod, Ginette Martenot, Boston Symphony Orchestra, conducted by Leonard Bernstein
Duration   75 minutes
Publisher   Durand: study score
Recordings   RCA SB 6761–2 (Seiji Ozawa); HMV SLS 5117 (André Previn)

Réveil des oiseaux

Orchestra   4.3.4.3 – 2.2.0.0 – piano solo, celesta, xylophone, glockenspiel, 2 percussion – 8.8.8.8.6
Composition completed   1953
Dedication   'A la memoire de l'écrivain et ornithologue: Jacques Delamain. En hommage à Yvonne Loriod, qui a doigté, et joué de façon géniale la partie de piano solo de cette oeuvre. Aux merles, grives, rossignols, loriots, rouges-gorges, pouillots, fauvettes, et à tous les oiseaux de nos forêts.'
First performance   11 October 1953, Donaueschingen; Yvonne Loriod, Südwestfunk Orchestra, conducted by Hans Rosbaud
Duration   20 minutes
Publisher   Durand: study score, solo part
Recording   Supraphon SUA ST 50749 (Yvonne Loriod/Vaclav Neumann)

Oiseaux exotiques

Orchestra   2.1.3.1 – 2.1.0.0 – piano solo, glockenspiel, xylophone, 5 percussion
Composed   5 October 1955 – 23 January 1956
Dedication   'à Yvonne Loriod'
First performance   10 March 1956, Petit Théâtre Marigny, Paris; Yvonne Loriod, Domaine Musical, conducted by Rudolf Albert
Duration   13–14 minutes
Publisher   Universal: study score, solo part
Recordings   Véga C30 A65 (first performance); Supraphon SUA ST 50749 (Yvonne Loriod/Vaclac Neumann)

Chronochromie

Orchestra   4.3.4.3. – 4.4.3.1 – glockenspiel, xylophone, marimba, 3 percussion – 16.16.14.12.10
1 Introduction   2 Strophe I   3 Antistrophe I   4 Strophe II   5 Antistrophe II   6 Epode   7 Coda
Composed   1959–60
First performance   16 October 1960, Donaueschingen; Südwestfunk Orchestra, conducted by Hans Rosbaud
Duration   22 minutes

Publisher Leduc: study score
Recording HMV ALP 2092; ASD 639; ZRG 756 (Antal Dorati)

Sept haïkaï

esquisses japonaises
Orchestra 2.3.4.2 – 0.1.1.0 – piano solo, xylophone, marimba, 4 percussion –
8.0.0.0.0
1 Introduction   2 Le parc de Nara et les lanternes de pierre   3 Yamanaka-
cadenza   4 Gagaku   5 Miyajima et le torii dans la mer   6 Les oiseaux de
Karuizawa   7 Coda
Composed 1962
Dedication 'à Yvonne Loriod, à Pierre Boulez, à Madame Fumi Yamaguchi, à Seiji
Ozawa, à Yoritsuné Matsudaïra, à Sadao Bekku et Mitsuaki Hayama, à l'ornitho-
logue Hoshino, aux paysages, aux musiques, et à tous les oiseaux de Japon'
First performance 30 October 1963, Odéon, Paris; Yvonne Loriod, Domaine Musi-
cal, conducted by Pierre Boulez
Duration 20 minutes
Publisher Leduc: study score, solo part
Recording Adès 16001, Everest SDBR 3192 (Yvonne Loriod/Pierre Boulez)

Couleurs de la cité céleste

Orchestra 0.0.3.0 – 2.4.4.0 – piano solo, xylophone, xylorimba, marimba, 3
percussion
Composed 1963
First performance 17 October 1964, Donaueschingen; Yvonne Loriod, Domaine
Musical, conducted by Pierre Boulez
Duration 16–17 minutes
Publisher Leduc: study score, solo part
Recording Erato STU 70302; CBS 72471 (Pierre Boulez)

Et exspecto resurrectionem mortuorum

Orchestra 5.4.5.4 – 6.4.4.2 – 3 percussion
1 Des profondeurs de l'abîme, je cris vers toi, Seigneur: Seigneur, écoute ma
voix!   2 Le Christ, ressuscité des morts, ne meurt plus; la mort n'a plus sur lui
d'empire   3 L'heure vient où les morts entendront la voix du fils de Dieu   4 Ils
ressusciteront, glorieux, avec un nom nouveau – dans le concert joyeux des étoiles
et les acclamations des fils du ciel   5 Et j'entendis la voix d'une foule immense
Composed 1964, Petichet
First performance 7 May 1965, Ste Chapelle, Paris; Domaine Musical, conducted
by Serge Baudo
Duration 29 minutes
Publisher Leduc: study score
Recording Erato STU 70302; CBS 72471 (Pierre Boulez)

Des canyons aux étoiles . . .

Orchestra 4.3.4.3 – 3.3.3.0 – piano solo, glockenspiel, xylorimba, 5 percussion –
6.0.3.1
1 Le désert   2 Les orioles   3 Ce qui est écrit sur les étoiles   4 Le cossyphe
d'Heuglin   5 Cedar Breaks et le don de la crainte   6 Appel interstellaire   7 Bryce
Canyon et les rochers rouge-orange   8 Les ressuscités et le chant de l'étoile
Aldebaran   9 Le moqueur polyglotte   10 La grive des bois   11 Omao, leiothrix,
elepaio, shama   12 Zion Park et la cité céleste

Composed 1971–4
First performance 20 November 1974, Alice Tully Hall, New York; Yvonne Loriod,
   Musica Aeterna, conducted by Frederic Waldman
Duration 100 minutes
Publisher Leduc: full score
Recording Erato STU 70974/975 (Marius Constant)

III VOCAL

Deux ballades de Villon

Scoring voice and piano
   1 Epître à ses amis   2 Ballade des pendus
Composed 1921, Paris

Trois mélodies

Scoring voice and piano
   1 Pourquoi?   2 Le sourire (Cécile Sauvage)   3 La fiancée perdue
Composed 1930, Paris
First performance 1930, Paris; Louise Matha, OM
Duration 6 minutes
Publisher Durand

La mort du nombre

Scoring soprano, tenor, violin and piano
Composed 1930, Paris
First performance 1931, Paris; Georgette Mathieu, Jean Planel
Duration 12–13 minutes
Publisher Durand

Mass

Scoring 8 sopranos and 4 violins
Composed 1933, Neussargues

Vocalise

Scoring soprano and piano
Composed 1935, Paris
Duration 4 minutes
Publisher Leduc

Poèmes pour Mi

Scoring soprano and piano
   1 Action de grâces   2 Paysage   3 La maison   4 Epouvante   5 L'épouse   6 Ta
   voix   7 Les deux guerriers   8 Le collier   9 Prière exaucée
Composed 1936, Petichet
First performance 28 April 1937, Paris; Marcelle Bunlet, OM
Duration 28 minutes
Publisher Durand
Recording Everest 3269 (Lise Arseguest, OM)

Orchestrated 1937, Paris
Scoring soprano; 3.3.2.3 – 4.3.3.1 – 3 percussion – strings
First performance 1946, Brussels; Marcelle Bunlet, Belgian National Radio Orches-
   tra, conducted by Franz André

Duration   28 minutes
Publisher   Durand: study score
Recording   Argo ZRG 703 (Felicity Palmer/Pierre Boulez)

O sacrum convivium!

Scoring   SATB choir; or soprano and organ
Composed   1937, Paris
Duration   3½ minutes
Publisher   Durand

Chants de terre et de ciel

Scoring   soprano and piano
   1 Bail avec Mi (pour ma femme)   2 Antienne du silence (pour le jour des Anges gardiens)   3 Danse du bébé-Pilule (pour mon petit Pascal)   4 Arc-en-ciel d'innocence (pour mon petit Pascal)   5 Minuit pile et face (pour la mort)   6 Résurrection (pour le jour de Pâques)
Composed   1938, Petichet
First performance   6 March 1939, Paris; Marcelle Bunlet, OM
Duration   28 minutes
Publisher   Durand

Choeurs pour une Jeanne d'Arc

Scoring   large and small choirs
   1 Te Deum   2 Impropères
Composed   1941, Neussargues
Note   Not performed

Trois petites liturgies de la Présence Divine

Scoring   36 women's voices; piano solo, ondes martenot solo, celesta, vibraphone, 3 percussion, strings (8.8.6.6.4)
   1 Antienne de la conversation intérieure (Dieu présent en nous . . .)   2 Séquence du Verbe, cantique divin (Dieu présent en lui-meme . . .)   3 Psalmodie de l'ubiquité par amour (Dieu présent en toutes choses . . .)
Composed   15 November 1943 – 15 March 1944, Paris
First performance   21 April 1945, Paris; Chorale Yvonne Gouverné, Yvonne Loriod, Ginette Martenot, Orchestre de la Société des Concerts du Conservatoire, conducted by Roger Désormière
Duration   40 minutes
Publisher   Durand: study score
Recording   Pathé PDT 190–4S (first performance)

Harawi

chant d'amour et de la mort
Scoring   dramatic soprano and piano
   1 La ville qui dormait, toi   2 Bonjour toi, colombe verte   3 Montagnes   4 Doundou tchil   5 L'amour de Piroutcha   6 Répétition planétaire   7 Adieu   8 Syllabes   9 L'escalier redit, gestes du soleil   10 Amour oiseau d'étoile   11 Katchikatchi les étoiles   12 Dans le noir
Composed   15 June – 15 September 1945, Petichet
First performance   24 June 1946, Macon; Marcelle Bunlet, OM
Duration   60 minutes
Publisher   Leduc
Recording   Argo ZRG 606 (Noelle Barker, Robert Sherlaw Johnson)

Cinq rechants

Scoring   3 sopranos, 3 altos, 3 tenors, 3 basses
Composed   December 1948, Paris
Dedication   'à l'Ensemble Vocal Marcel Couraud'
First performance   1949, Salle Erard, Paris; Ensemble Vocal Marcel Couraud,
   conducted by Marcel Couraud
Duration   17 minutes
Publisher   Salabert
Recording   Erato STU 70457 (Marcel Couraud)

La Transfiguration de Notre-Seigneur Jésus-Christ

Choir   s.s.m-s.a.a.t.t.bar.b.b   (10 voices to each part)
Orchestra   7 soloists: piano, cello, flute, clarinet, xylorimba, vibraphone and
   marimba; 5.4.5.4 – 6.4.4.2 – 6 percussion – 16.16.14.12.12
   Premier septenaire: 1 Récit évangélique 2 Configuratum corpori claritatis
   suae 3 Christus Jesus, splendor Patris 4 Récit évangélique 5 Quam dilecta
   tabernacula tua 6 Candor est lucis aeternae 7 Choral de la sainte montagne
   Deuxième septenaire: 8 Récit évangélique 9 Perfecte conscius illius perfectae
   generationis 10 Adoptionem filiorum perfectam 11 Récit évangélique 12 Ter-
   ribilis est locus iste 13 Tota Trinitas apparuit 14 Choral de la lumière de gloire
Composed   28 June 1965 – 20 February 1969
First performance   7 June 1969, Lisbon; Gulbenkian Chorus, Yvonne Loriod,
   Mstislav Rostropovich, Michel Debost, Henry Druart, Alain Jacquet, Jacques
   Delécluse, François Dupin, Orchestra de Paris, conducted by Serge Baudo
Duration   90 minutes
Publisher   Leduc: full score
Recording   Decca HEAD 1–2 (Yvonne Loriod, Janos Starker/Antal Dorati)

IV CHAMBER AND INSTRUMENTAL

Thème et variations

Scoring   violin and piano
Composed   1932, Paris
First performance   1932, Paris; Claire Delbos, OM
Duration   10 minutes
Publisher   Leduc

Fantaisie

Scoring   violin and piano
Composed   1933, Paris

Quatuor pour la fin du temps

Scoring   violin, clarinet, cello and piano
   1 Liturgie de cristal 2 Vocalise pour l'ange qui annonce la fin du temps 3 Abîme
   des oiseaux 4 Intermède 5 Louange à l'éternité de Jésus 6 Danse de la fureur,
   pour les sept trompettes 7 Fouillis d'arcs-en-ciel, pour l'ange qui annonce la fin
   du temps 8 Louange à l'immortalité de Jésus
Composed   1940–1, Görlitz
First performance   15 January 1941, Stalag VIIIA, Görlitz, Silesia; Jean Le Boulaire,
   Henri Akoka, Etienne Pasquier, OM
Duration   49 minutes
Publisher   Durand: score and parts; study score

Recording DG 2531 093 (Luben Yordanoff, Claude Desurmont, Albert Tétard, Daniel Barenboim)

Le merle noir

Scoring flute and piano
Composed 1951, Paris
Duration 6 minutes
Publisher Leduc

V ORGAN

Esquisse modale

Composed 1927, Paris

Le banquet céleste

Composed 1928, Fuligny
Duration 6 minutes
Publisher Leduc
Recording EMI 2C 153 16291/6 (OM)
Note Related to *Le banquet eucharistique* for orchestra

L'hôte aimable des âmes

Composed 1928, Fuligny

Variations écossaises

Composed 1928, Paris

Diptyque

essai sur la vie terrestre et l'éternité bienheureux
Composed 1930, Paris
Dedication 'à mes chers maîtres Paul Dukas et Marcel Dupré'
Duration 12 minutes
Publisher Durand
Recording EMI 2C 153 16291/6 (OM)

Apparition de l'église éternelle

Composed 1932, Paris
Duration 10 minutes
Publisher Lemoine
Recording EMI 2C 153 16291/6 (OM)

L'Ascension

1 Majesté du Christ demandant sa gloire à son Père   2 Alléluias sereins d'une âme qui désire le ciel   3 Transports de joie d'une âme devant la gloire du Christ qui est la sienne   4 Prière du Christ montant vers son Père
Composed 1933, Neussargues (Nos. 1 and 4); 1934, Paris (Nos. 2 and 3)
Duration 26 minutes
Publisher Leduc
Recording EMI 2C 153 16291/6 (OM)

La Nativité du Seigneur

neuf méditations

1 La Vierge et l'Enfant   2 Les bergers   3 Desseins éternels   4 Le Verbe   5 Les enfants de Dieu   6 Les anges   7 Jesus accepte la souffrance   8 Les mages   9 Dieu parmi nous

Composed   1935, Grenoble
First performance   1935, La Trinité, Paris; OM
Duration   55 minutes
Publisher   Leduc
Recording   EMI 2C 153 16291/6 OM

Les corps glorieux

sept visions brèves de la vie des ressuscités

1 Subtilité des corps glorieux   2 Les eaux de la grâce   3 L'ange aux parfums   4 Combat de la mort et de la vie   5 Force et agilité des corps glorieux   6 Joie et clarté des corps glorieux   7 Le mystère de la Sainte Trinité

Composed   1939 (completed 25 August), Petichet
First performance   15 April 1945, Chaillot; OM
Duration   46 minutes
Publisher   Leduc
Recording   EMI 2C 153 16291/6 OM

Messe de la Pentecôte

1 Entrée (Les langues de feu)   2 Offertoire (Les choses visibles et invisibles)   3 Consécration (Le don de sagesse)   4 Communion (Les oiseaux et les sources)   5 Sortie (Le vent de l'Esprit)

Composed   1949, Tanglewood – 1950, Paris
First performance   Pentecost 1951, La Trinité, Paris; OM
Duration   28 minutes
Publisher   Leduc
Recording   EMI 2C 153 16291/6 OM

Livre d'orgue

1 Reprises par interversion   2 Pièce en trio I   3 Les mains de l'abîme   4 Chants d'oiseaux   5 Pièce en trio II   6 Les yeux dans les roues   7 Soixante-quatre durées

Composed   1951
First performance   23 April 1953, Villa Berg, Stuttgart; OM
Duration   42 minutes
Publisher   Leduc
Recording   EMI 2C 153 16291/6 OM

Verset pour la fête de la Dédicace

Composed   December 1960, Paris
Duration   9 minutes
Publisher   Leduc

Méditations sur le mystère de la Sainte Trinité

1–9, untitled

Composed   1969
First performance   20 March 1972, Basilica of the Immaculate Conception, Washington, DC; OM
Duration   77 minutes
Publisher   Leduc
Recording   Erato STU 70750–1 (OM)

VI PIANO

La dame de Shalott

Composed   1917, Grenoble
Duration   5 minutes

La tristesse d'un grand ciel blanc

Composed   1925, Paris

Préludes

1 La colombe   2 Chant d'extase dans un paysage triste   3 Le nombre léger
4 Instants défunts   5 Les sons impalpables du rêve   6 Cloches d'angoisse et
larmes d'adieu   7 Plainte calme   8 Un reflet dans le vent . . .
Composed   1928–9, Fuligny
Dedication   'à Mademoiselle Henriette Roget'
First performance   1931, Paris; Henriette Roget
Duration   34 minutes
Publisher   Durand
Recording   Erato STU 70433 (Yvonne Loriod)

Fantaisie burlesque

Composed   1932, Paris
First performance   1932, Paris; Robert Casadesus
Duration   7 minutes
Publisher   Durand

Pièce pour la tombeau de Paul Dukas

Composed   1935, Grenoble
Duration   5 minutes
Published in   Revue musicale,   No. 166 (1936)

Rondeau

Composed   1943, Paris
Duration   3 minutes
Publisher   Leduc

Visions de l'Amen

For 2 pianos
1 Amen de la création   2 Amen des étoiles, de la planète à l'anneau   3 Amen de
l'agonie de Jésus   4 Amen du désir   5 Amen des anges, des saints, du chant des
oiseaux   6 Amen du jugement   7 Amen de la consommation
Composed   1943, Paris
Dedication   'à Yvonne Loriod'
First performance   10 May 1943, Paris; Yvonne Loriod, OM
Duration   48 minutes
Publisher   Durand
Recordings   Contrepoint CO 1–6 (78 rpm); Véga C30 A368 (Yvonne Loriod, OM;
different performances)

Vingt regards sur l'Enfant-Jésus

1 Regard du Père   2 Regard de l'étoile   3 L'échange   4 Regard de la Vierge
5 Regard du fils sur le fils   6 Par lui tout a été fait   7 Regard de la Croix   8 Regard

des hauteurs   9 Regard du temps   10 Regard de l'Esprit de joie   11 Première communion de la Vierge   12 La parole toute puissante   13 Noël   14 Regard des anges   15 Le baiser de l'Enfant-Jésus   16 Regard des prophètes, des bergers et des mages   17 Regard du silence   18 Regard de l'onction terrible   19 Je dors, mais mon coeur veille   20 Regard de l'église d'amour

Composed   23 March – September 1944, Paris
Dedication   'à Yvonne Loriod'
First performance   26 March 1945, Salle Gaveau, Paris; Yvonne Loriod
Duration   125 minutes
Publisher   Durand
Recording   Véga c30 A60–2 (Yvonne Loriod)

Cantéyodjayâ

Composed   1949
First performance   23 February 1954, Paris; Yvonne Loriod
Duration   12 minutes
Publisher   Universal
Recording   Véga c30 A139 (Yvonne Loriod)

Quatre études de rythme

1 *Ile de feu 1*   2 *Mode de valeurs et d'intensités*   3 *Neumes rythmiques*   4 *Ile de feu 2*

Composed   (No. 1) 1950, Paris; (No. 2) 1949, Darmstadt; completed the following winter, Paris; (No. 3) 1949, Tanglewood; (No. 4) 1950, Paris
Dedication   'à la Papouasie' (Nos. 1 and 4)
First performance   1950, Tunis; OM
Duration   No. 1 – 3 minutes; No. 2 – 2½ minutes; No. 3 – 7½ minutes; No. 4 – 4 minutes
Publisher   Durand
Recordings   Columbia LFX 998–9 (78 rpm) (OM); Erato STU 70433 (Yvonne Loriod)

Catalogue d'oiseaux

1 Le chocard des alpes   2 Le loriot   3 Le merle bleu   4 Le traquet stapazin   5 La chouette hulotte   6 L'alouette lulu   7 La rousserolle effarvatte   8 L'alouette calandrelle   9 La bouscarle   10 Le merle de roche   11 La buse variable   12 Le traquet rieur   13 Le courlis cendré

Composed   October 1956 – 1 September 1958
Dedication   'à ses modèles ailés, à la pianiste Yvonne Loriod'
First performance   15 April 1959, Salle Gaveau, Paris; Yvonne Loriod
Durations   No. 1 – 13½ minutes; No. 2 – 9½ minutes; No. 3 – 13½ minutes; No. 4 – 16 minutes; No. 5 – 8 minutes; No. 6 – 9 minutes; No. 7 – 30½ minutes; No. 8 – 5½ minutes; No. 9 – 11½ minutes; No. 10 – 19 minutes; No. 11 – 9½ minutes; No. 12 – 8½ minutes; No. 13 – 11 minutes; *overall duration* 165 minutes
Publisher   Leduc
Recordings   Véga VAL 11; Erato STU 70595–8 (Yvonne Loriod, different performances)

La fauvette des jardins

Composed   1970, Petichet
Dedication   'à Yvonne Loriod'
First performance   7 November 1972, Espace Cardin, Paris; Yvonne Loriod
Duration   34½ minutes
Publisher   Leduc

VII ELECTRONIC

Fête des belles eaux

Scoring　6 ondes martenot
Composed　1937, Paris
First performance　1937, Paris
Duration　31½ minutes
Recording　Adès 21 007 (Sextuor Jeanne Loriod)

Deux monodies en quarts de ton

For ondes martenot
Composed　1938, Paris

Musique de scène pour un Oedipe

For ondes martenot
Composed　1942, Paris

Timbres-durées

For tape
Composed　1952
Realized by　Pierre Henry
Duration　15 minutes
Note　Withdrawn

Bibliography

MESSIAEN'S PUBLICATIONS

With others: *Vingt leçons de solfège moderne* (Paris, Lemoine, 1933)
'Ariane et Barbe-Bleue de Paul Dukas', *Revue musicale*, no. 166 (1936), pp. 79–86
'Le rythme chez Igor Strawinsky', *Revue musicale*, no. 191 (1939), pp. 91–2
Vingt leçons d'harmonie (Paris, Leduc, 1939)
Technique de mon langage musical (Paris, Leduc, 1944; English translation, Leduc, 1957)
Preface to André Jolivet: *Mana* (Paris, Costallat, 1946)
'Maurice Emmanuel: ses "trente chansons bourguignonnes"', *Revue musicale*, no. 206 (1947), p. 108
Conférence de Bruxelles (Paris, Leduc, 1958)
Conférence de Notre-Dame (Paris, Leduc, 1978)
Traité du rythme (Paris, Leduc, in preparation)

BOOKS ON MESSIAEN

Ahrens, Sieglinde, Hans-Dieter Möller and Almut Rössler, *Das Orgelwerk Messiaens* (Duisburg, Gilles und Francke, 1976)
Borum, Paul, and Erik Christensen, *Messiaen: en handbog* (Copenhagen, Egtved, 1977)
Goléa, Antoine, *Rencontres avec Olivier Messiaen* (Paris, Julliard, 1960)
Halbreich, Harry, *Olivier Messiaen* (Paris, Fayard/SACEM, 1980)
Hohlfeld-Ufer, Ingrid, *Die musikalische Sprache Olivier Messiaens, dargestellt an dem Orgelzyklus 'Die Pfingstmesse'*, with Almut Rössler, *Zur Interpretation der Orgelwerke Messiaens* (Duisburg, Gilles und Francke, 1978)
Johnson, Robert Sherlaw, *Messiaen* (London, Dent, 1975)
Mari, Pierrette, *Olivier Messiaen* (Paris, Seghers, 1965)
Nichols, Roger, *Messiaen* (London, Oxford University Press, 1975)
Périer, Alain, *Messiaen* (Paris, Seuil, 1979)
Reverdy, Michèle, *L'oeuvre pour piano d'Olivier Messiaen* (Paris, Leduc, 1978)
Rostand, Claude, *Olivier Messiaen* (Paris, Ventadour, 1957)
Samuel, Claude, *Entretiens avec Olivier Messiaen* (Paris, Pierre Belfond, 1967; English translation, London, 1976)
Waumisley, Stuart, *The Organ Music of Olivier Messiaen* (Paris, Leduc, 1968)

OTHER LITERATURE

Barraqué, Jean, 'Rythme et développement', *Polyphonie*, no. 9–10 (1954), pp. 47–73; especially pp. 58–63

Boulez, Pierre, 'Olivier Messiaen', *Anhaltspunkte* (Stuttgart and Zurich, Belser, 1975), pp. 154–62

Drew, David, 'Messiaen: a Provisional Study', *The Score*, no. 10 (1954), pp. 33–49; no. 13 (1955), pp. 59–73; no. 14 (1955), pp. 41–61

Evans, Adrian, 'Olivier Messiaen in the Surrealist Context: a Bibliography', *Brio*, xi (1974), pp. 25–35

Heiss, Hellmut, 'Struktur und Symbolik in "Reprises par interversion" und "Les mains de l'abîme" aus Olivier Messiaens "Livre d'orgue"', *Zeitschrift für Musiktheorie*, i/2 (1970), pp. 32–8.

Hold, Trevor, 'Messiaen's Birds', *Music and Letters*, lii (1971), pp. 113–22

Melos, xxv/12 (1958), Messiaen issue

Messiaen Festival Programme Book (Paris, La recherche artistique, 1978)

Musik-Konzepte, no. 28 (1982), Messiaen issue

Smalley, Roger, 'Debussy and Messiaen', *Musical Times*, cix (1968), pp. 128–31

Indexes

INDEX OF WORKS BY MESSIAEN

GENERAL INDEX